A Monk in the SAS

Paul Sibley

Note for Librarians: A cataloguing record for this book is available from Library and Archives Canada at www.collectionscanada.ca/amicus/index-e.html
ISBN 1-4120-8635-3

Printed on paper with minimum 30% recycled fibre.
Trafford's print shop runs on "green energy" from solar, wind and other environmentally-friendly power sources.

TRAFFORD
PUBLISHING™
Offices in Canada, USA, Ireland and UK

Book sales for North America and international:
Trafford Publishing, 6E–2333 Government St.,
Victoria, BC V8T 4P4 CANADA
phone 250 383 6864 (toll-free 1 888 232 4444)
fax 250 383 6804; email to orders@trafford.com
Book sales in Europe:
Trafford Publishing (UK) Limited, 9 Park End Street, 2nd Floor
Oxford, UK OX1 1HH UNITED KINGDOM
phone 44 (0)1865 722 113 (local rate 0845 230 9601)
facsimile 44 (0)1865 722 868; info.uk@trafford.com
Order online at:
trafford.com/06-0391

10 9 8 7 6 5 4 3

This book is dedicated to my mother,
without whom none of this could have taken place.

Contents

Foreword   7

Chapter One   Contact!   9
Chapter Two   Childhood Years   11
Chapter Three   De La Salle   23
Chapter Four   21 SAS   33
Chapter Five   R Squadron 22 SAS   45
Chapter Six   Iran   63
Chapter Seven   Operation Storm, first trip   72
Chapter Eight   Operation Storm, second trip   95
Chapter Nine   Marriage and exercises   113
Chapter Ten   Operation Storm, third trip   121
Chapter Eleven   More exercises   133
Chapter Twelve   Operation Storm, fourth trip   150
Chapter Thirteen   Between armies   159
Chapter Fourteen   Firqat Force   163
Chapter Fifteen   Civil Aid Department   197
Chapter Sixteen   Camel trip and other stories   233
Chapter Seventeen Musandam   249
Chapter Eighteen   Musandam DevelopmentCommittee   252
Chapter Nineteen   MDC stories   269
Chapter Twenty   More MDC stories   279

Glossary   298

Appendix 1   Development Of The Insurgency   302
                   Firqat Names As At 1976   321
                   Bibliography

Appendix 2   Military courses completed   324

Foreword

This book is my autobiography. At the outset it was never intended for publication. It was for my grandchildren and their children, to give them some idea of how I spent my life. It charts my early, formative years, mainly spent Libya and Hong Kong, and then my time with the De La Salle Brothers, followed by the Special Air Service. It continues with my service as an officer in the Sultan of Oman's Armed Forces during the Dhofar War, and my subsequent activities among the mountain peoples of Oman. It was only when I found how much there was to write about, that I realised that it may have a wider audience. The title refers to my time with the De La Salle Brothers, and the fact that whilst in the SAS my nickname was 'The Mad Monk'.

It comprises my recollections, supported by the many notes and documents I collected during the period. I have only written about those events of which I have personal knowledge. I am sure that if there are any inaccuracies they are minor in nature. All views or opinions expressed in this book are mine alone, and I accept full responsibility for them.

I would like to thank Bruce Niven, who kindly gave me permission to use the photograph which forms the frontispiece of this book, and Ian and Mazzie Holt, who unstintingly gave their time, patience and advice in the early stages. Finally, to my son John, who persuaded me to write it in the first place, and to my wife Maggie, who patiently put up with me shutting myself away in the study when I could have been more usefully employed elsewhere.

The cover photograph is of the author at Medinat al Haq, Dhofar taken by Bruce Niven.

Chapter One

Contact!

Nothing moved in the village which lay in a hollow four hundred yards away. The warming rays of the dawn sun trickled over the ridge and illuminated the circular stone walls and bee-hive shaped thatch roofs of the houses. We could smell the characteristic mixture of wood-smoke, perfume and dried animal dung that drifted slowly down-wind towards us. We had marched half the night to reach this place, a village known to be sympathetic to the enemy. The patrol had split into four small groups to cover the exits of the village, and I lay looking over the sights of my Armalite rifle waiting for the first signs of enemy movement.

Suddenly a baby cried, a hungry baby, and we could hear the mother's voice as she prepared to feed it. Shortly after, thin skeins of wood-smoke began to percolate through the thatch as the fires were lit to prepare the morning brew of strong, sweet red tea, and we could hear the rattle of pots and the bronchitic coughing of the old folk as the households awoke.

Then the young women appeared, ducking as they came out through the low doorways, heading towards the low stock-houses. They wore black robes and brightly coloured head-shawls and had nothing on their feet, and they called to each other in their high, sing-song voices. They opened the doors and streams of small, snow-white goats trotted out, bleating, eager to find what nourishment there was in the bleached sun-dried grass on the hills around. The women herded them by clicking their tongues, and as they spread out from the village they came straight towards us. We flattened ourselves in the grass as the goats came through. The women didn't look in our direction as they passed by, still calling out to each other in Arabic and Shahri (The local dialect). Despite, speaking both, I couldn't work out what they were saying, and they soon disappeared out of sight.

There was no other movement in the village as we lay in wait while the sun climbed slowly in the clear blue sky. Then suddenly, the air was rent by several long bursts of Kalashnikov fire. Contact! The sound was deafening as the rounds cracked low overhead and ricocheted off the rocks around us. They knew exactly where we were, having been pin-pointed by the women, and had come in close. We couldn't see them, but we could see the smoke from the muzzles of the AK47s, and aimed below it. There was a pause in the firing as they took stock of the situation and redeployed, and then we heard the Bump, Bump, Bump of a mortar being fired. Instinctively we noted the direction of the sound, and timed the flight of the bombs heading our way, to work out where it was firing from. The mortar bombs screeched in. Crack, Crack, Crack, the bombs exploded viciously thirty yards away, each with its characteristic bright red flash and puff of oily black smoke. It was a 60mm mortar, and I buried my head in the grass as the red hot shards of shrapnel sizzled by. The hunters had become the hunted and we were going to have to fight our way out of it.

Chapter Two

Childhood Years

I was born on the 9th September 1946 in Pinner in Middlesex. My father had served as a lieutenant in the Royal Armoured Corps during WW2. My earliest memories are living with my grandparents at 20, Gayton Road, Harrow. Pampy (My grandfather) was a mechanical engineer and had been in charge of Battersea power station during the War. Before that he had been the chief engineer responsible for building a railway in South Africa. There was a large, inscribed, silver and crystal fruit bowl in the dining room commemorating this. He always seemed to me to be distant. Danny, (My grandmother) was something senior in the Red Cross, and ran an immaculate house. There were strict protocols regarding meal times – you could set your watch by them. The hall was tiled and always cold, and there was a grandfather clock, which ticked loudly, and chimed.

About this time we went to visit my mother's parents in Beaufort Avenue, Altrincham, near Manchester. The house was a large semi-detached at the end of a dark, damp, tree-lined avenue. The hall was always dark and cold. My grandmother Nanna, was a warm, caring Mancunian. The kitchen was gloomy, and had a large coal-fired range, with a rocking chair beside it. I used to sit in that chair to listen to 'Listen with Mother' on the radio. There was an iron grill outside the back door, which led to a small garden with rhododendrons in it, where I played when it was fine. In the attic were trunks with granddad's belongings from World War 1 in them. He had been commissioned in the Seaforth Highlanders and had taken part in the Christmas truce of 1914. He was given a memento in the form of a wooden bell surmounted by a cross, which my mother later gave to me.

I started at Harrow Infant's School – St Annes, in 1950. I don't remember very much about that except the smell of the cloakroom – that universal musty smell of mice that all children of that age seemed to have.

In 1952 my father, having left the Army and rejoined as a captain in the Royal Electrical and Mechanical Engineers, was posted to Libya. We flew from RAF Northolt in an Avro Lancastrian – a converted Lancaster bomber. I was sick all the way. King Idris, who ruled Libya at that time, travelled around in a big limousine with three Landrovers full of armed guards fore and aft, and three motorcycle outriders likewise. Any vehicles, which did not immediately get off the road on his approach, had their tyres shot out.

Libya had been an Italian colony during the War, and thus at that time was occupied by the British, although local rule had been restored in 1951. A lot of former German servicemen had remained, largely because they had nothing to go back to, and they worked as civilian employees of the British Army. My father was very clever with his hands, both as a pianist and a model maker. He made a twelve foot long model of a tug and used two of these Germans, Werner and Heinz, as ballast for it when he initially launched it in one of the camp water tanks.

We had a Ford Anglia car. Every now and then we would go swimming off the harbour mole. It had been the scene of much action during the war, and the concrete breakwater was littered with unexploded shells and flares. One day Alan (my older brother) and I decided to light one of the cordite flares. It was in a yellow canvas container with the fuse sticking out of the top. It was too windy to light, so we placed it in the lea of the car where it ignited splendidly. I have never forgotten the sight of my father leaping around the car trying to get in to move it as the enormous sheet of flame engulfed it. Fortunately it did little damage. The locals used to shave the cordite in these flares and wrap the shavings up tightly in brown paper, tied up with wire, and sell them. They were about an inch and a half in diameter, and exploded with a satisfying bang when hurled at a hard surface.

My brother and I got on quite well, except in the back of the car, where we quarrelled incessantly. One day during a long trip across the sand and gravel plain behind Benghazi, my parents got so fed up that they threatened to put us out if we did not stop. We didn't, so they stopped the car, put us out and drove off. We reasoned that they would not leave us, so we ran off the road and hid. We then spent the next two hours watching as they drove frantically up and down trying to find us. Eventually we got bored and came out. They were too relieved to punish us, but we were never put out again.

There was a sunken ammunition ship in the harbour, a leftover from the war. Divers were removing the munitions when the whole lot blew up. We were living in a flat near the harbour at the time, and I remember being told by my father to stand against the corridor walls as the whole building flexed with the blast. The Libyans had less reason to be thankful for Italian construction methods. At the end of our road (Via Misurata) there was an old palace which needed to be demolished. The method adopted was to attach a cable to the highest part of the building, attach the other end to a lorry, and drive away. At first, when the cable tautened, it lifted the rear wheels off the ground, so they filled up the back with rubble. This generally worked, but on at least two occasions the taut cable pulled the lorry backwards in time to meet the falling masonry, and the drivers were killed.

We moved to an older house with cool marble halls and walls. One day the sewer blocked and a Greek plumber was summoned. I watched, fascinated, as he went to work with his rods and plungers. When he had finished I asked him what the problem had been. "Two incha pipe, six incha arsehole" was his unforgettable response.

Opposite us lived a wealthy Libyan, Mr Qanoon. He was very fat, and used to sit in the shade in a specially made steel chair. One day his kitchen servant was demonstrating to his numerous children how people are hanged. Having secured the noose around his neck in the kitchen, he then fell off the chair. The knot must have been in the wrong place, because he survived, and I remember him showing off the livid bruising on his neck.

Every building had a *ghaffir*, or doorman. One day, for some reason or other a mob decided to stone me. The *ghaffirs* saved me, but I had some lumps on my head for a few days. Vendors used to come to our door selling vegetables, chickens etc. The birds were always alive, and the vendor would say that he would kill and dress the selected bird, and agree a price on his return. What they did was to inflate the carcass with a bicycle pump so that a higher price could be extracted. We did hear that some people had put the birds directly into the oven, with a subsequent explosion, but I don't know if that was true.

I used to play with the children of an Irish vet called Harry

Orr. They lived on a small farm on the outskirts of Benghazi, which I remember mainly for the dust, the musty smell of the donkeys, and the prickly pear cactus, which we were encouraged to eat, but never really enjoyed. One Christmas, Harry obtained a turkey which he gave to his Arab cook to prepare. Halfway through the morning he went into the kitchen to see how he was getting on and was enraged to find that it had been skinned instead of plucked. He threw the cook out, and spent the rest of the morning first plucking the skin, and then stitching it back onto the bird before cooking it.

Most of the children out there developed ulcers on their arms and legs, which were known as desert sores. I used to dread going to a clinic to have hot poultices applied, almost boiling, from the autoclave. I was luckier than Harry's boys however; he used to scrub theirs with a stiff brush, which must have been agonising. There was an enclosed children's swimming area at the beach. I was swimming there with them one day when I was suddenly dragged under. There was a shelf on the bottom, and one of them had got out of his depth. Seeing me swimming over he grabbed me. Fortunately my parents spotted my hair on the surface, and we were both rescued.

We left there in 1955, flying back to England in an Avro York, which was a derivative of the Lancaster bomber. As I had arrived, so I left, vomiting all the way.

My father's next posting was as adjutant in a Territorial Army unit on the outskirts of Edinburgh. We lived in Cramond, a quiet little village on the banks of the River Almond, west of Edinburgh. We had a new quarter in Cramond Place, directly opposite what is now part of Heriot Watt University. I went to the village school, which was only about three hundred yards away. The teachers were terrifying. They were all female, of various ages, shouted a lot, and were quick to use the tawse, a thick leather strap about 18 inches long and 3 inches wide, split down the middle. One of the more vicious ones was also the youngest. She was blonde, and used to wear a blouse and a woollen tartan skirt. She used to use both arms, brought back over her head in order to exert maximum force. We would have to stand in front of the class with both hands stretched out in front, one on top of the other, as punishment was meted out. One day, one of the boys pulled his hands back at the last moment. She hit herself across the legs with the tawse, and fell crying against the wood and glass partition that separated the two classrooms.

In late 1956 my father was posted to Hong Kong. We sailed from Southampton on a brand new troopship, the SS Nevasa, in January 1957. The Suez Canal was still closed following the Suez Crisis of 1956, and so we went via the Canary Islands, Durban, Colombo and Singapore. The voyage took about a month, and I was thoroughly rattled to find that there were school lessons on board.

In Hong Kong we initially stayed in the Belvedere Hotel on Boundary Road in Kowloon. It was at the time that the new Hong Kong airport, Kai Tak, was being built. Because flat land was at a premium, they had decided to extend the existing RAF runway out into the harbour. In order to obtain the fill to do this, they had located a small mountain near to Lion Rock. They then constructed a flyover out of bamboo over the houses, and the heavy lorries roared backwards and forwards all day. It was clearly visible from the hotel. I remember they used an old Vampire fighter with its wings loaded with sandbags to test the hardness of the impacted soil.

After a couple of months we moved to a hiring out at Lai Chi Kok. My parent's bedroom was the only air-conditioned room in the house. Consequently in summer, I developed Prickly Heat, a form of heat rash, which itched frantically. I scratched it so much, especially at night, that I was raw. The treatment applied by my mother, was to rub it with Eau de Cologne which stung with a vengeance. That year there was a monsoon. I had never seen one before – it rained and rained. The water rushed down the hill overflowing the drains and where each driveway crossed the drain to the road, it was thrown back up into the air some three feet high. There were houses on the other side of the valley from us. On the third day I was looking at one of them, which had the front supported on concrete stilts, when it suddenly moved. It slithered down the slope and collapsed in the valley bottom.

We had two Chinese servants there; Ah Jik, who did the cooking, and Ah Soo, who did the housework. They lived over the garage next to the house. I was on our roof one day, when I saw Ah Soo sitting on her balcony knitting. She had a ball of wool in her hand. I had a catapult in mine. I decided to knock the ball of wool out of her hand with a marble. The range was about 30 metres. I took deadly fiendish accurate aim, and loosed the marble. It seemed to wobble in flight, and hit her straight between the eyes. She didn't move for a moment, then slowly fell over backwards, her black pyjama-trousered legs, rising above the parapet, before they too disappeared out of sight. I was panic-stricken. I ran downstairs into the sitting room, and sat pretending to read a book. Shortly after, I heard a terrible commotion out at the back. "Oh Missy. Oh Missy" as she came in calling for my mother. I heard them talking for a moment, and then they came into the sitting room. Ah Soo had a swelling on her forehead, and she pointed accusingly at me. I denied all knowledge of it, and swore that I had been reading. I got away with it, but Ah Soo hated me ever after.

Ah Jik didn't have very much reason to like me either. I had noticed that he was a heavy smoker, so I bought some cigarette squibs. These were supposed to be put into the end of the cigarette and explode shortly after it was lit, to every one's amusement. I added a refinement to it. I damped the squib, and partially dried it before inserting it into the end of a cigarette. I offered it to Ah Jik in such a way that he would put the squib end into his mouth. He was pleased to accept it, and lit it immediately. I watched, fascinated, as he smoked it. When the hot tobacco reached the squib, instead of exploding, it went off like a miniature Roman-Candle into his mouth. He danced around the kitchen trying to get to the tap to put out the flames in his mouth while I legged it.

Explosive caps did not come in rolls, like in the UK. They came in red sheets of stiff paper, about five caps wide by about twenty-five long. They were three times the size of the UK caps, and could be struck individually. The trick was to detonate as many as possible at one go. One day one of the boys had a folded up sheet of them in his pocket when he fell. The whole lot went up in a great sheet of flame, and his leg was badly burned.

We moved into a fifth floor flat of a seven-storey block overlooking the Happy Valley Race course (19A 5, Ventris Road). In Benghazi, two of my father's friends had shown me how to make a water bomb out of a sheet of paper, and this gave me the ideal opportunity to bomb people from on high without being seen or caught.

I started at Victoria Junior School on Hong Kong Island. It was here that I did my 11 Plus exam, which decided whether I would be streamed into Grammar or Secondary Modern education. I passed, just, in July 1958, and then went to St George's School, which was on the mainland. This entailed a return trip on the Star Ferry across the harbour every day.

This was a frequent service, and I always travelled on the top deck, so as to get a better view of the harbour. Wherever I looked there were junks and sampans, both under sail and motor driven, laden with bales and crates, most with a little cage hanging over the stern containing several chickens, and screeching seagulls wheeling around in the wake. There were huge freighters and warships, and the air was full of the sound of hooters and klaxons, horns and whistles as they jockeyed for position, negotiating their way around the harbour.

I started formal piano lessons with a Chinese lady called Maple Quon. She made me work hard, and insisted on an hour's practise every day. I had to maintain a record book to prove it to her on my weekly visits. When she thought I was good enough she entered me for the British Music Examination, Grade one. The exam was to be held in the Queen Elizabeth School on a Saturday. On the appointed day I went to the Queen Elizabeth School in Kowloon only to find it shut. There was another school of the same name on Hong Kong Island. I rushed over there and arrived after the exam had started. After hearing my tale of woe, they allowed me to take part. Somehow I passed with an 'A'.

My father, who had always been interested in religion, decided to convert to Catholicism, and mother and I followed suit. I went every week to the Wah Yan College to see Father J P McCarthy. He was a Jesuit with a hunchback. His skin was a waxy white, and he had a prominent blue vein running down his forehead. The Catechism was all very interesting, but the highlight of every visit was the appearance of a bottle of Coca Cola and a packet of digestive biscuits. During the Second World War he had been in Macau. The colony's electricity generators ran on oil, but because of the war no oil was getting through. He experimented on oil extracted from shark's livers, and produced an oil compatible with the generators. He spoke and wrote Cantonese fluently. At the time I knew him his job was to analyse the news, which came out of communist China. He produced a weekly journal, which had a very limited circulation. He became involved with a fisherman who had lost his sampan due to an accident. He fought for the case in court, and won. As a mark of gratitude, the fisherman had a 3 foot long scale model of his new sampan constructed by the shipyard, which had made his new boat. Fr McCarthy's religious vows prevented him from keeping it, so he gave it to me.

My parents decided to adopt a little girl. We visited several orphanages, which were full of little girls, due to the social and financial pressures of Chinese society. They were depressing places full of cots with babies of all ages in them some standing monotonously banging their teeth against the rail, or just lying there. One of them smiled at my father, so he chose her. She was four months old, and her head was a mass of boils. She had been found at the age of four days wrapped up in newspaper in the gutter in Tsim Sha Tsui in Kowloon. She was called Jan. Whilst the adoption was taking place we were visited regularly by a Chinese Health Visitor. When she got to know my mother, she asked her why, if she wanted a little girl, she did not swap one of her sons (me!) with a friend's daughter. That is what she said she would have done.

In January 1961 my father's posting was up and we returned to the UK. We left Hong Kong Island in an Army landing craft for the last trip across the harbour. We sailed on the SS Empire Fowey, which, had previously been the German liner 'Potsdam', and had been used by the Germans during the invasion of Norway. We sailed down to Singapore, across to Colombo and Aden, then up the Red Sea to the Suez Canal. After that it was across the Mediterranean to Malta, through the Straits of Gibraltar and back to Portsmouth.

We moved several times, as my father's military career came to an end. At Liss, near Petersfield, I remember there was a man who used to wear a hat which looked like a cloth beehive. It was widely believed that it covered an extra face on top of his head. I went to Petersfield Secondary Modern, which was a seven mile bike ride away. I fought my way through that school. The trouble was that for most of my childhood I was always the new boy, and therefore a target. Punching a boy one day, I broke a bone in my hand. My father took me to our GP who looked at it, observed that it was broken and would heal, and told me to learn how to hit people properly! Today I would have been sent to Casualty where it would have been X-rayed, put in Plaster of Paris and followed up in clinic.

We moved to Pinner, in Middlesex and I started at Headstone Lane School in September 1961. Here I joined the Cross Country running team, and became used to the smell of sweat and liniment. I also became interested in Judo, and did my basic course at the Renshuden club in London. There were two older boys at this school who used to bait me with shouts of "Jew, Jew" and other pleasantries. When it became physical I attacked one of them in the school corridor. After that they stayed away from me, but they were always looking for ways to be unpleasant. I never told my parents. I had a crystal set, on which I used to listen to Radio Luxembourg, and an air rifle. I discovered that a Bengal Match would fit in the breach, and when fired would ignite as it travelled down the barrel. It had a range of about 50 yards and I used to try and set fire to things in other people's back gardens.

My father had a job in a bank, which he hated. He resigned three months later, and became a Housemaster in an approved school in Berkshire. The school was called St Benedict's, at Wokefield Park, and was run by the De La Salle

Brothers, a Roman Catholic teaching order. We moved into a school house which he called "Farthings", because he had a pound's worth (240) in a bag. I went to a local school which encouraged cross country running to the extent that the PE teachers would regularly make all the boys who were not in the cross country team run up and down a hill in the nearby park until they were sick, so that they would understand the sacrifices of the team runners. It didn't bother me because I was in the team. It was here that I punched a boy in the dining room because he pinched my dessert. We were both hauled up in front of the headmaster who offered us a choice of the cane, or lines. I chose the cane, the other boy chose lines. Because I had 'bravely' chosen the cane, I was let off. The other boy was caned for cowardice.

In the meantime, I was impressed by the De La Salle brothers to the extent that I wanted to join them. After being interviewed, I was taken to St Cassian's Juniorate, at Kintbury, near Newbury for a visit. It was a beautiful old house in extensive grounds with about 40 boys there aged from 13 to 16. It was such a happy place that it confirmed my intention to join the Brothers.

Chapter Three

De La Salle

My parents were encouraging throughout, and I started at St Cassians in March 1962. It was only years later that I discovered that they had been distraught at my wish to join a religious order. The De La Salle Brothers are a teaching order founded by St Jean Baptiste De La Salle in 1684. There are five vows – Poverty, Chastity, Obedience, Stability (Meaning staying where you are sent), and Teaching the poor gratuitously.

The school was run along the lines of a grammar school, but with some significant differences. Parents were only allowed to visit once during the entire time spent there, and that was for three days during the first year. The boys were only allowed home for five weeks during the summer holidays. The weekdays started at half past six and finished at nine thirty, the time in between being a mixture of prayer, study, and housework. Wednesday, and Sunday afternoons were devoted to sport, and Saturday afternoons to gardening. Some Sunday afternoons we were allowed out, and when that happened I went off on my bike with some of the other boys. The resident priest was Father Davies, a kind old man who used to say Mass every morning, and hear confessions once a week. No matter how heinous the sin we confessed to, the penance was never more than one Hail Mary. We were convinced that even if we had confessed to murdering the Pope, he would still tell us not to do it again, and give us the usual penance.

Many of the boys were Irish, so Hurley was popular, along with rugby and cricket. Some of the Brothers had a quite muscular approach to Christianity; Brother Anthony once told me, that sometimes the kindest thing you can do for someone is to punch them straight between the eyes. It saves any possible misunderstanding.

Sometimes, during the summer holidays, we would walk down to the Kennet and Avon canal for a swim. It was lovely, being in the cool water, watching the occasional water rat returning to its hole in the bank. The only downside was having to pick the leeches out from between our toes afterwards.

I had a particular friend from Salford, called Pat Evans. We were given lots of odd jobs about the place, such as scraping and painting the school gates, and helping old Brother Henry build a garage. It wasn't long before we were both made joint Head Boys, not that that carried any great responsibility – it just meant that we were left alone a bit more than the others. The winter of '62 was an especially hard one, and the school was snowed in. I was given the job, with Pat, to walk the mile or so into Kintbury to buy bread, the only thing that the school had run out of. The cast-iron drain pipes of the main building froze, and Pat and I were given the job of clearing them. After we had exploded two by pouring boiling water down them we were taken off the job.

There were three large rectangular water storage ponds behind the school, where in summer we used to observe wild life. This winter they froze solid, and we used the biggest one for playing ice-hockey (Hurley sticks, no skates, and a wooden block as the puck). The games were hard-fought, and there were many injuries, mainly to fingers and knees. Initially there were no goal posts. There were however, plenty of dead pigeons around. We made goal posts by placing a pigeon on the ice, pouring cold water on it so that it froze in place, putting another one on top of it and repeating the procedure until we had posts five feet high.

Initially, the headmaster (or Brother Director, as he was known) was Brother Leander (All the Brothers adopted names other than their given names when they took the Holy Habit). He was a severe Irish man with white hair. I am sure he was a kind man, but he always frightened me. He was replaced by Brother Alfred, who famously claimed, after images of an American beauty contest were accidentally screened during a reel change at a film show, that he could look at women's bodies all day without his composure being disturbed. He brought two Alsation dogs with him. I am not sure how that fitted in with the religious life, but he had permission. Over the fields from St Cassian's was St John's Novitiate. This was where we all destined to go after completing GCE's. It was the religious hothouse, where the novices all wore the Habit, had taken new names, and was seriously holy. On 5th November, after the bonfire on which was burnt an effigy, not of Guy Fawkes (He was a good Catholic) but Ian Paisley (who is not), some of us had got our hands on some fireworks. We went over the fields in the dark and let them off under the window of the refectory where they were just finishing the reading of a religious text. We ran back to St Cassian's with less than holy imprecations ringing in our ears, and let off some more around the school buildings. Br Alfred was furious, not only because of the complaint he received from St John's, but mainly because his dogs had been frightened. He made me put my hand one of their chests, so that I could feel the rapid heart rate. I don't know whether it was because of this, but shortly after his superiors told him to find another home for one of the dogs, presumably because he was getting too attached to them. He was clearly very upset.

Mealtimes started with Grace, after which the boys took turns to read a passage of a suitable book, after which we were allowed to speak. The Brothers sat at High Table, from where Br Alfred controlled the proceedings by means of a bell. One day we were all tucking in, when the bell rang; everyone stopped eating and looked up. "Where are High Table's peas?" he said. In the silence that followed old Br Henry was heard saying "Oh well, no peas for the wicked". Br Alfred wasn't amused as every one in the refectory burst out laughing.

A frequent item at meals was liver sausage, which was presented in a variety of ways. We had it so often that some of the boys complained. By way of teaching us to be content with what we were given, Br Alfred bought a huge quantity of brawn, which we hated. He said that we would go back to liver sausage when all the brawn was eaten. It took weeks, and it finished up in the flowerbeds outside the refectory, in the teapots, pockets, in fact anywhere it could be removed from the table.

We had butter only on Sundays. During the rest of the week we had a mixture of margarine and butter produced by squeezing the two together through a pump, and cutting the one-inch diameter extrusion into quarter inch long pieces. One week the boys on kitchen-duty did not introduce margarine into the machine so we had neat butter. We ran out of butter quickly, and in the meantime the margarine had become rancid. When Br Alfred found out he refused to order any more butter until all the rancid margarine had been eaten. Most of it followed the brawn.

In the summer of 1963 having attended 14 schools during

the course of my education, I took the GCE exam in English Language, English Literature, Maths, Physics, Biology, Divinity, Chemistry and French. I passed all except the last two, coming second overall in the group. That was a testament to the class size (9), and the teaching skills of the Brothers.

On the 11th July 1963 I went over the fields to St John's at Inglewood to become a Postulant with eleven others. Unfortunately my great friend, Pat did not come – he had decided that the religious life was not for him. The atmosphere was very different to St Cassian's. This was a religious powerhouse, and very much more serious than the relatively light hearted feeling at St Cassian's.

The Director of Novices was Brother Amedy Xavier, a severe man who used to be a professional footballer. He had a glance, which could whither, and he generally gave an impression of scarcely controlled violence, although he never was in any way. It was just the impression that he gave. The Deputy Director of Novices was Brother Philemon, a very warm man with a rich Irish brogue. He was the perfect foil for Br Amedy. Without him the atmosphere would have been repressive.

At first we wore our own clothes, but two months later, on 11th September 1963 was The Taking of the Holy Habit. There was a ceremony in the chapel during which we were presented with our habits. The habit consisted of a black serge gown with two pockets at the sides. At the collar we wore a stock which supported a 'rabat' – this looked like two white playing cards and formerly was made of linen, but now was made of celluloid. On our heads we wore a skullcap called a 'calotte'. Over the top, in winter, we could wear a cape called a mantle. Underneath we wore trousers and t-shirt, and shoes. Around our necks we wore a large crucifix (about 4" long) under the habit. We were also required to adopt a religious name. I chose Brother Paul Aelred. Paul, because that is my name anyway, and Aelred, because that was the name of one of the Brothers at Wokefield Park, where my father had worked, who I particularly liked, and who was my sponsor.

Initially when we went there we all slept together in a big dormitory known as The Barn, although later on we were given individual cells with just enough room for a bed, bedside locker and chest of drawers. Lights out was half past nine. We were awoken the following morning at half past five by the tolling of the bell. It was considered a fault not to leap out of bed as if on a spring, at the first sound.

One of the rules of the house was keeping silence. This did not mean only not talking; it meant not communicating in any way whatsoever, doing everything as quietly as possible. It even meant not looking up at passing aeroplanes, for example. Silence was maintained at all times, except during the vocal bits in chapel, during lessons, football, and the person doing the reading in the refectory during mealtimes. The only time we could converse was after supper in the evenings, when we walked in the grounds. Even then, we had to start with a religious topic before going on to lighter matters. Another rule was that on entering a room, one paused, did the Sign of the Cross, and said a short prayer. Posture was also very important, as was the way we did things such as moving chairs, for which both hands had to be used. Permission had to be gained for everything: talking, going into a different room, going to the lavatory etc. We had to be humble, obedient, and tactful. In short we were being groomed to live in serenity, according to strict rules.

The day started with Morning Prayer and Meditation. The meditation was carried out following a format so that it had some structure. You could stand, sit or kneel, depending on personal choice, and the battle to stay awake. The Novices were always at the front, the Scholastics (Those who had completed their Novitiate and were studying A levels before going to university) behind us, and the older Brothers at the back. It had its lighter moments. One morning one of the Novices fell asleep standing up and did a forward summersault over the pew in front. Fr D'Andria, a short fat Italian priest, celebrated Mass afterwards, always at break-neck speed, giving rise to mixed feelings of scandal and relief. The novices used to assist. One morning as Danny, as we referred to him, was standing at the centre of the altar with his hands together, waiting whilst the server walked up the altar steps to carry the Missal from one side to the other. Unfortunately, he tripped on the top step, and instead of picking the Missal up he pushed it, and it shot in front of Danny and came to a halt, miraculously exactly where it should have done. We noticed Danny's head turning as he followed its progress, without comment. The mortified server returned in confusion to the bottom of the altar steps.

Once a week before lunch we had the Particular Examen. This was more commonly referred to as Notification of Faults. It took place in the Common Room with Br Amedy sitting at the desk at the front, and the novices sitting at their desks. After a prayer we would take it in turns to walk to the front and kneel down. The other novices would then criticise him. The format was very strict: "It seems to me, my dear Brother so and so, that sometimes you, ---------"whatever the criticism was. Nobody was allowed to have more than three criticisms levelled at them before returning to their seat. Br Amedy would keep his eyes down throughout the process. Only once do I recall him looking up at one of the Novices to ask," Is this true?" to which the terrified Novice could only concur, on the basis that you were not allowed to deny anything. As a form of public humiliation it was remarkably effective, and reminds me now of methods the communists use to attain conformity.

In the afternoons we went to the chapel with Brother Philemon to perform the Little Office, which consisted of chanting a series of psalms. Unfortunately Brother Bernard, a Yorkshireman, was completely tone-deaf, and the noise he made was more reminiscent of a cow giving birth. It used to reduce us to hysterics, made all the more worse because you shouldn't laugh in church, we were all trying desperately not to laugh, so the tension was unbearable and Brother Philemon was becoming enraged by our dissipated performance. It was terrible. Even during the silences between verses you could feel the vibrations of hysterical bodies through the pew. Gradually Brother Bernard was prevailed upon to turn the volume down, and piety was restored.

The food was prepared for us by an Italian couple, and was excellent. The only downside was Friday breakfast, which instead of being cooked, was bread and cheese (no butter), eaten standing, in silence. The texts read out during meals were a lot heavier than at St Cassian's, and when there was no reading there was silence. The only exception was on Feast Days, such as Christmas, Easter, Founder's Day etc, when we followed a Sunday routine, and talking was allowed at mealtimes.

Sometimes on Saturdays we went swimming at Douai College which was a few miles away. The school had an indoor heated pool, and it was a great luxury to go there. One day I saw a body on the bottom of the pool. I dived down and pulled him to the surface. It was Brother Edmund, and he was resuscitated on the side. He said afterwards that I had saved his life, and he would pray for me every day to the end of his life. I wonder if he did, it is a nice thought.

In the evenings after supper we would go and walk in the gardens. A trick in the evening gloom was to separate from the group, put your *rabat* on back to front, and run backwards from around a tree towards the main group. The appearance was spooky, and the first time anyone did it the group nearly ran.

Early in 1964 I realised that all was not well at home. My mother used to write to me, and although she never said anything in her letters, I just knew. When I asked her, she told me that my father had left her for another woman he had met whilst on a course from St Benedict's, and that she would have to leave the home at Wokefield Park. She did not know what she was going to do, especially as Jan was only five. I decided that my duty was to leave St John's, and help out in whatever way I could. I left in tears in April 1964, saying "Goodbye" to all the other novices individually at the Common Room door.

De La Salle Novitiate 1963. Author seated far right.

Chapter Four

21 SAS

Having left the Novitiate, I went to London to live with my Mother in South Kensington. I got a job as a clerk in the City, and either walked the five miles to work each day, or ran around Hyde Park, before catching the tube. I joined the Budokwai Judo Club.

The club had been founded by Gunji Koizumi in 1918. He still used to appear in the *dojo*, teaching a small group of his friends. He was a charming old man, and in his spare time was advisor on Japanese ceramics to the British Museum. We were stunned to hear in 1965 that he had killed himself by pulling a polythene bag over his head because he did not wish to become a burden. The chief instructor there was Kisaburo Watanabe. He was a fifth Dan black belt, and a former All-Japan champion and Asian Games champion. He was very powerfully built, and demanded aggression from his students. If you tried hard enough, and if your technique was correct, he would allow you to throw him. Part of the etiquette in judo is that the junior grade approaches the senior grade to request *randori* (practice). It is the senior grade who determines how long the *randori* goes on for, never the other way round. One evening, while I was there a visitor to the club, a Brown Belt wearing a dirty outfit, approached Watanabe for *randori*. We noticed him, not just because he was a stranger, but because of his dirty clothes and startlingly, he was so casual in his approach to Watanabe. He just wasn't making any effort, which was insulting. To cap it all, when he had had enough, he bowed, signifying the end of the *randori*. Watanabe was having none of it. He grabbed him back and indicated that he should continue. He wouldn't. Watanabe then gave us a demonstration of all the techniques in the book. All other *randori* stopped, as Watanabe went through his paces with the Brown Belt. I don't know how long it went on for, but at the end of it, with the Brown Belt almost unable to move, Watanabe stepped back, bowed with a beaming smile, and left the *dojo*. We never saw the Brown Belt again. So far as I knew, Watanabe never spoke English. All his instructions were by sign. One occasion he was demonstrating an arm-lock on the mat. I was the subject. When he was satisfied with his demonstration he indicated that I should try and get out of it. I arched my back, slipped out of his hold and stood up. Watanabe's face was always inscrutable, but I saw a flicker of disbelief. He repeated the hold, this time more fiercely. Same result. That was how he discovered that I had very supple shoulders. I enjoyed judo, and went to the Budokwai five evenings a week. However, another, more time-consuming interest took my fancy.

In 1964 the Territorial Army ran a recruitment program for all the TA units in the London area. I was at a bit of a loose end, so I sent away for further details. There were lists of all the units, and the two which attracted my attention were the Intelligence Corps, and 21st Special Air Service Regiment (Artists) TA. I had never heard of the latter, so, out of curiosity I asked for further information. In due course I was directed to the Artist's Rifles drill hall in Dukes Road, Euston. I was immediately attracted by the bustle of activity, the photographs of parachuting, canoeing, and rock climbing, so I enlisted.

The selection course started in January 1965, and finished in May. 75 hopefuls started, and 18 were accepted for further training. At the very beginning we were taken to the Artist's hut at Bisley and taught the basics – how to wear a uniform, build a *basha* (A Malay word for Bivvy) etc. The Regimental Sergeant Major (RSM) was Jesse James, a ferociously hard looking Liverpudlian. We were formed up into three ranks and he gave his address. One of the things he said I have never forgotten. "You men are assembled here to try to join the best regiment in the British Army, probably the best regiment in the world. You are supposed to terrify the Russians, but right now some of you lot wouldn't frighten the cock off a chocolate mouse." We were in silent hysterics, but dared not show it. Jesse had a knack with words. Years later I was standing with him on a pavement waiting for a Land Rover to come and pick us up. A hippy came along on a bicycle, towing a small trailer, with a cat balanced on his shoulders. Jesse watched him go by in silence. Then "Look at that. His hair is so fxxxxxg long he's not got lice, he's got mice!" On another occasion, I had upset him about something or other and he said "Sibley, if you don't stop fxxxxxg about I'll put this stick up your arse and eat you like a lollypop"!

During the final test week in the Brecon Beacons I arrived at the penultimate RV (Rendezvous), planning to pause for an apple and a mug of tea. I noticed that one of those doing this selection as a warm up for the regular selection, and one of the PSI's (Permanent Staff Instructor who later became Squadron Sergeant Major in D Sqn. during my time there, and later still became a Beefeater at the Tower of London) were about to set off. I knew they would tab fast, so I decided to accompany them. They set off at a cracking pace, and I was hard put just keeping up with them. My previous map study told me that we were heading in the right direction, so I rarely referred to the map. After about an hour of this, we reached the brow of a hill, and a long wide valley opened up below us. They paused and I slumped. The PSI noticed that I had not looked at my map – a heinous sin in the SAS, because everyone is supposed to know exactly where they are at any given moment. "Where are we Sibley?" he barked. I looked up across the valley, and about 3 kilometres away I spotted a castle I recognised. I had read an historical novel about it ten years previously, and there had been a pen and ink sketch of it in the front. I said "See that castle? That's Carreg Cennen". He looked at his map. "So it is. Well done, young Sibley". I told him this several years later – "If I had known, I would have failed you there and then."

At the end of the final test week in Brecon, we were told that the Royal Horse Artillery were parachuting onto Sennybridge Ranges, with all their heavy equipment, so we went to watch. It was a hot, sunny day, and we lay on the grass and watched as the Beverleys and Hastings came over dropping Land Rovers, field guns and soldiers. I had never seen military parachuting before, and lay there taking photographs. I noticed that shortly after each soldier jumped out of the aircraft, he dropped his equipment, which was suspended some twenty feet below him. One of them did not drop his equipment, and he seemed to be falling a lot faster than anyone else. I took photographs of him. He hit the ground about a hundred yards away with a thump like a sack of potatoes, and a cloud of dust flew up. For a moment there was stunned silence, and then the Drop Zone staff ran over to him. After a few minutes one of them came back and asked if anyone had a camera. I had the only camera, so I was told to go over and take pictures. He was lying on his back, and seemed very short. There was an abrasion on his left cheek, and he was very pale. His left hand was still across his reserve parachute, a position I later found to be the exit position for leaving the aircraft. I photographed him and the knot in his rigging lines. I was then told to hand over the film, and I subsequently made a statement for the Court of Inquiry. I never got my film back, which was a shame, because I had other pictures on it which I had wanted. The finding of the court was that the centre base tie of the new PX parachute had snapped too soon, which had enabled the canopy to develop before the rigging lines deployed, causing them to knot. Had he looked up as he jumped, and checked his parachute, he would have been aware of this, and could have used his reserve.

In September the same year I was sent to No 1 Parachute Training School at Abingdon. I did my first jump on my 19th birthday, and completed the course. Some years later, listening to some PJIs (Parachute Jump Instructors) talking about the PX fatality, they said that the people who had witnessed it were given special treatment during their parachute courses. I racked my brains for some time trying to think what special treatment I had been given, and then I remembered.

It was a misty morning at Weston on the Green, the dew was on the grass, and the RAF ground crew were wearing green anoraks. The balloon was tethered to the ground, and beneath it was suspended a rectangular wicker basket with a canvas roof. A few yards away, the winch lorry was parked, the crew standing around it. We drew parachutes from a Bedford truck nearby, took them out of their cardboard boxes, and fitted them. We were organised into "sticks" of four men each, and ordered into the basket. We hooked our static lines onto the strong point inside, and then the single metal bar, which served as a gate was shut across the entrance. The dispatcher called out "Balloon 800 feet, four men jumping". This was echoed by the ground crew, and with a lurch, the balloon rose into the sky. It stopped with a jerk at 800 feet, and all was silent. The dispatcher opened the gate, called the first man forward, "Stand in the door!" and checked his static line. "Goooo!", and with a slap on the shoulder, the first man leaped out, causing the basket to lurch. I was last to jump, and, standing in the door, in the exit position, with my right hand on the door frame, and my left across the top of my reserve, staring ahead, I heard the dispatcher say "We are all alone up here. It's just you and me. Give us a kiss darling." As I turned to look at him in horror, he bellowed "Goooo!" in my ear, slapped me on the shoulder, and out I went without a second thought. That was the special treatment!

I parachuted whenever possible and by the time my army career was over had logged over 400 jumps. Most were at night with equipment. These were excruciating, because they entailed being up all day, then trying to stay awake by drinking coffee which caused indigestion. We would draw and fit parachutes, only to be told by the Crabs (RAF) that the jump was delayed or cancelled. The walk out to the aircraft was exhausting, wearing a 28 pound main parachute, a 14b pound reserve, and carrying over 80 pounds of equipment (Bergen rucksack, rifle, belt kit) on your shoulders. Everything dug in, and it was a relief to jump out of the aircraft into the cold night air. Collisions with other jumpers were frequent because of the speed of exit due to the need to land close together. Sometimes it was just bumping into each others rigging lines, but if you finished up walking across somebody else's canopy it could be more dangerous because inevitably the canopies would collapse alternately as they stole each other's air, and whoever hit the ground first would be injured. I jumped out of transport aircraft, helicopters and balloons. I liked balloon jumping the best because they were always during the day, without equipment. I used to ask the Dispatcher if I could dispatch myself (ie, no order to jump being given – just stepping out when I chose) I enjoyed the falling sensation, and both hearing and feeling the nylon ties in my parachute pack snapping as it deployed. Parachuting into water was tricky because it entailed unclipping the harness whilst in flight, and the moment your feet hit the water you slipped out of it, arching your back like a banana so as to resurface away from the canopy as it settled. There have been instances when parachutists misjudged their height over water and fell several hundred feet to their deaths.

In the summer of 1966 I was at a bit of a loose end, so I joined a Temp agency. They sent me to the Shell head office on the south bank of the Thames. They had a copying department, and the sole operative had not been on leave for a long time. He trained me for a week on the big copiers, what chemicals to use, in what proportions etc. The following week he sat and watched me operating the system, and on Friday 10th June he went on extended leave abroad. That same evening I went on Exercise "Sailor Girl". This was a parachuting exercise, emplaning into a Beverley transport at RAF Brize Norton, and jumping out in the early hours of the Saturday morning over DZ (Drop Zone) Fox Covert on Salisbury Plain. When I hit the ground, I felt a stab of pain in my right ankle. When I tried to stand, it hurt even more, and I heard and felt the crepitus, as the bones grated. I sat down again quickly, pulled my parachute around me to keep warm, and waited to be found. I had landed across a rutted track, and the ground was baked hard. In due course I was found, and loaded onto the DZ Land Rover ambulance with another casualty, and transported to the British Military Hospital (BMH) at Tidworth, where I was

X-rayed, and went straight to Theatre. When I awoke in the ward the following morning there was a large plaster cast on my right leg, and I was told that I had sustained a "Pott's" fracture. On investigating my bed space I noticed that I had been prescribed Pethidine, for pain. I immediately complained of pain, and was rewarded with an injection which quickly transported me through the clouds. When I woke up on the Sunday morning, I washed and shaved, put on my uniform shirt, trousers, stable belt, and one boot, and hopped around the ward, visiting the other patients. The ward sister came in. "You are incorrectly dressed". "No I'm not". "Yes you are. All walking wounded wear a white shirt, not a khaki one". "I haven't got a white shirt". "Oh yes you have. You were issued with one on admission". "No I wasn't. I was admitted in the small hours, and the Stores weren't open". "Either get correctly dressed, or get back into bed". Recognising defeat at the hands of a lunatic, I retired to bed. That afternoon, Yank, one of the PSIs from 21 SAS, and Jesse James, came to see me. I said "You have got to get me out of here, there are all mad". Jesse went and distracted the ward staff, while Yank helped me out into a Land Rover, and took me back to London. The staff at Tidworth were very upset about this, and complained, but to no avail. The following day I phoned up the Temp agency and told them. I don't think they believed me, and it must have cost Shell to hire someone from Rank Xerox to operate their machines. I presented myself at St Georges Hospital, Hyde Park Corner for further treatment. After I had broken my cast twice, by running around on it, they gave up, put me into a support bandage, and told me to report twice a week for physiotherapy. It was during one of these sessions that the physio, an attractive redhead, asked me how I had done it. I told her. She said "Oh, my brother was hurt parachuting. He landed on his head". I burst out laughing, because 'landing on your head' is an expression for whiplash injury following a fast back landing, but she had taken it literally. "It wasn't funny. He was seriously hurt" she said as she rotated my foot through 360 degrees. I recovered uneventfully and went on exercise with the Regiment in Germany in July and September.

In November I received a letter from BMH Millbank, referring to my claim for residual disability, and inviting me to attend for an examination. I was intrigued, because I had not claimed; I had made a full recovery. I turned up on a cold frosty day, wearing slacks and a roll-neck pullover. I was directed to a door, which I knocked, and was called in. It was a long room, with a brown, highly polished lino floor. At the end was a table with three Lieutenant Colonels sitting at it. I walked down the room and greeted them. The middle one said coldly "I hardly think you are correctly dressed to attend an interview". I replied naively "Oh, I am sorry. I didn't think you wanted to interview me. I thought you only wanted to look at my leg." The other two burst out laughing, and the ice was broken. They completed the examination, agreed that I was very fit, and sent me on my way. I thought that was the end of it, but a month later I received a letter putting me on six months half pay, even though I was back at my civilian job.

In January 1967 there was an exercise in Norway. I remember it particularly because the entry was to be a night parachute drop onto a frozen marsh. We had to wear heavy parkas for the jump, because of the risk of anybody injured freezing to death. When the green light came on I jumped out of the Argosy into the freezing night air. As usual I had my head back, watching the rigging lines and parachute deploy. As soon as they had done so I checked below and dropped my CSPEP (Carrying Straps Personal Equipment Parachutist) and immediately hit deep snow. Instead of the usual 1,000 feet, we must have jumped at about 400 feet. The walk off the DZ was exhausting because, with over a hundred-weight on my back, the snow crust was firm enough to enable me to step up onto it, take my weight, before breaking through and going down 18 inches. Every step. The marsh was dotted with frozen fir trees. Several of the other's Bergen rucksacks had hit these and split irreparably, putting their owners out of the exercise. They were lucky that they hadn't hit them themselves. Speaking to the aircrew after the exercise, they told us that our Argosy had bits of pine tree in the engine cowlings when they landed from the trees on the high ground around the marsh.

In February 1967 I went to Malaya to do my jungle training. The training camp was near Grik in northern Malaya, and was run by the RSM, known as "Gloom". The only time I ever saw him smile was when he was giving an order which he knew would entail someone suffering. He later committed suicide – by hanging, I believe. One of many pieces of equipment I was introduced to was "Drawers Dracula". These were green linen boxer shorts. They had a draw cord instead of elastic, because that perishes in the jungle. They had buttons at the front, and proportionately they had a tiny waist, large backside and skinny leg holes. One of the unkindest things that could be said of someone was that their Drawers Dracula fitted them. Having said that, I don't think anyone actually wore them - I never did. After jungle training we went on a training operation. That meant a consolidation exercise in an area known to be still used by communist terrorists (CTs), so we carried five magazines of ball ammunition for our rifles. Our patrol consisted of Lord M, Robbo, Jack and myself. We flew to Fort Kemar, and our patrol was to be a circular one to the South West of Kemar. On the 6th day we reached the summit of Gunong Ulu Sepat, shown as 7091 feet high on the map. At the summit we found the remains of some old *bashas* (Bivvies). Some years previously a mountain survey team had visited by helicopter, escorted by the Malayan Special Branch. They had left a large blue flag with SB in white on it. I considered that I had the greater right to it, having walked there, so I took it. The following afternoon, coming off the mountain by the north-east ridge, Robbo was lead scout. He indicated that the way ahead was blocked. Lord M was tired and irritable, and pushed past him, only to fall down a fifty foot cliff, which was what Robbo had been trying to tell him. We climbed down to him, and found that he was unconscious, and had a deep laceration by his eye. We made him comfortable while Jack tried to get through on the radio which Lord M had been carrying. It was damaged, so no contact was made. We decided that Robbo and Jack would walk out to Fort Kemar to get help, and I would stay with Lord M. By this stage he was semi-conscious and moving all limbs, so we put him in a hammock, and Robbo and Jack departed. That night I sat by Lord M to make sure he didn't wander off. The following morning he was awake, but had lost his memory. Later that day he remembered who he was, but did not know what he had been doing. We were on a slope by an old *ladang* (cultivated clearing). On the basis that I expected to be rescued by helicopter, I started clearing an LZ (Landing Zone). That night I sat by Lord M as he started at his very earliest memories and talked me through his life, in an attempt to regain his recent memory. Afterwards people said I should have told him he was Trooper Sibley and I was Lord M! After the second night I was very tired, and continued working on the LZ. About mid morning I saw some movement at the far side of the *ladang*, about a hundred yards away – brown men in green uniforms. CTs! (Communist Terrorists) I dropped into a firing position and waited until I had a clear shot. The third man out into the *ladang* was wearing a British Army shirt. I recognised our doctor. What a huge relief. The brown men were Gurkhas. Very shortly afterwards I heard a helicopter approaching. Lord M and I were winched out, - so much for my LZ! I was dropped off at Fort Kemar, while Lord M went to the military hospital at Butterworth. I didn't think any more of it, and continued with the trip.

On my return to the UK, I decided to go and see the new HQ. 21 SAS had moved from Dukes Road to the Duke of York's in King's Road. I was wearing shorts and a tee shirt. When I walked in the Adjutant was aghast – "Why aren't you properly dressed?" "What for?" "Didn't you get the letter?" "What letter?" Jesse James was retiring as RSM of 21 SAS, and was being presented with a ceremonial sword at a reception. At the same time, I was to be presented with the Green Tie for "having saved Lord M's life" It was very embarrassing going onto the stage in front of a lot of people in dinner jackets, wearing shorts and a tee shirt. I scuttled off as fast as I could. The Green Tie is a legacy from the Artist's Rifles, and is normally only given for such things as ten years undetected crime in the stores. I am pleased to be able to wear it, but I only did what I was supposed to have done.

Following all this excitement I went to stay with my mother in Chelsea. She had been having a bit of a problem. A restaurant had opened in King's Road, not far from her. Their telephone number was one digit removed from hers. She repeatedly received phone calls intended for the restaurant. Not only that, but when she told the callers they had the wrong number, they were frequently rude, and asked her for the correct number. She had complained to the management, to no avail. I took several of these calls. "You'd like a table Sir? For eight people? Friday night? Nine o'clock? On the balcony? Certainly Sir. We look forward to seeing you." It must have caused mayhem and they changed their number shortly afterwards.

Chapter Five

R Squadron 22 SAS

In 1967 R Squadron was formed. This was part of 22 SAS, and was intended to support the regulars as and when required. I joined as a founder member. We had to do the test week of selection again, after which we were in. R Squadron had its headquarters at Bradbury Lines, in Hereford, and all our training was done from there, instead of London.

In August 1967 there was an exercise in Alberta, Canada, the enemy being provided by Princess Patricia's Canadian Light Infantry. We appalled them on the first morning by walking straight across their parade ground to the cook house (Regular regiments consider the parade ground to be the Holy of Holies). We didn't have the chance to do it again because the following day we went off on exercise. I was the patrol signaller, and I was infuriated to find that one of the other patrol signallers always failed to 'listen out' before broadcasting. In effect this meant that if I was on the air he would blank out my message, and I would have to repeat it – a needless time-consuming exercise when you are in a hurry. I had my revenge though. We reached our laying up point two days early. I kept my radio-set open all day, and each time I heard this signaller opening up I just leaned on my morse key. It took him hours to send messages, and the rest of his patrol nearly lynched him.

The PPCLI were excellent hosts, and laid on a magnificent barbecue for us at the end of the exercise. Before leaving for the UK we went on a brief tour of the area, which took in the Athabasca Glacier and Calgary. The coach which carried us to the glacier did not have enough power to get up the hills, and we had to get out and push it. They also tried to educate us by visiting the Edmonton Opera House, of which they were obviously very proud, but it was wasted on us.

In February 1968 I went with a regular squadron to Sharjah in the United Arab Emirates for a desert exercise and boat training. Dubai was only just down the road so we paid it a visit. At that time it just consisted of the creek, a few small shops, and a traffic island with a clock on it comprised of three flying buttresses. It looked bizarre at the time because it appeared to be in the middle of nowhere. Now, of course it is in the middle of one of the most fantastic developments in the world. The boat training took place at Khawr Fakkan, on the east coast. The journey took eight hours, standing up in a Bedford three ton truck. Standing, because the state of the track made sitting impossible. It is now a dual-carriageway, and our campsite at Khawr Fakkan is now host to a power station. The subsequent exercise took place in the Wadi al Jizzi. We were the enemy to the Trucial Oman Scouts, who were mounting an 'invasion' up the wadi from the coast. I chiefly remember it for the awful food. We had been told to buy our own rations, there being none available for us. I had chosen mainly corned beef, which I found most unsuitable in that hot climate.

Later that year I left my job as a clerk, and started at Hopwood Hall, a teacher training college run by the De La

Salle Brothers. My intention was to study for a Batchelor of Education degree in Physics and Biology. At the same time I was offered a place on the French military free fall parachute course at Pau. There were eleven from 22 SAS, sixteen Paras, and two Cambodians and a Swiss who joined us at Pau. We travelled by train from London to Paris, where we were accommodated in the Rue du Faubourg St Honoré for a few days before carrying on down to Pau. I had a list of places I wanted to visit, and methodically ticked them off. One day I was standing under the Arc de Triomphe when I bumped into Jock T. He wanted to know where the Metro was. I said I would ask someone. He refused. He would find out himself. He approached a typical French looking couple, she in tartan skirt and white blouse, he in slacks, shirt and black beret. In his broad Scottish accent he asked "Excuse me, but d'ye speak Anglash?" She said "Aye, A do." They were both Scots!

We continued down to Pau by train. I had brought my racing bike, for which I didn't have a ticket. The ticket inspector demanded to see a ticket for it. When he realised that I didn't have one, that I was English, and that I was a soldier with no French, he gave up. In fact, my French wasn't bad. On the basis that I had failed O level French at school, I had been made course interpreter, but he wasn't to know that.

We were all sergeants for the purposes of the course. This was to give us better accommodation than we would otherwise have been given. We had three instructors who were all very experienced free fallers, regularly doing several jumps a day from the squadron of Noratlas transport aircraft at their disposal (and under their control, unlike the UK, where the Crabs (RAF) reign supreme, giving the Army a dog's life). Every day would start off with PT of some kind, usually trampoline work to develop flight skills, or a cross country run. We were fitter than they were, and after the first couple of runs, when we had got to know the area, we would run past them, much to their annoyance and shouting, and get back to camp before them.

We did three jumps a day, two in the morning and one in the afternoon. They would observe us in flight, and at the *critique* on the ground afterwards, would fine us for our errors. Half the kitty went into a Friday lunchtime booze up, before the weekend. The cumulative other-halves went into a fund for a grand, end-of-course booze up. I was the only person on the course never to have free-fallen before. On my first two jumps I let go of my ripcord handle *(Poignée)*. The first time I didn't even notice until the French pointed it out and fined me. The second time, I remembered just as I let go, and watched distraught as it described a delicate arc through the air. Although I didn't repeat it, they referred to me as *Paul la Poignée* after that. Early on, the French discovered that I was a student. They had just had huge student riots in Paris in which considerable damage had been done and the security services called out. They were intrigued that they were training a student military free fall parachuting – were they going to attack from the skies next?

We noticed that the French trainee parachutists marched out to their aircraft singing martial songs with great gusto. We were amused to see them afterwards, hobbling miserably back, in silence. They seemed to have a high casualty rate. There was a hospital on the camp. The patients were all in plaster, and seemed to be very happy – probably because they couldn't jump. This was at a time when the French Paras were not allowed to wear their red berets – they had to wear a khaki canvas thing instead. This had been De Gaulle's punishment for their rebellion in Algeria and they didn't like it at all.

I decided to jump with my camera one day. I jumped,

pulled my rip cord, took out my camera and started clicking away. I made no attempt to steer towards the DZ – I was too busy. When I saw the ground coming up I realised that I would have to put the camera away but I didn't know which way I was going to land, so I attached it to my reserve parachute hook, and tucked it underneath. Due to my inattention, I came in for a fast back landing. As I rolled over I was smashed between the eyes, and felt the blood run immediately. It was my camera, which had swung up on its strap, and clobbered me. I was being dragged, so I rolled over and took another picture. At the *critique* the French told me off for not having my harness tight enough, supposing that it had been my altimeter and chronometer which had struck me, and fined me more. Had they known the real cause, it would have been tripled.

Many rubber bands were used in parachute packing, and they lay about all over the place. The French rolled them up to make hard rubber balls about the size of cricket balls, and then bounce them off the Noratlas wings. One rainy day, waiting for a jump, we did the same. Half a dozen of these things bouncing between the wings and ground had the whole aircraft shuddering. Had that been the RAF, the aircraft would have been grounded for a complete overhaul, and we would have been court-martialled, whereas the French didn't appear to mind.

We jumped during the day, we jumped at night, and we jumped into water. At night we had to carry navigation lights, because technically we became aircraft in our own right. We jumped into one of the lakes at Lourdes, which wasn't far away. When I reached the shore I saw that there were coach loads of pilgrims, all with something severely wrong with them. I thought it a bit sick, seeing the contrast between them and us. An Irish tour guide asked me, in French, if we were French

Foreign Legion. I told her that we were, which made her happy. I hope she didn't find out the truth.

We spent our weekends at Biarritz, just down the road. We were given French Army haversack rations, and they were brilliant – a *baton*, butter, paté, salami, fruit and a bottle of rough red wine. If that's what they carry to war it's no wonder they keep losing.

On one of the free weekends I cycled to Spain. The road zigzagged steadily up over the Pyrenées, and took me half a day. It was quite chilly at the border-point on the summit, so I went into a Spanish café, where I had a coffee and the worst piece of chocolate I have ever eaten. I barely touched the pedals on my way back to Pau, travelling at warp 9.

On the last day of the course there was a lunch party. The French free-fall heroes of yesteryear were there. The drinking was horrendous. We were to travel back to Paris afterwards, by train, in uniform. I was smashed, and lay down on my bed to wait for the coach. Curiously enough, I didn't feel sick or dizzy. However, after boarding the coach to go to Pau station, I began to feel my gorge rising. I desperately kept it under control, and when the coach stopped in the car park I leaped off, looking for somewhere to be sick in private. I spotted a French army truck. I marched briskly towards it, reached it, and as I walked behind it there was a pretty French girl sitting in a car. She saw me coming and gave me a lovely smile. As she did so, I vomited. When I had finished I smiled weakly at her white face, and marched off. Can't have done much for her self-confidence.

John Ridgway and Chay Blyth had been the first people to row across the Atlantic Ocean in 1966. On his return, Ridgway had set up an adventure school at Ardmore, in Sutherland, on the northwest coast of Scotland. A friend of mine, Richard was helping him set it up, and he invited me to go up there and help. I took the train up to Lairg, put on my skis, and set about walking/skiing the fifty miles or so to Ardmore. The weather conditions were good, but there was thick snow on the ground, and the going was slow. I was running out of time, so I decided to cheat and caught the mail coach to Rhiconich, just down the road from Ardmore. The school itself was at the end of a rough track by the loch, and at that stage consisted of a large wooden hut with bunks and washing facilities. That is where Richard and I slept. Close by lived Rod and his wife Jeannie, in a converted wooden double garage. One half was the kitchen/living area, the other half their bedroom. The only access was through the kitchen. Outside and separate, was another garage, used as a store and the location of the chemical lavatory. The Ridgways lived in a croft on the other side of the loch. It was bitterly cold, and we didn't get very much work done. Jeannie very kindly cooked for us, and every morning saw us gathered in the cramped kitchen trying to keep warm, clouds of condensation hanging in the air, as Jeannie fried our breakfast. One morning, Jeannie had gone outside to the other garage. A little while later the door crashed open and Jeanie was standing there, her clothes in disarray, blue with cold. I looked down and carried on eating, to give her a chance to get dressed. After what seemed an age I looked up again. Not much had changed; she was too cold to move. I looked away again, as Rod, seeing what was happening, stepped adroitly over to shield her from my gaze. Richard had his back to all this, and afterwards asked me what had been going on. When I told him, he said "You are hallucinating. You've been up here too long already." The next day we swapped chairs. Jeannie went out. After a while the door crashed open, and I could tell by Richard's discomfiture that the scene was being repeated.

A few miles away lived a retired Army major with his wife.

They invited us round for tea. They had a croft with a fine view of the sea, and he had retired there because he was convinced that the Communist Chinese were going to invade Europe via northwest Scotland, and he spent hours every day looking out for them.

Richard and I decided to go for a walk for a few days. Foinaven wasn't far away, and was covered in deep snow. We spent the first night in a snow-hole, and the second in a nylon mountain shelter I had bought to try out. Unfortunately it produced huge amounts of condensation which ran down the sides, soaking every thing in its path. We spent most of the night mopping it up with a large sponge I had brought, suspecting that condensation may be a problem. The following morning we decided we had had enough of the great outdoors, and decided to return. We were walking across the frozen bog towards the A838. We were within a couple of hundred yards of the road. We were tired, and talking about going to the Kinlochbervie Hotel for a bath, when, to our dismay, we came across a fast-running stream running parallel with the road. There was no way around it. We would have to cross it. We determined to do so without getting wet. We decided we could just about jump it. We stamped out a ten yard runway in the snow, and threw our bergens over to the other side. Richard insisted I went first. I did a mighty run-up and hurled myself into space. I just reached the other side, buried my ice-axe in the snow, and slowly, agonizingly sat slowly back into the stream. Richard was in hysterics. I was cold and wet, but it didn't matter too much at that stage because we were so close to home. It was Richard's turn. I undertook to stand on the bank to make sure he didn't do what I had just done. He made his mighty leap, and got there. I grabbed hold of him, as promised, and pushed him back in, which I hadn't. I wasn't going to be the only wet one. Richard cursed me all the way back to Ardmore. I reluctantly returned to Hereford shortly afterwards, missing Rod and Jeannie's kind hospitality in difficult circumstances.

The following summer, Ridgway was running one of his management development courses. The first week would involve the candidates undertaking an outdoor exercise. Richard suggested I might like to help. I arrived by train at Lairg again, and this time decided to walk the whole distance to Ardmore. I camped by the Overscaig Hotel on Loch Shin, and the midges were terrible. Outside I had to keep a face-veil on to stop them flying up my nose, and the entry to the bar was surrounded by cans of aerosol for the use of people coming in. The exercise, when it started, had some aspects similar to the SAS selection process. The pleasurable part for me was that I was carrying a pocket-full of brown envelopes, to be handed out at certain map references at certain times. My job, it transpired was to be the Jonah. Whenever the candidates saw me I was carrying bad news for them. This meant that I could spend most of the week out by myself in the mountains, popping up only when required. The down-side, was that towards the end I think some of them wanted to kill me before I could hand out the brown envelope.

In July 1969 I went back to Malaya for further training, which started with an exercise. The briefing took place at Grik camp in the north of the country. The camp was composed of large wooden *bashas* (Huts) thatched with palm. The windows were large voids which could be closed with shutters when it rained. The Second-in-Command of the Regiment was to give the briefing. A tall eccentric man, we were sitting in the *basha* waiting for him. He strode in without a word and started rearranging everything on the table at the front. Suddenly he stopped said "It is much too hot in here." and walked out. We rose to follow him "Not you, me." he said.

We sat down again. He popped up at one of the windows and started to speak, then disappeared and popped up at another, and so the briefing went on.

We had been in the jungle for about ten days when we received a signal telling us to go to a certain RV (Rendezvous) by a given time, shaven. We were furious. We were in the middle of a beard-growing contest, and the thought of having to start all over again was galling. It turned out that the General Officer Commanding UK Land Forces in Malaysia was visiting with his entourage. They were accompanied by our RSM, Tanky Smith. The first thing I noticed, apart from their red tabs, was that none of them were armed, except for Tanky, who was carrying an Armalite. As they walked across the *ladang* I heard the general say to him "Sergeant-Major, you are carrying that weapon as though it was part of you." Tanky eyed him balefully for a moment, "So it should be Sir. So it should be."

Following the exercise I joined a jungle tracking course which I thoroughly enjoyed. The chief instructor was a Maori, and he taught us how to glean an enormous amount of information just from the signs that people leave behind them. Near our camp site was a large melon patch. As soon as we realised it was there nobody bothered to track their quarry from the camp – we knew where they had gone – the melons! We would pick up the trail on the other side of the melon patch. After a week's training there was a week-long exercise, tracking a group of 'terrorists' from the supposed site of an ambush. I have never forgotten what I learned, and still practice it now when I have the chance.

We were staying near a *kampong* (Aboriginal village), when we were told that the aborigines were going to have a dance that night. We watched as they split eight inch diameter bamboos until they could be unfolded into a sheet. They tied these onto a bamboo frame they had made, and then started dancing on it to a rhythm made by other abos banging pieces of bamboo cut to different lengths so as to produce different notes. I had been told to bring the patrol medical pack with me, but not why. The dancing went on for hours, and, becoming bored, got ready to go. I was persuaded not to, and then realised why. One of the abos appeared to have a fit, and was lying on the bamboo stage with his feet drumming on the bamboo. Several others went and inhaled his breath, and then they fitted. The edges of freshly cut bamboo are as sharp as razor-blades, and it wasn't long before there were multiple lacerations which we spent the rest of the night stitching.

At the end of the trip, four of us went to Kuala Lumpur for a day before boarding a train to Singapore. That was a lovely journey, travelling the length of Malaya sedately in an open-windowed carriage, drinking freshly crushed sugar-cane juice. At Singapore we were put into a transit camp at Nee Soon. We went out on the town, starting with the 'Brit' Club. The Britannia club was a club for members of the armed services. It had a swimming pool and a dance-hall with bar, and a restaurant. During the day, families would go there, but in the evenings it became largely the preserve of the animals. When we arrived, the bar was full of British and American sailors. The air was quite tense. The Americans were mainly from a destroyer flotilla which had come down from Viet Nam for some Rest and Recuperation. American ships are 'dry', that is, they do not have alcohol on board, and it showed. The six of us settled down at a low table with our Tiger beers and watched as the arguments developed into scuffles and then fist fights. When I went downstairs to the lavatory I found two Americans. One had his friend's head trapped under his arm. "Don't make me do it, John." And then smashed his head into the taps. He did this repeatedly. I couldn't work out what it was he didn't want him to do, so I left them to it, since they seemed to be enjoying themselves. When I got back upstairs there were fights going on all over the place. From where we were sitting we could see the swing doors, with their glass windows. We saw the arrival of the British and American Shore Patrols. The Americans were wearing steel helmets, and they all carried long batons. They were looking through the windows assessing the situation. We realised we would have to get out, but how, without getting a battering. Suddenly, the doors swung open, and one of the Brits came through. He was about seven feet tall and three inches in diameter, built like a drain-pipe. He blew his whistle. Some in the seething mob glanced up, but he was ignored. Next, the doors swung open again, and another Brit rushed in. He was a fearsome-looking creature, about five feet high and five feet wide. He had a huge, black, curly beard, and looked like a cave-man on a rampage. He was followed by the rest of the Shore Patrols charging in with batons drawn. Lew, our Troop Sergeant, reacted quickly. "Squad, on parade! Right turn! Quick march! Left! Left! Left Right! Left!" We marched briskly out and the Shore Patrols parted to allow us through, dumb-struck. When we reached the doors we legged it, before they realised what had happened. We got into rickshaws, and bribed the drivers to jump the traffic lights in a competition to get to Bugis Street first. Sadly, Bugis Street is now closed. This was an ordinary shopping area, but in the evening the shops closed and the pavements became covered with tables and chairs. The place was alive with people eating and drinking. In the crowd were the 'Kytais'. These were transsexual prostitutes. They could be identified in the distance by their incredible beauty, and close to by their deep voices. They were a lot of fun, and enjoyed banter. There were the shoe shine boys who actually did shine shoes, but their main source of income was noughts and crosses. They would challenge you to a game for ten cents. They would win the first game. You would see how they won it, and force them to a draw in the second game. They would win the third game using a different technique, and so on. As the money gradually drained through your fingers you learned all their techniques. When they realised this they would pack up and find some other mug. While I was there I was told that a restaurant called Zam Zams was worth a visit for a curry. Several of us went, and I ordered a chicken curry. When it came it was a leg. Judging from the size of it that chicken had stood four feet high! Clearly it was dog.

When we returned to the Brit Club the following night, it had been tidied up as if nothing had happened. The Americans were still there, but more peaceful. I was coming out of the lavatory with a friend, who hadn't washed his hands. An American in there noticed this and said "Didn't you Momma teach you to wash you hands after you've Been?" To which he replied "No. She taught me not to piss all over them in the first place."

In the jungle, malaria is a significant problem. For this reason we had to take Paludrine (an anti-malarial tablet) daily. We were responsible for taking our own, anyone going down with malaria being RTU'd (Returned to unit) as punishment. The rest of the Army had to attend a 'Paludrine Parade' every morning, when they took their tablets. I have no recollection of this, but after our night out, having returned to camp very well-oiled, we were sleeping in when the Transit Camp RSM burst through the door screeching "You have missed Paludrine Parade". I apparently rolled over, opened one eye and said "So f*****g what", rolled over and went back to sleep. He went purple, but never bothered us again. In the cook house, every table had a bowl in the middle of it containing salt tablets, vitamin tablets, Paludrine and contraceptives. They were

Durex Gossamer, and on the packing was a notice – "Don't leave this lying about in parks and streets it offends people"! I kept one as a souvenir.

One of the aspects of working in the jungle is that you have two sets of clothes. One for day, the other for night. The reason is that during the day your clothes get saturated with rain and sweat. You cannot sleep well in wet clothes, especially as it gets cold at night in the rain forest. When you have got your *basha* up, rigged your hammock and generally got sorted, you change into your dry set and go to bed. At some stage during the night as it gets cold, you will want a pee. But you mustn't get your clothes wet, so you pee over the side of your hammock, having made sure before you went to bed to put all your kit out of the way. In the morning you put on your freezing cold wet kit, and a new day starts.

At the end of this tour, a friend, Steve invited me to go home to his parent's house. We arrived there at about eleven o'clock at night. It was a big, well appointed house, and his parents had waited up for us. His mother had prepared a delicious meal, which we thoroughly enjoyed, having been living on army rations for the previous couple of months. When bed time came it was agreed that I should sleep in Steve's brother's room, as he was away. It was a lovely room, with all his things in it. The bed had an electric blanket – the first time I had ever slept with one.

The following morning I awoke early. I had thought I was still in the jungle, and when the call of nature came, had rolled over and pee'd in the bed. I was in misery, having moved to one side of the bed. I lay there trying to think of an excuse, to no avail. Eventually I gave up, realising that I would have to own up and offer to pay for the damage. While I was waiting for some sounds of movement in the house, I lay there and examined the room from right to left. It was immaculate, and all his things were neatly displayed; model aeroplanes, books, posters etc. When I reached the wall to the left of the bed I was surprised to notice an area of devastated plaster with two rawlplugs sticking out of it. I looked at it and wondered, since it was so out of keeping with the rest of the room. Then I remembered. I had woken in the night and seen something glowing. Thinking it was an insect; I had hit it and stuffed it down by the side of the bed. Unfortunately it was the control for the electric blanket. Misery heaped upon misery. I heard a sound out on the landing and went out. It was Steve. "Steve, I have an apology to make." I began. "No you haven't." he said. "I know what you have done. So have I." I told him about the wall, and offered to pay. He would have none of it. "I'll get you out of the house before my parents get up. I'll sort it out." And that was that.

In the Sergeant's Mess at Bradbury Lines there used to be a skull. The history was that during the Malayan Emergency the communist terrorists they were hunting were all known. When they killed one, they needed to be able to identify them from available photographs. Unfortunately, cameras did not last well in the humid jungle, and so it was the practise to decapitate dead CTs and carry the head out for identification. Jesse, had killed a CT, decapitated him, and was carrying his head in his Bergen when he himself was taken ill and medivac'd to Butterworth. He was still in hospital when the rest of the squadron returned to the UK, taking his kit with them. His kit was taken round to his house whereon Mrs J set about washing his kit. When she upended his Bergen, the rotting head dropped out onto the kitchen floor. Her screams brought the Guard out, who took the head. They boiled it to remove the flesh, mounted it in a varnished wooden stand, put a red light inside it, and had inscribed on the base "The Chinaman's Rest". It sat in a corner of the Mess for many years, until a visitor picked it up with the comment "Isn't it lifelike?" When told it was real, she dropped it, whereupon it shattered. That was the end of the Chinaman's Rest. Apparently he had been a middle ranking official by the name of Leu Kon Kim.

It was around this time that I thought it would be useful to get a driving licence. I had been driving army Land Rovers for years without one largely because I had been told to, but I thought now would be a good time to do things properly. I went to the Motor Transport Sergeant and asked for a driving test. He went mad, as he realised what had been going on – he had been signing vehicles out to me for years in the belief that I had a licence, and now here was I telling him that I hadn't. He took me for a test drive there and then and failed me on the spot. I went down to the TA in London and asked the Unit Tester to test me. He passed me and gave me the Pink Slip required to obtain a licence. I took it back to the MT Sergeant in Hereford and asked him to process it. He took it, saying it would take about a month. A month later I went back and enquired about my licence. He denied all knowledge of it. Said I hadn't given him a Pink Slip. What he didn't know was that I had taken a photocopy of it. I went straight to the Quartermaster, and told him of my problem, showing him the photocopy. He called the MT Sergeant in and suggested he find my Pink Slip forthwith, after which I got my licence.

In between all this I was continuing with my studies at Hopwood Hall. At the end of 1969 I had moved from my lodgings in Middleton to get away from a girl who had attached herself to me. The plan was to spend the last two weeks of the term sleeping on the floor of my friend Paul's room in college. On the third night there was a furious banging on the door. It was the Warden. We were ordered to see the Vice Principal the following morning. I couldn't quite understand what heinous offence we had committed, because he kept talking around in circles. Then it became clear. They had assumed that because we were sleeping in the same room we were gay. Fortunately Paul, my friend had been Head Boy at the school in Cardiff when the Vice Principle had been Headmaster. He knew that Paul wasn't gay so we got off with a caution. At the beginning of the January term I returned a day late because I didn't have any lectures until the following day. I was in the biology lab when I was summoned before the Principal and Vice Principal.

"Why didn't you return on the first day of term?"

"Because I didn't have any lectures on that day."

"Did you or did you not intend to return on the first day?"

"In those terms, no I did not."

"Make a note of that Brother." He said triumphantly. It was like the Spanish Inquisition.

"Have you seen this before?" he asked, throwing down an opened letter in front of me. It was from my friend Pat, and had been redirected from my lodgings of the previous term.

"No I haven't."

"Well I haven't read it but apparently it is disgusting. Who is the girl referred to?"

"A friend."

"Are you still seeing her?"

"Not that particular one, no."

"So you admit it?"

"What?"

"Having relations with women." By this time I was thoroughly fed up

"Of course I do."

"I suggest you consider your position in this college." I hadn't heard that expression before and asked him to clarify.

He wouldn't. He just kept on repeating it, staring at me with undisguised hatred. I left the room and looked for the college chaplain, who was supposed to be the student's mentor. I told him what had happened. He said he would investigate. The following day he came to me and said that if I voluntarily withdrew from the college I would be allowed to apply to any other training college. If I refused, I would be sent down and banned from every other college in the country. At the time I didn't realise that this was hogwash, and that the chaplain was obviously in cahoots with the two of them. At the same time as this two other students had been found guilty of cutting the painting of the college founder out of its frame in the Entrance Hall, folding it and rolling it up, thus effectively destroying it. They had been sent down for a term. How the Catholic Church is terrified of sex. Almost sent down for alleged homosexuality, sent down for heterosexuality! I phoned up Hereford and asked if anything was going on. I was told that if I could get there that day, I could go with G squadron to the Middle East. Paul saw me off on the train, giving me a hip flask as a parting gift, and we consumed most of a bottle of Martini waiting for the train to go.

Chapter Six

Iran

When we arrived at Sharjah, we stayed initially in the main British Army camp for a couple of days while we prepared for the training. I was lying on my bed after breakfast one day when Bird Man walked in. He was called this because of his interest in birds of prey. He looked at me for a moment then said "I want to run a four minute mile. Will you pace for me?" I agreed, and an hour later we were on the track at the sports ground. The plan was that I would run one minute laps, and then on the final lap he would overtake me. We set off, and ran according to plan. At the end of the third lap I pulled over and he ran past me. I let him get away a few yards, and then stayed with him. He ran 3 minutes and 58 seconds, and I came in at exactly four minutes. I wasn't particularly tired – could have run faster, but I never thought any more about it. It wasn't official anyway, the timing could have been wrong. I was more interested in the Army. In retrospect, maybe I could have been a runner. Our training camp was in the Wadi Shawkah, a terrible fly-infested place. I stayed there for a couple of months wondering what to do with myself. I decided to join up, so I returned to Hereford and signed on at the Hereford recruiting office into the Parachute Brigade. I never went anywhere near Aldershot, but instead went straight to Bradbury Lines.

As there was no Selection Course about to begin, I joined "Goon Troop". This was composed of people who had failed selection on a technicality, and were being given a second chance. In between courses they were kept usefully employed. I hadn't been there long before four of us were sent to the army chemical warfare establishment at Porton Down. Scientists were trying to discover exactly what it is that a tracker dog follows. Was it the person's smell? Was it the scent of crushed organisms in the soil? Did it attach to undergrowth? Was it affected by wind and weather? Our job was to lay trails and be followed. They had arranged a rectangular grid of wooden poles about ten yards apart over several hundred acres of countryside. Before each session we were told exactly where to start, in which direction, who was to branch off where etc, and at varying times teams of dog handlers with their dogs would follow us. At one stage, in order to rule out the crushed organism theory, I was suspended beneath a helicopter which then dragged me through the undergrowth without actually touching the ground. One of the first things that we noticed was that the handlers were all unfit, so when we were told to lay a trail through woodland, we headed for the brambles, got on all fours, and, using secateurs, cut tunnels, which we then crawled through. This left a strong trail which the dogs raced after, dragging their hapless handlers through the brambles. Lessons learned were that dogs get bored when they are tired, and pretend to be following a trail. The trail is affected by weather and type of terrain, and the wind can blow a trail to one side of the actual route followed. But the best way of putting a dog off is to exhaust the handler.

Before Selection started, we were sent off to do a week's

fitness training in the Eastern Black Mountains. We walked north from Abergavenny, but by the time we reached Llanthony Priory I was bored with the whole thing, and joined a local pony-trekking holiday for the rest of the week. The weather was lovely, and the other trekkers were slightly bemused by my habit of not carrying a flask and packed lunch, but brewing up and making a curry.

When Selection finally started, on one of the test walks (Target Recce) I arrived at the final RV (Rendezvous) where the instructor gave me the grid reference of the next RV, which was where I had just come from. I knew that I was at the final RV and argued. He threatened me with failure, so I set off, expecting any moment for someone to pop out from behind a hedge and tell me to get on the truck. This was a familiar ruse to see if I would give in. No one popped out and I walked all the way back to the previous RV. The senior instructor was surprised to see me, and when I told him what had happened he was livid. He told me to take it easy the following day. As it happened, the cloud was down, and visibility was no more than a couple of hundred metres, which made map-reading difficult. My navigation was spot-on, and I was first in at the final RV.

At the end of the Test Week of Selection there was an interview with a panel of SAS NCOs (Non-Commissioned Officers). The only bit of it I remember was the question "Having been a monk, why do you want to join the SAS?" I answered "When I was a monk, I used to pray for people to go to Heaven. In the SAS I can get them there quicker." The fact of the matter was that my time as a De La Salle brother had given me the self-discipline and mental resilience necessary for me to be an SAS soldier. That, and an innate bloody-mindedness.

I was subsequently posted to 17 Troop, D Squadron.

This was the amphibious troop. The troop sergeant, made it clear that he was anti TA, and did not want me in the troop. Consequently nobody spoke to me, unless to tell me to do something. This changed when we went to Iran in September 1970, when he realised that I was not going to go away, that I was very fit, and that I had useful skills learned on the many courses I had done over the years. We didn't know it at the time, but our visit to Iran was to prepare us in mountain desert warfare which we would need for a war that we hadn't yet heard about in Dhofar.

We arrived at Tehran airport, and the manifest was comprised of our *noms de guerre*. These were false names to be used in the event of a European war. However, the Iranians insisted on seeing our passports, with our real names on. Blown! Fiasco! We were hosted by the Iranian Special Forces who were based at Farahbad Barracks in Tehran. They were excellent hosts, and they had brought in chefs from one of the best hotels in Tehran, but we just did not enjoy Iranian food. The whole squadron started losing weight. I survived on a diet of hard boiled eggs, chappatis and pistachio nuts. When they asked what we preferred, someone said chicken and chips. After that, whenever we were in camp we were only ever offered chicken and chips, which we grew to hate.

While we were there, an intake of conscripts arrived in a fleet of coaches. They were lead straight away into sheds where their heads were shaved. They were then issued with one set of fatigues each, a steel helmet, a stool and a small blue plastic case. We saw them day after day, in squads of a hundred learning drill and dismantling weapons. They would spend an hour learning how to raise the left arm, then an hour raising the right arm, and then the third hour raising both arms alternately. Then they started on the legs and so on, until they could march.

There was a permanent guard on our accommodation. One day, someone had an electric razor stolen. A complaint was made, which resulted in the entire guard being sent to prison, and the guard commander, an officer, reduced to the ranks and put on permanent 24 hours a day guard, in the latrine. We used to find him, collapsed, asleep, in the laundry baskets.

Boat troop went into the Elburz Mountains north of Tehran for mountain training. We were in a tented camp with the Iranian Special Forces, who were all body builders. On our arrival they said that we should do PT "Iranian style" at six o'clock the following morning. We were horrified at the thought, and some bright spark suggested that since we were the guests, we should all do PT British style. The Iranians, generous hosts as ever, agreed. The next morning we took them on a ten mile run through the mountains. The Iranians staggered in long after we had finished. After a while, one of their officers came over and suggested that in future, we did our PT separately. We agreed, and thereafter slept in every morning.

The Iranians thought our use of ropes whilst climbing was for ninnies, and they refused to use them. After they had sustained several casualties in falls, they seemed to lose interest in climbing. Perhaps their idea of what constitutes climbing was different as well. They all had masses of American-style badges on their uniforms. When I pointed out one particularly lurid one and asked what it was, he said, "I am demolition expert". I asked when he last used explosives, he said "On my demolition expert's course, ten years ago".

Nearby were the reservoirs which had high cables slung over them which the Iranians said they had parachuted off during a visit by the Shah, and still continued to use. When we asked for a demonstration, we were told it would not be possible. Looking at the cables, it seemed to us that this was bravado, because the cables did not look as if they had been used for years.

We jointly laid on a firepower demonstration for the Shah. On the day, the Shah and his entourage were in medieval style tents on top of a hill. I was in a wadi nearby, part of a line of demonstrations ready to demonstrate Single Point sights, amongst other things. The demo started with helicopters, Pink Panthers (SAS desert Land Rovers, so-called because of the paint scheme) and Iranian .50 calibre Browning machine guns engaging a target, then the Iranian infantry charged in. The .50s were too close, and one of the Iranians got hit. Nobody moved, because the Shah had not inspected the medical tent. A senior officer ran up the hill, and obtained the necessary permission. The medics then descended on the hapless soldier. When they started, his feet were at ten to two. When they had finished they were at quarter to three, and the medics walked away rubbing the blood off their hands onto their uniforms. They then noticed an air ambulance helicopter nearby. But that hadn't been inspected either. Again the necessary permission was sought, and granted, and he was taken away. As a courtesy, we sent representatives to his funeral, where they were abused by the man's family. We found afterwards that they had been told that we had killed him, not the Iranians.

When we went to practice tactical manoeuvres using live ammunition (field firing), we noticed a lot of apparently recently deserted villages. Our squadron commander told us that when the Iranians had taken him to a prospective area for field firing he had said it was unsuitable. On the way back to Tehran he noticed a suitable area and said something like this would be fine. The Iranians had ordered all the civilians out, and that became our range. We noticed, when travelling about the country, that the Iranian army never paid for their drinks in roadside cafes. We always did. Perhaps that was another reason why the Shah was overthrown. On our first day on this range, Smiler (Because he was always smiling) and myself decided to go for a run. It was about midday, and we aimed at what looked like a trig (Triangulation) point we could see in the distance. After an hour in the burning heat, it was no nearer. We determinedly continued. After three hours we reached it. It was not a trig point, it was a 20 foot high column. We got back in time for supper, totally exhausted.

We went on an exercise with a parachute entry. It was out of an Iranian C-130 Hercules, with American rigs. Unfortunately the harnesses did not fit our CSPEPs (Carrying Straps Personal Equipment Parachutist), which were used to carry our Bergen rucksacks, belt kit and weapons when parachuting. The problem was that either one hook of the CSPEP popped off when the reserve parachute was hooked on, or vice versa. The problem was compounded by the fact that initially we were to jump out of both port and starboard doors, so people rigged their harnesses accordingly. Then it was to be a starboard exit, so half had to re-rig, then they finalised on a port exit, so we all had to change. Nobody was happy. When we flew down to the DZ (Drop Zone), and stood up ready to jump, the Iranian pilot threw the aircraft around like a fighter bomber, and we were falling around all over the place. I was last man out, and had to run up the aircraft to keep up with the rest. When my canopy developed, it did so with such a shock that I realised that the aircraft had been flying too fast for safe parachuting. I also noticed that I was travelling across the sky rather fast – it was very windy. I hit the ground with a thump, and was immediately being dragged. I was pulling on my lower lift webs to deflate the parachute, when an idiot Iranian appeared and started pulling on the upper lift webs so the canopy retained its relative shape. I cursed him roundly, and he disappeared. A lot of equipment was lost or damaged on that drop, not through our own fault. Never-the-less, on our return to the UK our leaders made us do several more jumps to bring our parachuting skills up to par.

We stayed in Iran for about six weeks, during which time we carried out various forms of training. We spent a while boat-training at Bandar Abbas. One of the more memorable experiences was finning through a shoal of jellyfish. They couldn't sting us, because we were wearing wet-suits, but it was like swimming through tapioca. At the end, we had a week off, and were offered various forms of amusement. I chose to go with a group to walk up Mount Damavand, which, at 18,900 feet was the highest mountain between the Himalayas and the Rockies. An extinct volcano, the snow on the summit was tinged yellow from the sulphurous gases still escaping. The last people up it had been the Japanese Women's Everest Expedition several years previously. Straight away we ran into problems – we couldn't go because no Iranian Army team had been up it. Then we could only go if we took an Iranian Special Forces mountain guide. Then we also had to take an Iranian Mountain Federation guide. Having resolved all these difficulties we set off. There was a dirt road which we used to drive up the first ten thousand feet. We started walking at mid morning, clad, inadequately as usual, in OG (Olive Green) trousers, Heavy Duty pullovers and windproof smocks (The Iranians had duvets, woolly hats – all the kit). We reached a mountain hut at about eighteen thousand feet in the late afternoon. This hut had apparently been airlifted by the Iranian Air Force several years previously. We rested there until about 2100, before setting off for the summit, all feeling wretched with altitude sickness. When we reached the snow line, the Iranians panicked, saying we should all go back; we were going to die etc. We told them to go back if they wanted to – we were going on, so they stayed with us. It was bitterly cold. When we reached the summit, there was a metal box. In the box we found a visitor's book. Nobody had anything to write with! There was also an aluminium tray with a painting of Mt Damavand on it, with the words "Iranian Mountain Federation" around the border. We took it to prove that we had been there. It is still in the D squadron interest room at Stirling Lines. We were back at the track-head before mid morning – we had done it in less than twenty four hours, whereas the Japanese women had spent several days acclimatising before going for the summit. It was at a cost though – we had one case of pleurisy, and several of minor frost bite.

We returned to the UK on an RAF VC 10. When the aircraft reached cruising altitude, the pilot came on the public address system and gave the usual information about aircraft, altitude, flight time etc then he said "Your first meal will be served in twenty minutes, and it will be chicken and chips". The aircraft shuddered as fifty men simultaneously jumped to their feet, bellowing with rage. He had clearly been briefed.

Chapter Seven

Operation Storm, first trip

In February 1971 D Squadron prepared to go on Operation Storm in Dhofar, the southern province of the Sultanate of Oman. Oman lies in the southern part of the Arabian Peninsula. Strategically it is important, because its northern province, Musandam, forms the southern part of the Straits of Hormuz, through which two thirds of the West's oil passes. If Oman was to become communist, or at least, anti-West, closure of the Straits would have a crippling effect on Western economies.

Dhofar is the Southern Province of Oman, nearly a thousand kilometres of sand and gravel plain to the south of Muscat, the capital. It is about the size of Wales, and the mountain area (Jebel) rises in places to about 5,000 feet. The jebel runs right to the sea along most of the coast line, except at Salalah Plain. Salalah is the capital of Dhofar, and the Plain is a semi-circle approximately 50 kilometres long, by 12 kilometres deep at its widest. The principle distinguishing feature of Dhofar is the monsoon, which runs from June to September. It rarely produces heavy rain and is more of thick, persistent cloud, producing drizzle which soaks everything.

A Monk in the SAS

The ground turns to mud, leather turns mouldy, and insect life flourishes. It extends from the coast inland as far as the northern edge of the jebel. Over the years the run-off has cut deep wadis in the pre-dominantly limestone rocks, and has also produced sink-holes, such as Tawi Atair. The seas rise, making sea journeys hazardous, and severely inhibiting the landing of goods through the surf. The result of all this water is to turn the jebel green for several months each year. The wadis are filled with lush primary jungle, and the hill tops are covered with grass three and four feet high. This supports wildlife normally found in Africa, such as porcupines, hyenas and leopards. It also enables the indigenous population to survive by breeding camels, cows and goats.

The former sultan, Said bin Taimur was distrustful of development, and had kept Oman in a medieval condition. This lead to a rebellion in the southern province, and in 1970, he was overthrown by his only son, Qaboos, in a palace coup.

During Said bin Taimur's rule many Dhofaris had left to work elsewhere in the Middle East, both to make money and to gain an education unobtainable in Dhofar. Others joined the armies of the Gulf States, in particular the old Trucial Oman Scouts, where they rapidly gained an enviable reputation. Others went to the Peoples Democratic Republic of Yemen, to attend schools in Al Ghayda and Hauf.As the rebellion developed, the rebels became more organised and formed themselves into the Dhofar Liberation Front (DLF), whose motto was 'Dhofar for the Dhofaris'. They were both conservative and Muslim.

In Yemen a hard core communist group initially called the People's Front for the Liberation of the Occupied Arabian Gulf (PFLOAG) became the People's Front for the Liberation of Oman (PFLO) when Britain withdrew its military forces from east of Suez. It was backed by China and Russia who gave it considerable assistance, in the form of weapons, money and training.

The DLF and PFLOAG soon joined company, despite the one being Muslim and the other communist. The highly motivated communists soon gained control, and established a network of cells across the jebel, whose aim was to indoctrinate the Jebalis (The people living on the Jebel). They attempted to destroy the tribal structure by a mixture of persuasion and torture. Children were taken from their parents and sent to the People's Democratic Republic of Yemen to be 'educated', and many young men were sent to Russia and China for training in guerrilla warfare.

By 1970, PFLOAG controlled the entire jebel. The Sultan's Forces had been pushed back to the plain around Salalah, Taqa and Mirbat, which PFLOAG used as sources of supply.

On the 23rd July 1970 Sultan Qaboos bin Said deposed his father and immediately instigated a civil development program. This was the turning point, and some of the original members of the DLF came down from the jebel in response to the general amnesty which Qaboos declared. The hard core of PFLOAG, however, remained, and on the 12th September tried to take over the DLF and ordered its members to disarm. Many refused, and after the ensuing fire fight, 24 of the DLF changed sides. It was about this time that the SAS became involved.

As part of our briefing our squadron commander told us to have our heads shaved. When asked why, he said "To make it easier for the surgeons when you get shot in the head." We visited the Royal Military College of Science at Shrivenham to look at the type of weapons which would be deployed against us, and to be able to identify the artillery pieces used when we found them in the caves. We were given to believe that the enemy was elusive, and would not stand and fight. We thought it would be a patrolling, arms cache searching sort of operation. How wrong this was we soon found out.

I, with three others, was sent on the short Arabic course at the Army School of Education at Beaconsfield. This was a six week course, intended to provide a vocabulary of about three thousand words and knowledge of the grammar required to learn the language on arrival in the Middle East. When we went into the cookhouse for lunch on the first day, in uniform, we attracted a lot of attention. I was in the queue for the main course, and when I approached the gorgon behind the counter she said "What course are you on?" The SAS are renowned for their reticence so I just looked at her for a moment, said nothing, and moved on. Jim was behind me. "What course are you on?" she asked again. Jim looked at her, and said slowly "Intercourse Ma'am," and came over and sat down. A few minutes later there was a crash as the doors flew open and the RSM (Regimental Sergeant Major) marched in. He came straight over to our table. "Which one of you lot said 'Intercourse' to the WRAC (Women's Royal Army Corps)?" Jim didn't bother to look up. He just waved his fork, which had a piece of meat on it, slowly in the air. The rest of us continued eating. The RSM drew up a chair and sat down. He was surprisingly pleasant. He explained that there was a big problem with the WRACs there. That there were a lot of them, and anything we could do to keep the peace would be appreciated.

We slept three to a room. Each room had three beds, three bedside lockers, three steel wardrobes, and nothing else. We were kept awake by a mouse. We couldn't find it. The cookhouse WRACs had a cat called 'Cooking Fat'. I stole it, and we locked it in our room when we turned out the lights. There wasn't a sound. When I got up the next morning

Cooking Fat was sitting by the side of my bed looking pleased with himself. There was no sign of a mouse. I told him that he was going to stay in the room until such time as he caught the mouse. I continued to get dressed. When I came to put my boots on, I felt something in my left boot. I took it off and shook it. Out rolled a gnawed mouse skull. Cooking Fat had made sure I couldn't miss it. I passed the course, and on the second of February flew out to Salalah via Cyprus and Sharjah in a C130, arriving on the third.

Stepping out of the gloom of the C130 into the blinding sunlight of RAF Salalah, and the stink of aviation gasoline, we collected our bergens (rucksacks) and aviator's bags and loaded them onto a waiting three tonner. In the distance we could see the jebel, and wondered what it had in store for us. RAF Salalah at that time was a primitive airfield north of Salalah on the Salalah plain. It was ringed by five 'hedgehogs' for defence. These were small forts constructed of old 'burmails' (80 gallon oil cans) filled with sand, and manned by various local units. Salalah was surrounded by a barbed wire fence on its landward side, and we were driven four kilometres east along the line of the fence to the camp at Umm al Ghawarif (UAG). The truck did not exactly follow the line of the dirt track, to avoid mines which were regularly laid. Umm al Ghawarif was the HQ of the resident plains battalion, and consisted of a little white fort, surrounded by tents, the whole being surrounded by a barbed wire fence with two gate houses, one to the north, the other to the south, on the town side. Because Harold Wilson had declared that no British forces were to be engaged in warlike operations East of Suez, we were not SAS – we were BATT (British Army Training Team). The BATT enclave was within UAG, and consisted of one brick building, which held the squadron commander's office, radio room, and the stores and armoury. The rest was tented. Our immediate neighbours to the East were the Oman Artillery. They had two 5.5" field guns, which fired interdiction shoots at waterholes and track junctions on the jebel. They were only a few yards away from our cook tent. They fired without warning, a deafening crash, always, it seemed, at meal times, and covered us all in a fine, sand-coloured dust. We slept in 180 pounder tents, and we looked like Mother's Pride grain-graders every morning as the fine dust was caked by the sweat of the night to our faces.

When Sultan Qaboos replaced his father many of the tribesmen came to declare their loyalty. They were disarmed, and their rifles and bandoliers were stored at UAG. I hadn't been there many days when I was invited to take my pick "But don't take too many. Remember others will want some". They were mainly Martini-Henrys with silver embellishments on the furniture, and the bandoliers were made of leather, and heavily studded. I took three of each, and gave away two to people later. One day I was called into the squadron commander's office to translate for him. He was known as Taweel, because he was tall (Taweel is Arabic for tall). I didn't understand a word! They were *jebalis* and didn't speak Beaconsfield Arabic. In due course I learned to understand them completely, even when they switched into Shahri. This was the original local language, and they often used it for secrecy when they knew that you understood Arabic.

We had two main aims. One was to raise *Firqats*. These were groups of Surrendered Enemy Personnel (SEPs). Essentially they were jebel tribesmen who had changed sides and wanted to fight for the Sultan. The function of the BATT was to raise, train, and administer them. Our function in the field was to provide them with heavy weapon support, and gain information from them. The first *firqat*, the Firqat Salahadin was multi tribal. There was much quarrelling, and subsequent *firqats* were based on single tribes. Our other aim was to provide local assistance to the civilian population (As CATs – Civil Action Teams) – in essence the families of the *firqat* members. This took many forms, running clinics, supplying fresh water, food, veterinary assistance, tents etc. They were very demanding. *"Ureed"* (I want) usually started most conversations, and they were persistent. We were never safe from them day or night, and we referred to them as "Firks".

While I was at UAG it was decided to send a convoy to Taqa, 27 kilometres east of UAG, on the coast. There was a Bedford truck full of supplies, with another full of infantry, three Commando Carriers (An American Armoured Personnel Carrier mounting a machine gun), with three man crews. There were three of us in a Land Rover with the bodywork cut down. Wearing rubber-soled boots, green trousers and shirt belt kit and bush hats, we were armed with semi-automatic rifles and a 7.62mm Light Machine Gun (Bren). We set off east through Salalah Plain, between the sea to the south, and the jebel Qara to the north. We passed the Dhofar Gendarmerie camp at Arzat as the plain became increasingly constricted. Along this coast there are brackish inlets, called *Khawrs* fed by springs from the landward side, and only separated from the sea by a short stretch of sand. We had crossed several of these, and when we reached Khawr Sawli we came under machine gun fire from the north. We stopped, deployed and took cover. The rounds crackled overhead, but we could not see where they were coming from. It wasn't really effective fire. The Commando Carriers fired into likely areas, and the convoy moved on without having been damaged.

This sort of contact was fairly typical in its style. When on the offensive, the *adoo* (enemy) were generally very hard to spot and their field-craft was of a very high order. They would often open fire at long range, whilst others carried out a flanking manoeuvre to close the range. They were lightly equipped and moved very fast. They were able to do this because they could break off a contact whenever they wanted and re-supply themselves from caches close at hand. When attacking at night some of them would lie in hollows flashing torchlights in time with the machine guns to draw fire. They would place *shemaghs* (Arab head cloths) under the machine guns to collect the empty cases so that finding where they had been firing from was difficult. In 1975, when I was an officer in Firqat Force of the Sultan's Army, I was briefing the officers of the Desert Regiment about a forthcoming operation. One of them asked "How will we be able to tell the difference between the *adoo* and the *firqat*". I said "If you can see them, they are *firqat*. If you can't, they are *adoo*".

Taqa had a population of about 2,000 people and consisted of two storey mud brick buildings with a palm plantation between the town and the sea, a Foreign Legion style fort on a promontory to the north, the *Wali's* (Mayor) fort on the eastern side, and the whole lot surrounded by the ubiquitous barbed wire. 17 Troop were housed in the BATT house opposite the *Wali's* fort. They were as miserable as sin. This sort of war wasn't what they had expected. The operations were taxing, against an aggressive, persistent enemy, and to come back and be harassed by the locals for various forms of assistance was wearing in the extreme, especially as we suspected that some of the people we were assisting were of doubtful loyalty. But then, 'Hearts and Minds' played a large part in this operation. I couldn't wait to unload and get out of the place, and we returned to UAG without incident.

Close to Arzat camp was the old sultan's summer house at Ma'murah. It was decided to raise the Firqat Qaboos there. This was to consist of Bait Jaaboob tribesmen, whose main tribal area was to the north on Jebel Naheez. The track leading to Ma'murah was lined with dead date palms. They had died due to lack of water when the *adoo* destroyed the *falaj* (aqueduct) which drew water from Ayn Arzat waterhole at the foot of the jebel. There were four of us altogether, and we equipped and trained some forty tribesmen. We tried to teach them infantry tactics. They humoured us as we taught them the principles of fire and movement, and the use of support weapons in the attack. As it turned out, they were absolute naturals in their own terrain. They expertly used cover and pepperpotted (The infantry principle of fire and movement) at speed. We should have realised – they had been fighting in this environment for hundreds of years – we had nothing to teach them, except net discipline with hand held radios. In a contact this went out of the window and they used them like telephones.

One night we received a message that one of the Dhofar Gendarmerie at Arzat had defected to the *adoo*, taking with him a Commando Carrier which he had driven out through the wire. We were told to engage it with the 84mm Carl Gustav anti tank launcher which we had. We were bemused. Although we had trained with the thing, none of us had ever thought we would be called upon to use it for real. As we took it out of its case, we had a feeling that we were making regimental history by using it. As it turned out, although we heard its engine in the distance, we never saw it, let alone get in range of it. It was found some years later, burned out in the bottom of the Wadi Arzat, with the radio and machine gun missing.

As the trip was thankfully drawing to a close, I was told that Taweel had persuaded his seniors that we should stay a month longer, because the jebel was about to fall "like a ripe plum". That went down like a lead balloon. We stayed, and it didn't fall at all, let alone like a ripe plum.

I was at Ma'murah for about a month before being

moved to Sudh, a small town on the coast, about a hundred kilometres from Salalah. I went to Rayzut harbour, west of Salalah, which at that time just consisted of a small jetty, and boarded a Sultan of Oman Navy *boom* (Wooden vessel). It was about sixty feet long, and armed with two .50 calibre Browning machine guns, and a small field gun (RCL). Also on board was a platoon from the Dhofar Gendarmerie. We sailed in the evening and arrived at Sudh the following morning. Sudh was a mud brick village built along the sides of a wadi which opened into a natural harbour. The BATT house was about half way along it. Inside were elements of 17 Troop, who had just returned from the jebel after recapturing the town in an earlier operation. They were exhausted, and didn't recommend the place as a holiday destination.

There were nine of us living in the BATT house, and we also manned a picket (Defensive position) above the village. The house was in a tumble-down state, and we rigged up a shower with a *burmail* (Empty oil drum). All the water had to be lifted from a well in the wadi bottom, the Jerry cans being filled by one of us and pulled up on a rope. It was then hand carried to the house. It was very brackish, and we used a local herb, recommended by the locals, to improve the taste. It didn't really improve it at all, and tea was ghastly. All the supplies had to be hand carried from the beach – about 400 yards of soft sand away. It was back breaking work, especially the 81mm mortar ammunition. The local traders, who also used the same route, were so impressed with our work output that they offered to pay us to shift their stores!

I was swimming in the bay one day when a large scaly head popped out of the water about six feet away and looked at me. I had swum half way up the nearest jebel by the time I realised it was a turtle. The sea life there was fantastic, and the beach was strewn with the heads of hammerhead sharks. The wadi bottom also stank of the smell of drying abalone. Pearls were also found there, and several years later I bought some from a fisherman.

Sudh was a hot, boring place to be in, with limited scope for patrolling. One of team, known as Smiler, who I had run with in Iran, used to drive us mad by playing his mouth organ tunelessly. We stole it from him, and when he went to man the picket, we used to play it to him over the radio. Some local light relief was also provided by the Dhofar Gendarmerie, who mounted their 3" mortar on a neighbouring roof. The roofs were strongly made of palm trees, and this one withstood the first few rounds, but when it gave up, the mortar suddenly disappeared into the sand below. They had a British officer (Geoff Mawle) who came to see us one day after a patrol. He saw that the Number One burner (cooker) was out and said "Oh, I am too late for a brew". "No, I said, the water is still warm. Put some in your mug and heat it up on a hexy (hexamine) cooker". I watched, fascinated, as he took out an Army black plastic mug, filled it with water, and put it on the lighted hexamine. Just as it started to melt, I said "If you look closely at the side, it says 'KEEP AWAY FROM HEAT OR FLAME'." Sadly he was killed at Taqa several months later when he stood directly behind a French 90mm anti tank gun, which we had installed, as he fired it. The recoil buffer failed, and the gun barrel came back and took his head off.

One day about forty armed men suddenly appeared in the town. They were in the wadi directly in front of the BATT house. They weren't causing any trouble, but we didn't like the fact that they could do. Ossie (the troop commander) said "You are the troop Arabist, Sibley. Go and disarm them". I said "You must be joking". "No, he replied, I will cover you with the Jimpie (GPMG – 7.62 General Purpose Machine Gun) from up here". There was no way out. I went down and politely asked them for their weapons. They looked at me as if I was mad, which I probably was. When they didn't do as I had asked, Ossie fired a burst across the wadi. They complied. As it was, they were friendly, and later joined the Firqat Gamal Abdul Nasser. Being the troop Arabist did have its compensations, however. When an Arab came to talk to me the troop would gather round asking what he was saying. I would make up something obscure and cryptic such as, "He said, before the sun is over Jebel Samhan the wadis will run with blood." Or "The ravens will not go hungry today." This got the barrage of abuse it deserved, but it did highlight what was most on our minds, namely, personal survival.

We were relieved in May, and returned to Salalah by helicopter. At UAG Taweel gave us a briefing about what was to happen next, and said there was a place on a Russian course, volunteers to see him after. I decided quickly that since the Russians would win the next war, I could at least get a job as an interpreter in a POW camp. I went to Taweel, and made my request. He looked at me for a moment, turned his chair towards the window, and looking into the setting sun, said "Sibley, your destiny lies in the Middle East". He did not say any more, so I walked out, had a quick think, and went back in, and asked to stay on with the next squadron. He could hardly refuse, and granted my request. The rest of 17 Troop were appalled – "For God's sake get on a CAT team." So far as I know, I was the only Sabre Troop member to volunteer for an extra tour there. When I left the Regiment several years later, to join SAF, despite 'my destiny lying in the Middle East' he put a six month block on my application, to try and stop me – "If I let you go, everybody will leave".

I was sent to Taqa with 13 of the relieving squadron. We manned the BATT house and the fort on top of the hill. During the day we provided civil assistance in the form of a clinic in a separate building, sprayed camels against black flies, which were extremely irritating, and used our Land Rover – the only wheeled transport in the place, to ferry water in plastic Jerry cans to families who needed it.

Rats were a serious problem. They destroyed food, and stores. They would sharpen their teeth on water bottles and mugs, gnawing them until they were useless. The SAF soldiers took their boots off at night. The rats would gnaw the calluses on their heels until they reached living flesh. At this point the soldier would wake up, but by this time the damage was done. Any weight on the foot would cause the wound to open. The only treatment was bed rest until the wound healed. We set traps for them at night, in the stores. These were squirrel traps which caught them alive. In the morning they would be so full of rats that it would have been impossible to squeeze another in. We took the cages down to the beach and drowned them. We never got on top of the problem.

We were re-supplied either by the kind of convoy along the coast, which was expensive in terms of forces required, by beach run, or by air. The beach runs were carried out at night by Land Rover or 4 ton Bedford truck. About four of us would go, and having negotiated the sand dunes, driving as fast as possible along the beach, on the hard sand temporarily left behind as each wave receded. It was a bit dodgy, because apart from the risk of being bumped by the *adoo*, if you got bogged down you were really stuck; the tide would come in and swamp the vehicle. This happened a couple of times, but fortunately I was not involved.

Air resupply was by Skyvan, the work horse of the Sultan of Oman's Air Force (SOAF). We used a dirt strip three kilometres to the east of Taqa called Tangmere. It was opposite Sumhuram on the Khawr Rawri. Sumhuram was reputed to be one of the Queen of Sheba's palaces. It had been partly excavated before the war, and we had patrolled round it a couple of times. We would be told by radio to expect a Skyvan, but never the time. We would go out with elements of the resident *Jaysh* (Sultan's Army) platoon, check the airstrip for mines, and then settle down in the sun to wait. There were old *sangars* (small defences made by stacking rocks) dotted around the edge which we never used, because of the mine risk. From time to time we came under fire, but it was usually long range, and not effective.

On one occasion we noticed a group of *Bedu* camped on the plain between Taqa and the airstrip. They were a wedding party from the jebel, come down to register the marriage with the *Wali* of Taqa. We were expecting a re-supply the following day, and we informed the *Jaysh* accordingly. The following morning the *Jaysh* platoon arrived outside the BATT house to go with us to the airstrip. At this moment a signal started coming in, so we told the *Jaysh* to go on ahead, and we would catch up with them when we had decoded the signal. The signal announced that the re-supply had been postponed until the following day. We had no direct communications with the *Jaysh*, so Flicker (so-named because of a nervous tick he had) and I got into the Land Rover and drove to the airstrip to inform them. As we approached the airstrip there was a loud explosion from the *sangar* which I usually lay near. Two of the *Jaysh* had gone into the *sangar* and lifted a rock which was in the middle of it. There was a mine with an anti-lift device. We drove over and reversed up to it. There was a strong smell of cordite and the fine dust was settling over the bodies as the blood soaked through. One was dead, and the other severely injured. Hoping that the *adoo* would not have laid two mines in the same *sangar*, we put the two of them in the back of the Land Rover, told the platoon commander that we would cancel the Skyvan (No point in telling him that it had been cancelled anyway), and returned to Taqa. We told the locals that there had been a vehicle accident (They didn't believe us, of course) and arranged a Casevac (Helicopter casualty evacuation).

We then returned to the scene of the mine incident to search the area for pieces of the mine for identification purposes. We probed around and filled our pockets with little bits of green plastic, springs etc. When we returned to the BATT house, we emptied our pockets out onto the table to examine our finds. Wally, the troop sergeant, picked up what looked like a piece of wire. "Electrically detonated", he announced. We looked hard at it. "Wally, that's a human tendon". He dropped it in disgust.

The following day we drove out without the *Jaysh* to receive the Skyvan. On the way we noticed that the *Bedu* wedding party had gone. I went to my usual place near the *sangar* where the mine had been. We came under small arms and heavy machine gun fire from the other side of the Khawr. They were out of range of the 81mm mortar in Taqa, and we replied ineffectively with the Jimpies (7.62 machine guns). We decided to bring the mortar out and set it up near the air strip. The target was quickly adjusted, and the *adoo* driven off. About fifteen minutes later I saw a group of people about two kilometres away, running towards the jebel. Because of my location, I was the only one who could see them, so I directed the mortar onto them. After the first couple of rounds of HE (High Explosive) I was on target, and ordered "Five rounds mixed fruit pudding". This was a sequence of HE, Smoke (White Phosphorous), HE, Smoke, HE. We had found this combination to be highly effective in rocky terrain. The group scattered, and ran even faster towards the jebel. I realised that they would shortly disappear out of sight behind a low ridge, so I ordered a large left switch, to land in front of them and drive them back into the open, where I could continue to stonk them. At this point the *firks* began to express concern. At Beaconsfield we had been taught that the word for civilian was *madani*. I asked the *firks* if they were *"madaniyeen"*. They said "No, maybe they are *mawataniyeen"*. I didn't realise then that a *madani* was a town dweller, which patently these people weren't, and that *mawatani* really meant civilian, so I continued the shoot. When the *firks* became agitated I stopped the shoot. At that point a civilian ran into our location from the east. He said "We are the wedding party. Stop shooting." Several had been killed and wounded. We waited until they brought the wounded in, treated their injuries, and arranged a casevac. One of the wounded was a girl of about ten. She had a leg blown off. When I discussed this incident with the *firks*, they said that the mine layers had used them for cover, and that it was Allah's judgement. I didn't think they would have been so philosophical had they been of the same tribe.

Ten years later, when I was working for the Civil Aid Department (CAD), I was on the jebel in the Wadi Darbat. The Wadi Darbat is a major wadi, and its outlet is the Khawr Rawri, near where this had happened. I spotted a *Bedu* tent and went over. They greeted me, and invited me in. They were very friendly and hospitable. There was a small fire going, and the women were sitting in a line behind it. The man of the house offered me coffee and dates, and told the women to arrange it. I noticed that one of them, a strikingly attractive girl of about eighteen, used a crutch, and was obviously missing a leg. I asked him what had happened. He shrugged and smiled and said "It was the war. *Allah kareem* (God is generous)". Although there had been lot of action in that area, I thought that this must be the same girl. I asked if they needed anything from the government – tents, food, whatever. He said that they were self sufficient. What need of those things was there?

This incident has stayed with me ever since. I have gone over it a thousand times in my mind. What could I have done differently? I can't think of anything. In the same circumstances, with the same information, I would do the same again. As the man said "It was the war", but I have never been able to get it out of my mind.

During the day, the *adoo* would shell us from Jebel Aram, to the north, using a 75mm RCL (Artillery piece). They would light a fire about a hundred yards from the RCL, and cover it with a cloth. Each time it fired they would lift the cloth allowing a billow of white smoke to rise thus confusing us as to its exact whereabouts. It was out of range of our 81mm mortar, so the crew, instead of using the normal maximum charge of three large augmenting cartridges and three small ones, would use six large ones and add petrol. This increased the range of the mortar. However it never actually achieved anything except to wear out the barrel, and make the mortar crew deaf. They would only fire about ten rounds at a time before withdrawing, so they would be gone before we could arrange a jet strike. On one occasion I was walking from the clinic towards the BATT house when the RCL began firing. For some reason I chose to go right, instead of left around the house. Lucky I did, because the next salvo landed in the alley I would have used. At that time, SOAF were equipped with Strikemasters. These were a military version of the Jet Provost, and carried two 7.62 machine guns, rockets and bombs. Despite the claims of the pilots, I always considered that their main advantage was in drawing enemy away from us when we were in a corner, thus allowing us to redeploy – there would be more kudos for the *adoo* in shooting down a Strikie. The skill of the *adoo* at concealment, and the nature of the terrain

– hilly scrub, covered in soil with scattered rocks, deep wadis with cave systems – meant that in the vast majority of cases, a direct hit was required to get a kill.

At night the *adoo* would come in close, using AK 47s (Russian Assault Rifle), Guryonovs, RPDs (Ruchnoi Pulemet Degtyarev, a Russian light machine gun, which used the same ammunition as the AK 47. The *firks* referred to these as 'Doktors', from the last part of the name.), and 60mm mortars. To reply, we had two GPMGs, an 81mm mortar, and our personal weapons. We were always short of mortar ammunition, because the Quarter Master for the Middle East, based in Cyprus said that we had used up our training allowance for the year! This meant that we had to severely ration ourselves in contacts, giving the *adoo* the advantage. It took months before he was put in the picture that we were actually at war. This was particularly irritating, because the RAF Regiment in Salalah, trialling a new Trilux (mortar night sight) sight, had unlimited supplies, and we were between them and the *adoo*. We eventually got the new Trilux sight – a vast improvement on the old battery system.

Early one morning there was a banging on the BATT house door. One of the team opened the window shutter and saw a *firk* standing there. "Go away. We don't open until nine o'clock", and shut the shutter. At 0900 the man returned. He was an *adoo* trying to surrender! He told us that he had been sent from the jebel as protection for a minelayer. What the *adoo* had not known was that the minelayer had killed a member of his family. As soon as they were off the jebel he had killed him, hidden their weapons, and come into Taqa. He went out to bring the weapons in, and was sent to Salalah for debriefing.

The monsoon ran from July to September. It didn't really rain very much, but there was continual heavy cloud and mist, which at times reduced visibility to a hundred yards. It was also very humid. These conditions favoured the *adoo*, and in that three month period we recorded over 70 contacts. Because of the need to be alert at all times we wore our boots day and night, so most of us had foot rot. We never took our belt kit off, and our weapons were permanently at hand. At night I kept my webbing braces on and used my belt kit as a pillow – when I stood up it dropped onto my waist and I only had to fasten it. During the day, several of us took to wearing a *futah* (local sarong), but instead of wearing it full length, folded it in two, so that it looked like a miniskirt. Boots, miniskirt, belt kit, OG shirt and Armalite – unfortunately I never took a photograph of this rig. When, in my medic role, I went on house calls, I would go into a large room where all the family were gathered, and after the traditional greetings would squat down. I quickly became aware that the women would gradually shuffle round the room until they were directly opposite me. This was to facilitate looking up my skirt! Once I realised this, I became adept at keeping my knees together, and changing which way they were pointing, so there was constant movement in the room as they tried to keep up with my manoeuvring.

Our doctor paid us a visit every month or so to see how we were getting on, and assist us when necessary. During one of these visits there was a knock on the door one night. It was an agitated man, asking us to come and see his wife who was pregnant and in pain. We set off down the dark and dusty streets and went into his house to find his wife lying moaning on the bed. The doctor questioned her via the husband, using me as the translator. When he said that he wanted to make a physical examination I said "There is no way he is going to let you touch his wife." "Just ask will you." So I did, and was surprised when he agreed. Having carried out the examination he then said that he wanted to carry out an internal examination. I said "There is absolutely no way he'll let you do that." "I can't confirm my diagnosis without it." So I asked again, and was amazed when after a few words to his wife, the man agreed. Not knowing the Arabic for 'lithotomy position' I cleverly said to him "Please ask your wife to position herself for sexual intercourse." He said a few words to her, and with a terrible groan, she rolled off the bed and bent forwards over it. The doctor went beetroot with embarrassment and rushed out into the night shouting "You bastard, Sibley." I had to run after him and calm him down before he returned to complete his examination.

In between helping the civilian population, every couple of days we would go out in daylight, hoping to catch the *adoo* on the hop, searching villages under the jebel, or just sitting there, knowing that they would come and have a go at us. This wasn't very nice, because they had the benefit of the high ground, and used to produce a Shpagin 12.7mm heavy machine gun. We used to bring the mortar out and set it up in dead ground to try and catch it but we never did. Having been pasted we would then retire to Taqa.

At night we mounted ambushes. They were never successful, because the town's people knew when we went out, and flashed torches towards the jebel. However, we tried. We would take Claymore mines and a Jimpie (machine gun) and lie out for hours on the rocky ground. I generally used to carry the Jimpie and 400 rounds of mixed link ammunition. On one of these we had been told that we would lift the ambush at 0100 hrs. The night was pitch black – low cloud and no moon. I couldn't see my hand in front of my face. I had the Jimpie. At midnight I became aware of movement in front of me. I nudged Flicker, who was next to me, pulled the Jimpie into my shoulder and took first pressure on the trigger.

I could hear footsteps coming slowly up the slope towards me. Then I heard the noise of plastic striking a rock. Our Claymore mines had plastic reels. I held my fire. Suddenly Mac, the troop sergeant came through where I was lying, reeling in a Claymore. The troop commander had become bored, and had pulled the ambush an hour early, and nobody had told Flicker and me. When we got back I told Mac that I had very nearly cut him in half. He was not a happy bunny at all, and had words with the boss.

Because we didn't have adequate defences we were provided with an old French 90mm anti tank gun. We set it up by the fort, and taught ourselves how to use it. It had a range of two thousand yards, and two types of ammunition – HEAT (High Explosive Anti Tank) – not very useful against personnel, and TPTP (Target Practice Tracer Projectile). This last gave off a hideous howling noise when it ricocheted, and we decided it would be useful to terrify the *adoo*, who would think we had banshees. It was fired by a long lanyard from the top of the fort at the nearest position the *adoo* were likely to use at the start of any contact. It was this weapon which subsequently killed Geoff Mawle.

One night I had gone to bed in the yard at the foot of the keep of the fort, dressed in shorts, boots and OG shirt, belt kit as pillow with a waterproof bag of spare clothes to soften it. I slept in a sleeping bag made of parachute nylon with my Armalite inside pointing towards my feet. I heard a single crack of a round passing overhead. I leaped out of my sleeping bag and ran up-stairs to the parapet. I had paused to draw breath and suss out the situation, when I heard the boom of the RCL. The next thing I knew was that I was on my back, and there was the pungent stink of cordite. I couldn't move my legs because they were covered in masonry, there was a large hole in the wall where I had been leaning, and there was a hail of machine gun fire coming though it. I pushed the masonry off my legs and realised that I couldn't use my left arm. I was also stinging down my left side. I ran downstairs to the room below where the rest of the BATT were gathered, doing a head count. We heard groans coming up the stairs and told the owner to shut up. We were busy. As it turned out it was a severely injured Baluchi soldier whom we subsequently treated and casevaced. It turned out that the *adoo* had brought their RCL down from the jebel and had set it up a thousand yards away. They just couldn't miss the fort at that range. It was hit several more times before we fought them off. The following day I was casevaced to the FST (Field Surgical Team) at RAF Salalah, where they found a minor fracture in my left elbow, and flash burns down my exposed left side. I returned to Taqa the same day on light duties – we were too short of Arabists for me to lurk in UAG. My sleeping bag at the foot of the keep was riddled with shrapnel, as was the waterproof bag I had been using as a pillow. If I hadn't moved as fast as I did, I would have been dead. I still use that sleeping bag and each time I do the memories come flooding back.

After this, we started to make our own mines, which we laid in suspected *adoo* fire positions at last light, and lifted the following morning. We never got anybody this way, although we did score an own goal when one of the relieving team managed to set one off as he was laying it, sustaining chest injuries.

When we had the opportunity we used to swim in the sea. The monsoon waves were mountainous, but it was invigorating. On one occasion I was swept out, which was frightening, not only from the drowning point of view, but because of the sharks, which were often visible in the waves just before they broke. I remembered that there is a cyclical motion along a beach, so I trod water, and in due course I was swept in again several hundred yards further down. Not so lucky was one of our doctors, who was swept out at what subsequently became known as 'Beer Can Bay' near Rayzut, and was drowned. I happened to be in Salalah at the time, and went to the service.

At the end of the tour we had piously hoped to be airlifted out. Instead we were told that the incoming team would arrive by land convoy, and we would go out on it. We didn't mind. It was the end of it all and we had survived. We were horrified to receive a signal on the morning of our departure, that intelligence had indicated that the Salalah to Taqa road had been mined. We were to leave our bergens etc in Taqa, and go out and clear the road. We went out, looking for signs of disturbed soil, prodding the ground with spikes. We didn't find anything, and were hugely relieved to get onto the three-tonner when it arrived. We celebrated our survival in the NAAFI at RAF Salalah that night, and returned to the UK on the 19th August 1971 by C130. We had two week's leave, some further training, and I returned to Dhofar on the 15th November with my own squadron.

Chapter Eight

Operation Storm, second trip

We arrived at Salalah on the 16th November 1971, and nothing had changed. Our camp at UAG was just the same, but we were furious that the Sappers, who were due to come out, were having built for them substantial, air conditioned accommodation.

A position on the jebel had been established at White City by two squadrons of BATT (A and G) after an exhausting march from the north. We went up by Skyvan. The landings were always white knuckle rides, because the Van had to circle tightly down within the perimeter of the position to avoid *adoo* (Enemy) fire. At the last minute the pilot would pull the nose up, the stall-warning klaxon would sound, and bang! we were down, bumping along the rough airstrip, whereon the pilot would apply reverse thrust, throwing us all forward, to stop it from running off the end. We dug in near the perimeter, and I shared a hole with Tosh, a friend. It was six feet long and five feet wide and three feet deep. It was bitterly cold at night, so I found a large cardboard box, put it in the hole, and slept in that. We were short of kit, so I also made a sort of duffel coat out of a blanket, with a hood.

Bruce Niven (Our Squadron Commander) photographed me wearing it for his book, which served to reinforce my nickname of 'The Mad Monk'. It was about this time that we were told that the Commanding Officer (CO) would be paying us a visit. 'Black Bill' had been a sergeant and was now commissioned. He called us together. "Now lads, you know that the CO is a bit of a stickler for discipline, so for Goodness sake, when he is around don't call me 'Bill', call me 'Boss', or 'Sir'." When the CO came up, he greeted us and sat down on the edge of a *sangar* with Black Bill. Tosh had put the burner on to make some tea. He approached them. "Hey Bill, I mean Boss, I mean Sir." He spluttered "Would you like a brew? And 'ow about you mate?" He said, nudging the colonel in the ribs. We fell around laughing. Black Bill put a brave face on it, and the CO pretended not to notice.

A and G squadrons showed us the ropes, patrolling out of the location, laying ambushes, and generally trying to induce the *adoo* to attack us on our terms. They didn't need very much inducing. They really didn't want us there. A good way of encouraging a contact was to escort the cattle owned by the *firks* to a waterhole to the west of us. These were hard fought engagements, and we had to picket both sides of our route, hold the ground over the waterhole until the cows had walked down, been watered, and come back, before withdrawing. We were within gun and mortar range of White City, so we mainly carried our own weapons, together with GPMGs, both SF (Sustained Fire, on tripods) and in the light role (Off tripods). I recall engaging a group of *adoo* on a ridge about six hundred yards away with my GPMG. Tosh was my number two. He became bored with passing ammunition, and opened fire with his rifle. Unfortunately for me, he was just behind me and immediately to my left. His muzzle was about six inches away from my left ear. The pain was intense as I rolled away from my gun, cursing him roundly. "Sorry mate!" I still have reduced hearing in that ear. Duke Pirie was a squadron commander at the time, and conducted these trips for the first couple of weeks. He was unfortunately killed on an exercise in France a little later. It was on one of these walks that we had a couple of Guardsmen along. They hadn't done Selection – the idea was that they would enjoy Dhofar so much that they would want to do it on their return to the UK! They enjoyed it so much that during their first contact they lay on the ground, refused to move, and when the cry, "Ammunition!" went up, they threw their belts of GPMG linked ammunition six feet forward onto the ground in front of them, necessitating someone else having to expose themselves to collect them. They didn't stay long.

One of the squadrons had been relatively newly formed, and they had taken some casualties. Their Squadron Commander made himself unpopular by stating that they only needed a few more casualties and they would have earned their place in the Regiment. One of his squadron retorted "It is a pity Chris died. He would have made a good squadron commander". "Why so?" "Because he had half his fxxxxg brain shot away".

When nothing was happening at night, we lay on the ground staring up at the clear skies. The number of satellites and shooting stars was incredible. It is no wonder that three of the great religions of the world came from the Middle East. During the day we worked on the airstrip, levelling and lengthening it by hand. Someone had the Good Idea of getting a baby bull-dozer up from Salalah. It duly arrived by Caribou. What they had forgotten, was that in order to load it at Salalah, they had supported the tail section of the aircraft. When they unloaded at White City there was no such support. When the baby dozer trundled down the Caribou's rear ramp, there was a horrible squealing, crunching sort of noise as the aircraft's nose lifted twenty feet into the air, and the tail buried itself in the ground. There was nothing for it but to continue unloading and assess the damage afterwards. Fortunately it was still airworthy (by whose standards I don't know) and it returned to Salalah for repairs.

The *adoo* mainly attacked at night, or just before last light, so we couldn't call up a jet strike. The hardest thing about any contact is when you don't have anything to do. If you don't have a target to fire at; if you are not manning a mortar or directing fire, then there is nothing to do except have your imagination run wild. Lying out on the ground, I knew that the small of my back was the size of Wembley Stadium, and every mortar round was heading straight for it.

Late one afternoon, being in a hedonistic mood, I wanted to sit in a chair for a change. There were only two chairs in the position. They were in the Quarter Master's (QM) tent, so I paid him a visit. He was known as Gypsy because of his origins. He greeted me hospitably, once he found I wasn't asking for anything, and offered me a mug of coffee. We were sitting in the chairs under the awning of his tent, looking out over the wadi to the north west, chatting, when suddenly came the unmistakable "Boomp" of an RCL artillery piece being fired from directly in front of us. The shell passed with a sound like an express train directly over the top of our tent, and impacted on the airstrip a hundred yards behind us. "Incomers", went up the cry, and we slid like two pieces of paper off our chairs onto the ground. We lay there, studying each other's faces, continuing to make small talk, whilst watching for giveaway ripples on the surfaces of our mugs of coffee, which we were still holding. Round after round passed directly overhead. The slightest change of trajectory would have wiped us both out. Gypsy had served in every campaign since, and including the Korean War, and he commented that in Dhofar, we were coming under heavier fire than any other British troops since the end of Korea. That made me feel better.

When it became obvious to the locals that we were here to stay, more and more of them moved in with their cows, and it was decided to move them from the jebel to the plain. It was clear that the *adoo* would not allow this to happen. There could be no secrecy, because the presence of several thousand cows was unsustainable, and the civilians needed to know what our intentions were. The main organiser was a man called Said bin Ghia, from the Bait Qatan, whose tribal area was to the west of us. Short and fat, he was a wheeler-dealer, who I got to know well when I worked for the Civil Aid Department (CAD) several years later. When the day came, we moved south east towards Shuheit, picketing the ground as we went. It was like a scene from the Wild West. Thousands of cows mooing and lowing, being driven as fast as possible by the *jebalis* in a huge cloud of dust, to the background of the crackle of Kalashnikovs and GPMGs and the whoomp of mortars. We escorted them as far as Aqabat Aram, overlooking the coastal town of Taqa. We saw them disappear over the scarp, before returning to White City. On later jaunts into the same area we found the graves of the *adoo* killed. There was a lot of grumbling that we weren't there to risk our lives for cattle, but that was wrong. Livestock was fundamental to the existence of the people we were there to help. It was part of the job.

After this, it was decided that we should go down to Shuheit again, and stay for a few days. Shuheit was situated between the Wadi Darbat and Wadi Ethon, both *adoo* strongholds, and we were sure to have a lively reception. We set off at midnight. Two kilometres short of Shuheit the column split into two. The other column went to hold a picket on Jebel Ghaidah, so that we could go right flanking below it onto Airfok, which directly dominated Shuheit. Unfortunately there was an *adoo* picket on Jebel Ghaidah, and a fire-fight broke out. I was carrying a GPMG, but there was no way I could open fire because I couldn't identify who was who. I lay there with my head behind the body of the jimpy, listening to the AK rounds cracking past, wondering how much protection it was affording me. When the *adoo* were driven off, it transpired that Connie had been shot through the spine. Our new priority was to get him out, and since the *adoo* knew where we were, there was little point in continuing with the original plan. He couldn't be moved, so we had to consolidate our position where we were. I was with Nick (He had quit his medical studies to join the SAS, and subsequently became a war camera man), and Lofty. We started building a *sangar,* but after about an hour, we were told to move further up the hill. We cursed and did so, starting a new *sangar.* We had worked on that for about another hour when we were told to move again. I refused, on the basis that it was almost light, and we didn't have time, so we stayed put. As it began to get light we were horrified to find that a hill which we had thought was a long way off, was in fact, only a couple of hundred yards away, and dominated us. If any *adoo* got on that we were dead men. We lay in our *sangar,* checked our weapons, ammunition, shell dressings and morphine syrettes, and waited. Fresh rations were treasured, especially fruit. I had an orange with me which I had intended to eat later. In the circumstances, that was looking increasingly unlikely, so I peeled it and offered it to the other two. We couldn't eat it – our mouths were too dry. It went to waste. We waited and waited. Nothing happened. We didn't know it then, but the *adoo* had taken casualties as well, and were sorting themselves out. The Huey 205 came in and took our casualty. As soon as it took off we started to pull back. This galvanised the *adoo* into action. Since they were mainly down wind of us we set fire to the grass to form a smoke screen and we had a long running battle all the way back to White City. It was text book stuff, moving in bounds like proper soldiers, in broad daylight (Unusual for us). I thought it looked most impressive.

All this running around took a toll on our kit. When we complained to the QM in Salalah that we needed more clothing, the response was "Take it off all the *adoo* you are supposed to be killing!" There wasn't a lot of love lost at times, between us on the Hill, and them in Base. We used to call them REMFs (Rear Echelon Mother Fxxxxxs) and they use to call us FEWBs (Forward Echelon Whingeing Bastards).

White City was renamed Medinat al Haq (The Town of Truth), and we were told that Sultan Qaboos was going to pay us a visit. We started arguing about who was going to get the gold watch. We needn't have bothered – white faces were not acceptable, only Omanis were to be seen. We all had to hide outside the position, except the mortar crew. They had to hide inside a bunker in case the *adoo* attacked, in which case they would come out and take over from the Omanis. In retrospect, I don't believe such an order would have come from the Sultan – it was probably some overzealous Brit.

During this time the *firks* presented us with an owl which had been shot through the leg. The mortar team took it, amputated the leg, and fashioned a prosthesis from ration box wire. It lived happily in their mortar pit, until one of the mortar crew took ill and was medivac'd down to the FST (Field Surgical Team) in Salalah. He took his owl with him, in a ration box. On arrival at the FST he put the box under his bed. It wasn't long before the staff found it and told him to get rid of it. In the grounds of the FST was a large aviary full of budgies. Our hero slunk out that evening and put his owl in it. The following morning, on their way into work the FST staff noticed that instead of a cage full of budgies, they had a lot of feathers, and a fat, dozy owl. They were not best impressed, and insisted that the owl be removed from the premises.

From time to time one of the *adoo* would surrender. They would be questioned by the Intelligence people in Salalah for any useful information, especially where their group was currently located. They were usually very keen to pass on this information, and a 'Flying Finger' would be arranged. This took the form of their arriving at White City in a helicopter, when they would be joined either by myself or Lofty (The other Arabist available). We would fly to the designated area, the ex-*adoo* would point out the location to me, and I would describe it to the pilot, who would then talk in a couple of Strikemaster ground attack aircraft which had been loitering out of earshot from the ground. They would then paste the target. The problem was that whilst the *jebalis* knew the jebel like the backs of their hands on the ground, from the air it was a different matter. Having them waving and pointing and shouting above the engine noise of the helicopter made for some interesting conversations with the pilot. It didn't take long for the *adoo* to realise that the jet strikes were being directed from the helicopter, and once they knew that their position had been compromised would give the heli everything they had. I used to keep the window open and only wear one side of the headset in order to be able to hear if the ground fire was getting too close and warn the pilot. I have forgotten how many I did, but it was a lot. On one occasion on a target on Jebel Ashawr, a bomb hit a waterhole. It cracked the aquifer, and it drained, never to refill.

Working with the *firks* was always very frustrating. We would say that we wanted to patrol a given area. They would say they couldn't go because they didn't have enough food.

We would say that they had been given a month's rations a week ago. "Yes, well it has all gone" (It had gone to their families). We would argue the point, and eventually they would say that they could muster half the number of men required. We would say that wasn't enough, and they would say that it was because there wasn't enough food, and so the argument would go around in circles, until they agreed. Another argument that they used was that they didn't have enough cow meat, whereas the *adoo* had as much as they wanted. They laid great store by this, and offered it as the main reason why the *adoo* were fitter than they were! We would agree to leave at midnight. At midnight we would be ready. No sign of the *firks*. I would go to their tents. They would all be asleep. "We are not going till four o'clock". Big row. Eventually, grumbling, they would be ready to go at about two o'clock. We would set off, and at first light would realise that we were not where we had expected to be. Quick reorientation, reset the mortar plotter boards, and wait for the show to start. Our QM once memorably remarked that the *Firks* were just a very expensive way of turning good food into shit. Unfair perhaps, but it indicated the level of frustration we experienced when working with them. Somebody else put it more kindly by borrowing W H Longfellow's "And when they were good they were very very good, and when they were bad they were horrid".

The order of column was usually the firks first, followed by ourselves, and then the *Jaysh* (SAF - Sultan's Armed Forces). This was because they knew the ground, and could make contact with any locals we may meet. It also meant that they would make first contact on any pickets occupied by the *adoo*. They came to Ossie, the troop sergeant, and said they wanted a GPMG (Machine Gun). "No way". "Well if we can't have a GPMG we want a member of BATT with a GPMG to go first". Ossie and the rest of the troop thought this was reasonable, especially since I carried the GPMG. I said that I would be happy to go point, provided there were three other members of the troop immediately behind me to help me if I got into trouble. Suddenly there was a change of heart, but having agreed it was a good idea, there was no way they could get out of it. Thereafter, when we were the lead troop, I would go point with my GPMG, and there would be three other BATT behind me.

Meanwhile, White City was being developed. The Civil Aid Department (Which I would join several years later) erected a hut close to my dugout, which was the first food store on the jebel. Ossie decided to brew some beer out of a beer kit he had brought with him, in a sawn off five gallon plastic Jerry can. We all watched it closely for a couple of weeks, then one day when we returned from a patrol, having left Vince in charge, we returned to find him smashed out of his brains, having sampled it. There were no more repetitions.

Taff was feeling lonely, so he had obtained a copy of "Forum" magazine. We watched him as he perused the advertisements, drawing up a short list of services he wanted to access. Eventually he selected the offer of a pair of soiled knickers, and posted his cheque. Every time the mail was delivered, he was first in the queue. One of the troop went down to Salalah, and whilst there, noticed the discarded clothing of the outgoing squadron, waiting to be burnt. He selected a pair of soiled "Drawers Dracula", wrapped them up in brown paper to make them look like an authentic parcel, and put it in the post for Taff. We all knew about it. When the next post was delivered, Taff snatched his parcel with delight, and scurried off. He came back five minutes later, looking crestfallen, to find us rolling about in hysterics. He was furious, because he hadn't realised that we were watching him. He was even more disappointed to receive a letter from Forum later telling him that the magazine he had used was old, and would he obtain a more recent issue.

Rats were a major problem on the jebel, as they had been at Taqa. I had brought out a Webley .22 air pistol with me, and used it to shoot them during my morning dump. I would regularly get four or five each morning. One day coming back to my dugout I saw something shining on a rock by it. I took a pot shot, and saw it fly off. When I reached it I was appalled to see that I had shot my Peterson pipe in half. I got a Meershaum up from Salalah to stand in while I sent to the UK for an urgent replacement. When we returned to the UK I was trying to get to sleep one night, but Chippy, whose bed-space was directly opposite mine flatly refused to turn his overhead light out. Still lying in bed, I took out my pistol and shot it out, showering Chippy with shards of fine glass. He wasn't happy, but at least I got to sleep.

In the rations provided to SAF were tins of Crosse and Blackwell Mackerel in Tomato Sauce. Every body hated it, and so it wasn't eaten. There were piles of tins of the stuff lying around. Some of the Baluch (SAF troops from Baluchistan) had the bright idea of making a sangar out of them. All went well until it took a burst of automatic fire. We ran over and saw that they were all covered in blood. At least it looked like blood. In fact it was tomato sauce, and they all stank! Another favourite was JEP. This was unsweetened lemon powder. When mixed with water and drunk, your mouth imploded. It seemed that no matter how much sugar was added to it, it never was sweet enough. There were piles of that lying around as well. Fresh meat came in the form of live goats. When they were transported by air they posed two problems. Firstly, stopping them from running around the aircraft, and secondly, stopping them from fouling it. Both problems were solved by a very simple means. Each goat was put in a transparent plastic bag, with it head sticking out, and tied around the neck. It was simple, efficient and humane.

Christmas came. We were told that the fresh Christmas rations would come up on the 23rd to fool the *adoo*, who would undoubtedly attack us on Christmas Day. This was just a ploy, because it coincided with an existing fresh day. The extra consisted of one Christmas cracker between six, two and a half eggs per person, a cubic inch of Christmas cake and two cans of beer. When I went down to UAG a couple of weeks later I was surprised to see the remains of several big burmail barbecues. On asking I was told about the huge feast the poor REMFS had enjoyed. That explained our wretched fair. Despite this, some of BATT had amassed some beer and got a bit drunk. Their Troop Officer, Mike Kealy, was furious.

We went to Shuheit again with two squadrons. We occupied Airfok, directly overlooking Shuheit, while our backs were protected by a strong picket on Jebel Ghaidah, to the north. We tabbed down in light order overnight (weapons/bullets/gallon water container/3 water bottles/brews/food/paperback/shovel) without incident. At first light the helis came in with our support weapons, water, food and kit. My job was to marshal them, which involved standing up in clear view with my hands raised giving them the hand signals required. I was told to wear a dayglow tabard! I said "You must be joking!" and refused. The LZ (Landing Zone) was almost in dead ground (Out of sight of the *adoo*), but not quite. With the arrival of the first heli the *adoo* woke up and gave us a hard time. It was uncomfortable marshalling in those conditions, and when one pilot ignored my directions, I pointedly turned my back on him and sat down. He quickly realised that he couldn't land among the rocks without direction, and went into the hover, as the small arms fire crackled by. I stood up and landed him.

I made myself a little *sangar* out of the water Jerry cans, a little funk hole. Trouble was, they kept on disappearing as people came for their water. Unsurprisingly, our two Irishmen, dug the deepest trench on the position. When the entire ration of fresh potatoes went missing we knew exactly where to find them. We noticed that instead of opening a four man box of compo rations on the top, and selecting a menu, they would open it from the end, and eat the cans in sequence of appearance regardless of what appeared first. One chap wouldn't leave his *sangar* – said that married pads (Married men) shouldn't have to do this; it was a job for single men. He was RTU'd (Kicked out). Pockets, a troop officer from the other squadron had been writing letters home to his wife describing in detail what we were doing. He came unstuck when he wrote to his insurance company asking them to confirm that he was covered whilst at war. Unfortunately, the Chairman was a golfing partner of an SAS brigadier, and he asked him what was going on. ' Pockets' was RTU'd in the field, and made to walk with all his kit, under fire, from the bottom position to the top position to be lifted out. The *firks* had brought a *mullah* with them. He insisted on standing up in his spotless white *distasha* and giving the call to prayer. He wore big boots, so we called him 'Puss in Boots'. He always attracted a lot of fire, and we marvelled that he didn't get hit sooner than he did.

The *adoo* definitely didn't want us there, and attacked day and night. Apart from personal weapons, we had a couple of 81 mm mortars, a 25 pounder field gun at White City, and the jets. Tiger Wright (From the *Jaysh*) got his hands on a Vickers machinegun, and its slow rate of fire and high trajectory made it ideal for dropping rounds into the wadis. Unfortunately he was killed in action a year later. I had got into the habit of carrying a spare gas plug assembly for the GPMG. The problem was that contacts tended to last all day, and when the gas plug fouls up it slows the rate of fire of the gun. By having a complete spare gas plug assembly I could change it without having the gun out of action for more than a few seconds, and clean the dirty one when I was able.

We weren't far from the Wadi Darbat, a very large wadi to our east. One of the troop sergeants decided to take six of his troop and look into it. We told him he was mad, but he insisted. He went to the edge at first light. The *adoo* quickly realised he was there. It took all the combined fire power available over five hours to extricate them. There were some very white faces when they got back to the position. Like ourselves, the *adoo* avoided leaving their dead on the battlefield. When we knew they had taken casualties that we couldn't reach, we used to mortar the area using white phosphorus. The intention was to make the bodies difficult to move, thus extending *adoo's* time in an exposed position so that we could engage them again.

One of the *firks* was Ahmed Mohammed Salem Al Umri, nicknamed "Kartoob", after the small growth on his left ear. He didn't like being called "Kartoob" — bit like calling someone "Warty". He was originally an executioner in the *adoo*. He told me that he used to carry a Tokarev (A Russian automatic pistol). He would walk into a village, and would be invited in for refreshments. After the usual exchange of news, he would ask the head man if he had any information on the following "traitors". Knowing who he was, the head man would dish the dirt on those on the list. When he had finished, Kartoob would say "Funnily enough, I have your name on a similar list", take out his Tokarev and shoot him. He claimed to have killed over a hundred men in this way. I think this was probably an exaggeration, but even so. Despite this, I liked Kartoob. He was intelligent, courageous, and had a good sense of humour. I got to know him well over the next few years. I once asked him, while we were sitting on the jebel, what he was going to do after the war. He said that there was terrific tourist potential in Dhofar and that Europeans would like to swim in the sea, but would prefer the cool of the jebel. He therefore anticipated tourist hotels on the scarp, connected by ski lifts to the beach. Unfortunately he was killed with Simon Garthwaite in 1974. The *adoo* obviously hated him, because they emptied several AK47 magazines into his body. Just before I moved down to Taqa, he had been on a patrol out of Shuheit. He was left handed, which was fortunate for him, because it made him hold his rifle 'the other way'. An AK47 round, which should have hit him between the eyes, travelled down the left side of his rifle and instead took off the tips of the fingers of his right hand. Before coming in for medical treatment, we noticed that he stopped short of the position to share out the loot they had captured. I caught up with him in Taqa, where he had a house, and continued the treatment to his hand. One day I took him to Salalah. We were driving through the town centre in a Land Rover, when we came to the cross roads by the Sultan's palace. There was a policeman on point duty, waving his arms all over the place. I ignored him and turned right to go to the RAF camp. Kartoob said "I think he is angry". I said "Why". He said "Because he is blowing his whistle". So I drove on. He said "I think he is very angry". I said "Why?" He said "Because he is chasing us in a Land Rover". So I drove on. The copper in the Land Rover careered past us and stopped in a cloud of dust, so I stopped. "Why did you ignore me?" I adopted the penitent attitude of the motorist, apologised, and said that I had misunderstood him. He demanded to see my driving licence. I said I didn't have it on me. He asked for my ID card. I said I didn't have it on me. He said he would take my number. Unfortunately he did not have any paper, so he took out a 100 Baiza note (Local currency) and a stub of pencil and tried to write on the bonnet of my Land Rover. Unfortunately for him, it was camouflaged with sand and paint, and was too rough to write on. He told me that I would have to accompany him to the police station. Up until this stage Kartoob had remained silent, sitting in the Land Rover. He said "Do you know who I am?" The copper looked at him with that traditional look of distaste universally employed by police all over the world. "No". "I am Ahmed Mohamed Salem Al Umri". The copper turned white, jumped back babbling apologies, ushering us on. I drove on, with Kartoob giggling beside me.

After we had been at Shuheit for a couple of weeks I was moved to Taqa with some others to man the forward airhead in support of Op Amatol. Apart from manning the LZ, we went out from time to time, taking the mortar with us to give fire support for Shuheit. On one occasion, we found that the town gates had been padlocked, stopping us from leaving with the three tonner. Having seen all the best movies, Nick took out his .45 Colt and shot the padlock three times. The rounds just ricocheted away. Eventually we just drove the Bedford through it. The *Wali* (Mayor) was livid on our return, but we told him that if his *askars* (Guards) had been doing their job they could have opened it for us. We were still doing the beach runs at night to Salalah. One of the jobs that we had to do was take *adoo* bodies with us and bury them in unmarked graves in the dunes. The idea was that the enemy would have no shrines to glorify their dead. More recent history in other countries has shown that this practise sometimes causes even more problems.

We were still using our Land Rover to ferry water around the town. The kids used to love riding on it, chanting "*Mr Sibley wagid zain* (very good)", or "*Mr Jess*", if he was driving.

This irritated the *Wali,* who banned it. So we would pick them up and unload them out of sight of his fort. Somebody must have bubbled us, because one day we found that he had put them all in his prison as punishment. Fortunately the cell had a window which looked out onto the street, so we gave them sweets and comics. The chants of *"Mr xxxxx wagid zain"* continued, this time much closer to the *Wali,* so he gave up and released them.

Despite the goings on at Shuheit, we were still being attacked on a regular basis, mainly long range machine gun, and 75mm RCL. Sometimes the rounds overshot the fort, which was their principle target, and fell in the town. There were civilian casualties. I attended a woman who had been hit in the face by a piece of shrapnel. She refused to be casevaced out to Salalah. A week or so later I was called back to her house – she could feel something protruding through the roof of her mouth. I had a look, and could see the shrapnel had migrated and penetrated her palate. I reached in and pulled it out. We were both happy – me the more so, because it had occurred to me that it could have been close to a blood vessel which could have bled and bled, with me unable to do much about it. In conversation with a doctor once, he was horrified when I told him what drugs we carried and routinely administered, and the treatments we undertook in the field. My response was that we wouldn't have had to if more doctors had the balls to join the SAS.

Towards the end of the trip, it was decided to push down from Shuheit to the Plain east of Taqa via the Wadi Darbat. I was told to take the Bedford 4 tonner to the bottom of Darbat Falls and collect them. I thought it was absolutely lunatic. Me, alone in a truck, only my Armalite, no radio, along a track known to have been mined, under the jebel where we had had many contacts, the *adoo* stirred up like hornets – only the previous day a Huey 205 had force landed at Taqa because it had been shot up flying low level in the same area. I was not a happy bunny, and my sole recollection is of the drive there. The actual pick up, and return to Taqa are a complete blank – there probably wasn't anything left in my mind to think with after that stress.

The operation around Shuheit and the Wadi Darbat had been a protracted affair, and had considerable success despite stiff opposition from the *adoo*. The aim, apart from killing *adoo* had been to penetrate the Wadi Darbat. This had been done, but we were unable to hold it, because we had insufficient troops and supplies. The bulk of those involved had been picketing the sides of the wadi, while a few (Those who I had picked up) could walk down it. Some wag at UAG sent a CQ (All stations) signal saying that a special medal was being struck to commemorate the event, made of melted down communist weapons. It would only be available to those who had actually set foot in the wadi bottom. This caused considerable discussion. Only one officer took the bait. He sent a long message arguing that although he had not actually set foot in the wadi bottom, those who had done so could not have done it if he had not been there picketing the sides, therefore, he deserved one. It was very long winded, and was put up on the notice board at UAG, much to everyone's delight.

In early March we were pulled out, and returned to Salalah. All our clothing was burned. We had a party in the NAAFI at RAF Salalah, and returned to the UK on the 14th of March 1972.

Chapter Nine

Marriage and exercises

On the 17th April 1972 we returned to Malaya for an exercise. It was a Quick Move. That is to say, from the order to go we had to be deployed and on the ground anywhere in the world within twenty four hours. We emplaned at Brize Norton and flew by C130 Hercules transport aircraft to RAF Butterworth in northern Malaya where we were briefed, issued with maps, ammunition and extra equipment. We drew and fitted parachutes, and within 24 hours of leaving the UK were floating down onto a secret DZ in the jungle at dawn. As I rolled my parachute a little Malay chap rolled up on a bicycle. "You like buy melon?" he enquired pleasantly. I asked him how he knew we would be there. "We know for months." We moved off into the jungle, and *basha*'d up that evening. The next morning I woke up and everything was green. "Who's painted the ceiling green overnight?" and then I remembered where I was.

I had been going out for some time with Maggie (a former Welsh schoolgirl hockey International, until someone discovered that she had been born in Manchester). We had met in the "Bunch of Grapes" in Hereford, and after a series of ups and downs decided to get married. The wedding took place in Hereford Registry Office on the 15th July. The Best Man was Laurence Gallagher, a big, airborne engineer who was killed in the Falklands with 19 others from the Regiment on the 19th May 1982, when the Sea King helicopter they were in crashed into the sea. Also on board was Phil Currass, who had sutured my finger in the jungle. We had a buffet in the cellar bar of a pub in Hereford, and on the 22nd July she gave birth to our son John. It would have been unfair to continue on long trips abroad, so I asked to be transferred temporarily to HQ Squadron, which effectively meant guarding the main gate. One of the permanent guards was a big chap called Cyril who had a habit of, instead of standing by the gate, standing on a branch in a tree above the gate. The unwary visitor, not seeing anyone, would tentatively approach, and then as he tried to walk through Cyril would drop down out of the tree, landing about an inch in front of him, demanding to know what he wanted. When accused of being mad, Cyril would say that he could prove he was sane because he had a certificate to prove it.

I had been trying to get on a diving course, and during my leave in September, I was having a beer in the Grapes when somebody asked what I was doing there. I was supposed to be on a diving course at Portsmouth. Nobody had told me, so I went back to camp and was sent to the Medical Room, where I was told that I needed a chest X-Ray before the course, and was sent to Hereford Hospital. I then went down to the Diving School at Portsmouth. The first few days comprised physical endurance tests, followed by a physical examination. I sailed through the endurance tests, and was last to go in to the physical examination. As I went in, one of the instructors said "Waste of time you going in there. You are the fittest here." The Surgeon Commander said much the same thing, except he added "You have had TB. There is no way you can do this course." I realised that the idiots in Hereford, having screwed up the administrative arrangements, had realised that the only way for me to have an X-Ray quickly was to say that it was an emergency because I was suspected of having TB. I explained this to the doctor, and pleaded with him to phone Hereford. He was adamant. He would only go by what he saw written in front of him. I was off the course, and returned miserably to Hereford. The only good thing to come out of it was that I spent more time with Maggie and John.

On the 25th October 1972 we went on exercise to Norway. The idea was that we would board a Norwegian submarine at Bergen and sail down the coast over-night. We would change into wet suits and swim ashore from about a mile out. On landing on the beach we would move at night to the vicinity of our target in a fjord on which we were to place explosive charges and then creep out.

The Norwegian submariners were very hospitable, and fed us well during the short voyage. When the time came to leave, we donned our wet suits and waterproofed our kit. The submarine surfaced, and the three other members of the patrol went up the conning tower, while I stayed in the control room. The idea was that they would lower a rope to me, and I would attach the Bergen rucksacks to it, and they would be pulled up one at a time. My other function was to ensure that the horns of the Bergen frames did not get stuck on the ladder. When the rope came down for the last Bergen, it had got quite cold in the control room, and I needed a pee. The great thing about wet suits is that you pee inside them, as a means of warming them up. I duly did so, and then became aware of a subtle change of atmosphere in the control room. The Norgies in their blue serge trousers, white roll neck pullovers and jaunty hats had all shuffled away from me. Looking down, I realised why. There was a large puddle around my feet. It was obvious what it was – they were swimmers as well. There was obviously a hole in one of my bootees. There was nothing to be done. I thanked them for their hospitality, scuttled up the ladder, and disappeared into the cold waves with a feeling of relief.

When we landed on the beach we were joined by our Squadron Commander (OC), who intended to accompany us. As he didn't have a wet suit we chose the wettest approach to our target – we were indignant that he hadn't swum ashore with us. The exercise went as planned, except that we found a secret Norwegian airfield. We realised that we shouldn't be there, so we did a quick reconnaissance and bugged out. We crossed the perimeter fence by climbing up one side, stepping onto the shoulders of the man in front, and then onto the ground. At this stage we would have been carrying about 60lbs of equipment. When it was the OC's turn, Taff stepped off the fence onto his shoulders and instead of stepping off, just stood there. With about fourteen stone on his shoulders the OC's knees gradually buckled. When he reached the ground Taff stepped off and walked into the darkness without a word. We had two days off in Bergen at the end. We found that the Brits were very popular. We were talking to an old Norwegian who said "I remember the SAS when they came here in 1945. They shoot the Nazis. They shoot the Quislings. They kill every bugger!" They were very hospitable to us, although we found the prices expensive.

On 25th November we went on an Escape and Evasion (E&E) exercise in the south of France. As there was a river crossing involved we had to practise our river crossing technique in the lake at Eastnor Castle. On the chosen day it was bitterly cold and there was snow on the ground. I stripped to my underpants, waterproofed my Bergen, strapped my rifle to it and stepped in to swim to the other side. Luckily it was only about fifty yards, because the cold very quickly got into me, and my strokes were becoming shorter and shorter as my breathing became more and more restricted. There was an urn of tea on the other side, but one of the group was shaking so much that when given a cup of tea immediately threw it over his shoulder.

The exercise plan was that we would do a night parachute jump with equipment on Pau Drop Zone, move non-tactically about five miles to the River Gave de Pau, carry out the crossing, pick up non-regiment personnel involved, such as aircrew, Intelligence Corps etc, and then move about another five miles to the start line, at which point we would become tactical and be hunted by French Paras with helicopters and dogs. We were to stay as a four man patrol, unless bumped by the enemy, in which case we were supposed to split into pairs and continue. It was a five day exercise, but we were only given three days rations because the exercise plan was that we would all be captured and interrogated, where, in theory, we would be fed. As usual, this was just a Quarter-Master's ploy to gain rations, because the amount of food given under interrogation was minimal.

The jump and the river crossing were uneventful. I was the signaller, and we picked up our fourth member as planned. He was a tall gangling creature from the Intelligence Corps. Whilst we were walking non-tactically towards the start line I decided to talk to him to get to know him as we were going to be together (in theory) for the next five days. It was bitterly cold, and the front of my smock was frozen solid. He said he didn't like our rations – he had been eating them on the flight over. I couldn't believe that anyone would break into his rations before he absolutely needed them – it was going to be a long five days. Then he complained of the cold. I said not to worry, because when it was light we would brew up. He said he thought we were supposed to be tactical. I said, flippantly, that there was nothing more tactical that a cup of tea. He then revealed that he had discarded all his Hexamine fuel. I was stunned; he had broken into the meagre rations given for the exercise, and not brought any means of heating his food in the Pyrenees in winter. He was clearly going to be an albatross. I at once decided that this was Darwin's Theory of Natural Selection in process. I shouted "Enemy! Go left!" They all went left, I went right, and carried on running until I was certain that they would never find me.

I carried on moving rapidly for two days until I reached a point high in the Pyrenees about two miles from the pick up point – the Col Ste Marie Blanc. Since I had three days in hand I decided to lie up under a fir tree. Knowing that the French were using tracker dogs, I did not move from under the tree, to avoid leaving any sign or smell. On the last night it thawed slightly. I became aware of it when I woke up with wet feet. Being half asleep, I just pulled my feet up to my chest a bit and went back to sleep. Then they felt wet again, so I did the same. The third time I woke up properly to investigate. To my horror I discovered that a little rivulet had formed and run into the top of my waterproof sleeping bag cover and pooled in the bottom. There must have been about two gallons in there. My goose down sleeping bag was soaked. This was a survival issue. I waited until first light and then brewed up. I sat on my Bergen, put my poncho on, and lit small pieces of Hexamine on the ground between my feet to keep warm. A couple of hours later I heard the French searching the woods not far away. I put out the Hexamine. Suddenly I heard a sound in front of me and saw a section of French Paras with a tracker dog coming straight towards me. I froze. They walked past within fifteen feet. They didn't see me and the dog didn't smell me because I hadn't moved from under the tree. When they were far enough away I moved off to the pick up point.

We were taken to a French barracks to sort ourselves out and get ready to go out for a few beers. Late in the day we were told that the regimental Parachute Jump Instructor was missing. We were to stay in camp and get ready to go out and search for him. He turned up the following morning – he was a day out in his calculations, and we weren't very happy. As the route of the E&E had been along the line of a Second World War escape route, a lot of the chatter was to do with BBC broadcast codes used during WW2 to the Resistance. People would walk up and say "Ze autumn leaves are falling", and a typical response would be "And ze cat ees on ze roof". That night Duke Pirie, a squadron commander was killed in a road accident. Dick was woken up with the statement "Ze Duke is dead". The response was "And ze Queen ees on ze throne". "No, you silly sod! It's Duke Pirie. He's dead". The following morning there was a muster parade for us to be told formally of the sad news. Our squadron commander gave it. It was quite a long talk, but there were two things he said which have stuck with me. One was "It is particularly tragic that he died in this way, because as a professional soldier he would have much preferred to die in action"! What planet was he on? I have never known a soldier who didn't want to die in bed. The other was "It is also very sad for xxxx (his wife). This is the second husband she has lost. She seems to be making a habit of it"!

It was shortly after this that I had my annual report with Mellor, my Troop Officer. It was all very nice, until I read in the middle of it 'Does not appear to take the Army seriously'. I said "I am not signing that." He said "But it's true." I said "Of course it's true. Nobody in their right mind takes the Army seriously, but you can't expect me to confirm it." He took it out.

I was sent on an Astro Navigation course at Hermitage. At that time the Regiment used theodolytes to track the stars so as to navigate across deserts. The course was for two weeks, and we spent our days learning how to use the books of tables and graphs to do the calculations needed to work out our position. The nights were spent getting stiff necks looking through our theodolytes, chasing stars, and timing them with chronometers. It is amazing just how quickly stars move when looked at through a theodolyte. One of the instructors had a glass eye. When one of the students was close to hysteria trying to locate a given star, he would take out his glass eye, place it against the theodolyte eye piece and say "I see no problem." It was quite tricky. On one occasion I managed to move a motorway service station from one side of the road to the other.

On my return I was in camp at Hereford when we were asked to help a local Convent move to another building. The nuns wore distinctive black and white habits, and several of us went along with a Bedford truck to carry out the move. With us was 'Joker', the Regimental wit. All was going smoothly when Joker, parking the Bedford, spotted the Mother Superior. He ran up to her and said "Do you have any nuns about two feet high?" She looked at him for a moment before saying "No, I don't." "Thank goodness for that," he said, "I must have just run over a penguin." She stared at him for a moment before saying "I shall pray for you."

Chapter Ten

Operation Storm, third trip

On the 20th February 1973 I returned to Dhofar. I was on the advance party and went straight from Umm al Ghawarif (UAG) to Tawi Atair, in the Eastern Area. The ground was very broken, and covered with scrub, enabling the *adoo* to get in close. It was also the tribal area of the Al Umri, the largest tribe on the jebel. Consequently it consisted of a large number of sub-tribes, leading to endless wrangling. Because of problems of re-supply caused by the mist and rain, the position had been withdrawn at the start of the previous monsoon, and it had been reoccupied since. The problem was that the *adoo* would have mined the *sangars*, so second best locations had been selected for our stay. We were to relieve one of the other squadrons, and I went on several patrols with them to familiarise myself with the area.

Tawi Atair was so-named because of the sinkhole. *Tawi* means well, and *Atair* means birds. The hole itself is over 600 feet deep and 150 yards in diameter at the top. There are pools at the bottom. Traditionally one of the *jebalis* would climb down to the bottom, the women would lower a rope with a goatskin attached, he would fill the goatskin with water, and they would pull it up, about six women to a rope. The full skin would then be carried by a single woman another 200 feet up to the cattle troughs. These skins weighed in excess of 60 pounds, and they would do this all day, otherwise the cattle would die of thirst.

The position itself was a sausage shaped feature with steep sides about 800 yards long, running south east to north west. There was an airstrip on the south side, which was short and bumpy, and several aircraft crashed there. To the north, south of the *tawi* itself was the *firks* position. Each position was separately surrounded by barbed wire.

The other ten members of 17 Troop arrived a couple of weeks later, including Mellor, the troop officer, who was keen to make a name for himself. He insisted that we *sangar* up together, on the basis that since I was troop arabist I would be able to keep him informed, and in any case, he needed to be able to think! As a lure he told me that we would not have to do stags (night sentry duty) at night like the rest of the troop. I quickly realised that this would not do very much for my popularity within the troop, and insisted on doing stags, cumulatively exhausting though they became for all of us. When I dug the *sangar* I made it sausage-shaped, so that we would sleep foot-to-foot. He didn't offer to help. When it was completed, he returned to find me filling empty 81mm mortar ammunition boxes with rubble, and placing them where our feet would be. He asked me what I was doing. I said, "I am building a blast wall so that when you get fragged I won't get hurt." Minutes later he offered me a mug of tea, the first and last time he ever did so.

We settled into a routine of patrolling the area. The format consisted of negotiating with the *firks* about where to go, moving off at about 0100hrs, grazing our legs on the dragon-tooth rocks which abounded the area, until we reached the chosen location, usually with a village in view. We chose villages because the *adoo* were local tribesmen, and their families lived there. We would set up an area ambush, making small *sangars* for defence in the event of the inevitable day-time contact. At first light there would be no movement. Then the smoke would begin to percolate through the thatch roofs of the *baits* (local houses), as they prepared their morning brew. Then the women would come out with the goats, split into several small herds. We would hear them calling to each other in their sing-song voices, as they spread out around the village, checking the approaches. When they had driven their herds through our locations they would disappear. Then about an hour later, the *adoo* having been briefed as to where we were, the contact would start. They usually used AK47s and RPD machine guns. They kept their heavy weapons secreted in the deep wadis for their own planned attacks because of the time it took to deploy them. We would reply with GPMGs and whatever support weapons were within range from Tawi Atair. Then at about midday, the *adoo* would decide it was time for lunch, we would decide it was getting too hot, and so we would all go our various ways. Sometimes we inflicted casualties, and sometimes we didn't. The intention was to unsettle the *adoo*, to demonstrate that they could no longer move with impunity, and for us to learn the topography of the area – the maps at that time were very poor.

One of my fears from the previous trip was that in a fast moving contact I could have been left behind by the rest of the BATT, and then have a stoppage with the GPMG leaving me defenceless. In Hereford I had an old bicycle which I used to pedal around the camp. A friend of mine, Nick, who used to work for a gunsmith in London, and whose chief claim to fame was that in the film "The Battle of the Bulge", it had been his hand which was seen passing a belt of ammunition to Telly Savalas, coveted it. I asked him what he proposed to swap for it. He asked me what I wanted. I told him, a side arm. He agreed, and told me to get a firearms certificate. I duly did, and became the proud owner of a Walther PPK pistol. I carried this in the top left inside pocket of my smock, and although I never had to use it for real, it was like a Linus rag to me. When I graduated to carrying an AR15 Armalite I didn't really need it, and it was becoming an encumbrance. On a later trip, Kartoob noticed it and he also coveted it. I agreed to swap it for an Omani *khanjar* (Traditional knife) with a giraffe horn handle, encrusted with silver. On my return to the UK I wrote to the Chief Constable at Hindlip Hall, and informed him that I no longer had the Walther, without telling him what had happened to it; I couldn't really – Dhofar was secret. I had a nasty letter back demanding to know what had happened to it. I went to the unit Intelligence Officer and told him about my predicament, and he told me I was in deep trouble. Anyway, he got me out of it. A few years later, when I worked for the Civil Aid Department in Salalah, I used to go round to Bob Brown's house every now and then to exchange notes. He was Head of Intelligence for Dhofar. On one occasion, he was complaining how unreliable his agents were. He said that one of them had come in to be paid. He asked to check the weapon assigned to him, and instead of producing his Makarov, he produced a Walther PPK. When asked where the Makarov was, he said that he had swapped it with Kartoob, who had since been killed. I asked to see it. It was mine. I told him the story of the swap, and said that I would swap an old bicycle for it. He refused. Bob's house was heavily protected with a steel front door, bolts, spyhole, pump action shotgun etc. On another occasion we were sitting having a wee dram, when we heard a noise around the back. We drew and cocked our pistols as Cyril Baxter, an elderly Scottish employee of the British Council came in from the kitchen. "How did you get in?" demanded Bob. "Weell, the front door was locked, so I came around the back."

From time to time, battalion sized operations were carried out. These usually took three or four days, and the aim, apart from the usual one of killing the enemy, was to search a given wadi in the hope of finding arms caches. We would set out around midnight, as usual. Three or four groups of *Jaysh* infantry, each headed by the *firks* and BATT, in a single column which would separate at drop–off points along the way. It never failed to amaze me that when in column, the people at the front are moving slowly and cautiously, while those at the back spend their time kneeling down waiting for movement, and then having to run like rabbits, cursing and falling over the rocks, to catch up with the rapidly-disappearing group in front of them.

We would picket a large wadi complex, and during a lull in the initial contact, would have our mortars and other heavy equipment brought in by heli. We would probe. The *adoo* would probe. They would bring out their heavy weapons. We would reply in kind. We would get the jets up to bomb selected targets – the effect of five-hundred pound bombs in a narrow wadi was interesting – if nothing else they made our ears ring – Lord knows what they did to the *adoo*! When everything settled down after a couple of days, the wadi search would begin. The *firks* would sweep down with ourselves in close support. The *firks* knew where to look because they were all ex-*adoo* themselves. They had an interest in finding equipment because the government paid a reward for arms finds – to them, not to us. Consequently we often didn't know what they had found, which was a nuisance, because we really needed to know. It was on one of these in 1974 that Kartoob was killed with Simon Garthwaite when they took the wrong junction and went down an unpicketted *wadi.*

On one three day operation, we had walked back to Tawi Atair, carrying all our heavy equipment. We had just got back to Tawi, and I was dismantling my radio pack, when we heard a terrific roar of fire to the South West. Elements of the Jebel Regiment (JR) had been withdrawing across the narrow isthmus which connects Jebel Ash Shawr to the hinterland, when they had been ambushed. They were about four kilometres away. We grabbed our kit and ran towards them. We crossed a deep wadi and got ourselves onto a ridge about a kilometre away from them. We didn't go any further because light was failing by then, and we could have got ourselves into trouble. In any case, we were picketing their line of withdrawal. The jets were up, and everywhere I looked I could see people running around, although we were the furthest forward. I heard orders for a jet strike going in, being given by a Royal Marine officer in SAF and checked the grid on my map. I recognised it. It was mine. He had identified us as *adoo.* "Stop. Stop. Stop. Tiger callsign location." The two Strikemasters continued their run, but did not drop their bombs. Instead they banked over to eyeball us. Having confirmed our location they withdrew out to sea. We waited until JR had withdrawn to safety before returning to Tawi after dark.

Because of the cost of British 81mm mortar ammunition, SAF had purchased Indian mortar ammunition. We continued to use our own, but SAF of course, used the Indian. It was of low quality, and the rounds went all over the place. When being used in close support, this is less than ideal. They decided to dispose of them, and the method they chose was to fire them off on charge primary, the smallest charge. The intention was to avoid civilian casualties. The result was to pepper the position with shrapnel. So they gave up on that one, and instead, made a large pile of several hundred of them in the middle of the position, interspersed with nuggets of Plastic Explosive. We said it wasn't a good idea, and offered to do the job properly. They refused. They knew better. When they told us they were going to blow it we left the position, and sat down several hundred yards away. There was a loud explosion, and we watched fascinated as a shower of unexploded mortar bombs rained down. The ground was littered with the things, mainly tail-less, scorched, and smouldering. We went over to the *Jaysh* and told them that if they didn't clear the position we would leave altogether. They asked us for help! We refused on the basis that we had already offered it and been turned down. "Your mess. You sort it out." And they did – very unhappily.

One quiet day we were strolling around doing whatever needed doing when the *adoo* opened fire with a DSHK 12.7mm heavy machine gun. They were right on target, and we dived for cover and grovelled. Three of us finished up in the tiny radio *sangar*. We tried to get through to the guns on the A41 radio, because we could see where it was firing from. We couldn't get through, and grovelled lower. Then it was all over. Closer examination of the A41 revealed that I had managed to kick out the coaxial lead in my haste to maintain life. It isn't like that in the films!

It was on this trip that I saw one of the most horrible things I have ever seen. There was a tree just to the west of my *sangar* where the *firks* used to sit in the shade. One day I saw them bring a cow to the other side of it. Suddenly they slit its throat, and pushed it over onto its side. Before it was dead they started to skin it, punching the hide off. When they had done this they proceeded to butcher the poor animal on its own hide, so the meat wouldn't get dusty. When they disembowelled it, a pregnant womb dropped out. It started contracting, and pushed out a perfect little calf. As its head appeared, one of them leaned over and cut its throat. Welcome to the world. I was shocked. I knew that there was no point in talking about cruelty, so I asked them why they had killed a cow knowing it to be pregnant. "Because we are hungry", was the answer. I said "If you had waited a bit you would have had two cows." (Appealing to their greed). "But we are hungry now." I had no answer to that logic.

The local badgers were a problem. They were very inquisitive, and would come into the position at night and steal whatever they could. When cornered they were vicious, and if you threw something at them, they would run away until the object landed, and then they would run along side it to see if it was edible. I got some nice pictures of them by tying some dried meat to the end of an ammunition tins by my sangar, when I heard them I sat up and took a flash picture. The trouble was that each time I did it the whole position stood to, thinking they were under attack.

A senior member of the Firqat al Umri (FAU) was Ali Said Ali. He was an intelligent, fine-looking man known for his courage. He had recently got married at Mirbat, when he came to me and asked me to arrange for him to go to the FST (Field Surgical Team) in Salalah. I asked him why, but he wouldn't tell me. I told him that in order to get him an appointment there I would have to give a reason; otherwise they wouldn't even look at him. He told me that he was no use to his new wife. Big problem. When I next went to UAG to collect the *firks* pay, I popped into the FST, and asked if they would see him. At first they were doubtful, but then agreed. I got a message to Tawi, and he came down the following day. They examined him, and found nothing physically wrong. His problem was psychological, and he was desperate for some kind of treatment. We got into a huddle and hatched a cunning plan. I would tell him that he would get the treatment

Brits get for this problem, which is absolutely sure-fire. He was prepared, as for an operation and was sedated with sodium pentothal. While he was in this state I sat by him and told him what kind of man he was going to be afterwards. It is difficult enough talking filth at length in English, let alone Arabic. I managed to keep going for half an hour. When he came round, he immediately lifted his theatre gown and was disappointed not to see a scar. I had to explain as convincingly as I could that this was a special kind of operation which left no scar. He returned to Mirbat and wasn't seen on the jebel again for a month. When he returned he was a happy man.

Towards the end of the tour we decided to go east, with a view to collecting some arms the *firks* knew about, and in the hope of precipitating a contact with the *adoo*. About eight members of the BATT together with about forty *firks* set out around midnight. We travelled east through the thick scrub and bushes, collecting an old *adoo* mortar aiming post on the way. So much for the arms find! We continued east, past the hockey pitch feature (so called because it was a flat grassy area about 300 yards by 100 yards, and dominated to the north by a low ridge) and set up an area ambush. At first light we realised that the *firks* had put us in a hopeless position, heavily dominated by a ridge only a couple of hundred yards away. We had to move, and the *adoo* spotted us. An untidy contact developed for about an hour, of confused dodging around in the bushes, during which Mellor kept on forgetting his rifle whilst trying to control the jets. After the first time we told him to go back and find it himself, while we waited for him. It was a shambles, so we decided that there was nothing to be gained, and set off for home.

We broke off the engagement and headed west. The *firks* leading, with me amongst them, and the BATT behind. The *firks* were fed up, and as they so often did in similar circumstances, switched off and lost interest. When we reached the hockey pitch feature the *firks* walked straight across the centre of it, rifles over their shoulders. I was appalled. If there was anybody on the ridge to the north, they were all dead men. I hung around in the bushes and watched. Nothing happened. The leading elements reached the far side without incident. My job was with the *firqat*, so I followed on. I got about fifty yards out when I thought I was having an hallucination. The air started humming and quivering around me. Then the dust rose up around me and I heard the deafening roar of automatic fire. I ran in an anticlockwise circle and spotted a rock about the size of my head. I dived behind it, listening to the racket. Then training kicked in, "Win the fire-fight." I looked up and saw movement in the bushes about fifty yards away with the grey smoke from the muzzles drifting away. I fired a series of double taps at them, and paused to change my magazine. As I did so I looked to my left and saw one of the *firks* lying about five yards away. He gave me a thumbs-up. I gave one back and continued firing. When I looked again, he had gone. My position was distinctly uncomfortable, and I was wondering how to get out of it when I remembered I was carrying a Squadcall. This was a radio about the size of a large packet of cornflakes with a range of about 20 Kilometres. I knew the jets were standing off to the south so I called in a jet strike. I didn't go through the normal formalities, instead – "Hello SOAF jet this is Tiger 23 Lima, I have a mission for you. I am at grid 456903. Large grassy area to the north. Low ridge north of grassy feature. Enemy on ridge. That is your target, Over." "Copied, commencing run, Out". As the jets screamed in I heard the rest of the BATT shouting to me from the bushes "Run!" I wondered how much a Squadcall would protect my back from a hail of AK rounds. Then I did, leaving tatters of my clothes on the spiky bushes as I did so. We pulled back through to the mortar position where, our squadron commander, and, the incoming squadron commander were observing - I knew him from TA days. "Hello Sibley, showing off again?" We laughed and carried on.

The *firks* had taken casualties. The bodies were taken to the mortar position where they were heli'd out together with the mortar. The bodies were covered with empty mortar ammunition boxes in the panic. I later heard that when it landed at Mirbat, one of them sat up, complained bitterly and then died properly. More to the point, Kartoob bugged out with the casualties, leaving the *firqat* without any effective leadership. The BATT and the *firks* pepper-potted back independently of each other.

We continued withdrawing, under fire, to Tawi Atair. On the way we reached a small rocky wadi. Mellor, the troop commander shouted for us to cover him while he went ahead. I relayed this back to the rest of the BATT, shouting above the noise of the jets which were low overhead. Tikus shouted back "Call me that again and I'll knock your f******g head off." I wondered what he meant. We crossed the wadi and reached a small area of dead ground. I was last over, and the rest of the troop had slumped down on the ground. I walked over to him, dropping my belt kit and rifle on the way, and said "Who is going to knock whose f*****g head off then?" The rest of the troop looked alarmed. Here we were in the middle of a contact, and a fist fight was about to break out. He said "You called me a silly old c***." I denied it. It was clear he didn't want a fight, and it would have been silly of me to have stuck one on him, so it fizzled out. We kissed and made up, and returned to Tawi without further incident.

When I returned to Tawi at the start of my next tour in April 1974 I went to the *firqat* position. The *firks* all lined up to shake my hand in greeting. I reached two who I didn't recognise. "I don't know you." "We know you." They said. "We were shooting at you in that ambush last year." "Rubbish." I said. "Oh, yes we were. You were wearing the camouflaged stripe jacket (I wore an old faded French para jacket) and carrying a radio. You escaped when the jets came in." I said "Well if you can't hit a man in the open with an AK47 at fifty yards, I'm not sure that I want you in the *firqat*. They said "Don't worry. When we defect to the *adoo* we will drop a grenade in your sangar to make sure." We all laughed happily and I moved on.

We returned to the UK on the 3rd June 1973.

Chapter Eleven

More exercises

After a week's leave we went on a NATO exercise in Greece, leaving on the 18th June. We were initially put into tented accommodation on the airfield at Thessalonika. We watched in envy when the Americans turned up. They erected a huge camp on the other side of the airstrip which had air-conditioned accommodation, PX, gravel paths, cafes etc. We were further infuriated to find that the RAF aircrew involved were living in an hotel in town. It was to be a night parachute entry. The first night it was cancelled at the last minute due to bad flying weather – our hatred of the Crabs increased. The following night we drew and fitted parachutes, and boarded a C130 for the short flight through the mountains to the DZ. Just four of us in the cavernous hold. Uncomfortable in our tight harnesses, steel helmets, 80 pounds of equipment strapped into the CSPEPs between our knees, and suffering with indigestion. This was not helped by the low-level flight in bumpy conditions through the valleys. The RAF crew wouldn't fly above the cloud because it would be too dangerous to descend to parachuting height in a mountainous area. They tried valley after valley, being forced back by low cloud, the aircraft banking steeply as it turned tightly without warning in the darkness. We were all feeling sick and tired and frightened. When I am like that I retreat into myself and go quiet. Not so my neighbour, Bernie, the patrol commander. His face was sweaty and his eyes were like raisins. He wouldn't shut up. He was driving me mad. He had been one of the most vociferous critics of the Crabs before we took off. Then he came out with "I don't mind the Crabs living in four star hotels if it helps them to fly safely"! I didn't laugh at the time, but I did after. Funny how fear can change people's opinions! The exercise went as planned and we returned to the UK on the 27th June after a couple of days R&R in Thessalonika.

Later that year 17 Troop went boat training at Oban on the west coast of Scotland. We spent hours finning in the sea lochs. Every now and then a seal would pop its head out of the water and look at us. We asked the locals if they were dangerous. They said only when the bull seals are in rut! We canoed until our arms dropped off, and sailed. The weather was good, and we enjoyed ourselves. We also practised in Geminis. These were inflatable craft underpowered by a Johnson 40 horse-power outboard engine. We used old Spitfire compasses to navigate with, in their boxes, pushed up against the bulwark. On one occasion we spotted a sheep cut off by the tide against a cliff. "Fresh mutton for supper!" was the cry. We went in and caught it. It baa'd. "Okay, Lofty, cut its throat." "No, you do it, Johnny." It baa'd again, its big brown eyes rolling. It knew what we were talking about. "Go on Pete, you do it then." "Why don't you?" The four steely-eyed killers headed for shore, and let it go.

In September four of us from 17 Troop (A sergeant, corporal, lance corporal and me) were sent on a Coastal Navigation course at Southampton. The intention was that we would be able to navigate and manoeuvre ships up to

120 feet in length. I found the chart work fascinating, and learning to manoeuvre around Southampton harbour great fun. The final exercise was to take a Motor Fisheries Vessel (old trawler) across to Alderney, which we did without incident. The weather on the return was appalling, and I only managed to stop myself from being seasick by standing up in the bows which were going around in a corkscrew motion like a roller coaster gone mad. At least I had the wind in my face and I had to concentrate so hard to stop myself from being thrown overboard that I didn't have time to think about being sick. After the final exam we were marched (!) into the Commanding Officer's office to get our results. We stood to attention as he read them out in rank order. When finally he came to me he said "You have made a mistake. You are top of the group." We were dismissed. On the 'About Turn' we all went in the wrong direction and crashed into each other before falling out through the door in a complete shambles. I was to meet him again several years later.

On the 19th October I was sent to Brecon to do the Junior NCO's Section Commander's Battle course. It was to be the last one run by the Parachute Regiment – subsequently it was taken over by the School of Infantry. Brecon camp was on the outskirts of Brecon. It was an old-style wooden-hutted camp left over from the Second World War. It was to be my introduction to the REAL ARMY. Never having gone through Regular Army Basic Training, much less Parachute Regiment Basic Training, this was to be an eye-opener for me. Twelve beds to a wooden hut with a potbelly stove in the middle. This was never lit, even in the depths of winter, because it was more trouble to get it clean each morning. The ablutions were in another unheated hut. Large troughs to wash in, no hot water and no doors on the lavatories. Due to the usual poor administration at Hereford, I arrived late together with

Nobby and Dave. We were separated on arrival, and I was assigned to a hut. I walked in with my kit, enquired as to the availability of an empty bed, and started to sort myself out. There were eleven Paras in there, who looked at me curiously, but they were friendly and helpful. On that first evening I was sitting on my bed sorting my kit when the door burst open. Somebody bellowed "Stand to attention!" as the man marched in. I stayed on my bed as eleven sets of heels crashed into the floor. He came over to me and identified himself as the Divisional Sergeant Major (DSM). I stood slowly, more as a social politeness than anything else, and introduced myself. He seemed friendly enough, as he welcomed me to the School, offering me any assistance needed in view of my late arrival. While the conversation was going on I gradually leaned against my 6 foot steel locker. He finished what he had to say and walked out. There was a bellow of "Stand easy!" followed by the crash of heels I was to come to know so well. They came over to me. "How the Hell did you get away with that?" "What?" "That. Leaning against the locker when the DSM was talking to you". I said "He seemed pleasant enough". They retired in awe, shaking their heads.

The place was completely Army Barmy. Only on the parade ground did people march. Movement around the camp was by doubling (Running) in a squad. The place echoed to the crunch of boots and hoarse bellows of command. The course was very physical, and each day started either with PT or a battle run in full kit with steel helmets and ammunition pouches filled with sand. These runs were usually only a couple miles, and weren't so much runs as 'Brecon shuffles', from the way a squad of heavily laden men run. The first few weeks were largely theory – learning how to teach according to the handbook, signals/jungle tactics etc. It was here that I came across the TEWT – Tactical Exercise Without Troops! This was only surpassed by JEWT – Jungle Exercise Without Trees! Wonderful. Only the Army could have dreamt up that one.

One week of the course was devoted to Northern Ireland training. This consisted of a sleep-deprived routine comprising street patrols/riot control/road blocks, and vehicle searches. The 'enemy' was supplied by the Royal Irish Regiment. In the confrontational situations they were armed with baseball bats and half-bricks. They threw themselves into it with great gusto, and focussed my attention greatly. The road block exercise involved setting one up on the main gate into camp, catching all the morning workers coming in. These were mainly civilian employees, and they hadn't been warned. Needless to say, their reactions were realistic as well. Once I realised their antagonism I found an empty mortar-bomb container which I put into the boot of one of the cars, and then claimed to have found it. Immediately the hapless driver was dragged out and thrown, spread-eagled up against the nearest wall, to be subjected to an immediate interrogation. Not a happy bunny. I hope there was something in his contract of employment rendering him liable to this sort of treatment.

Each morning we formed up on the road outside the Armoury to collect our weapons. One frosty morning we had formed up and were waiting for the Senior Division to collect theirs. Fortunately they were between us and the gate. One of our instructors drove in, having partially cleared his windscreen of ice. Dazzled by the morning sun, he drove straight into the Senior Division, severely injuring Don, who had been with me at White City in 1972. It put an end to his active military career.

The course commander was an American 10th Special Forces major, who had served in Viet Nam. He was a very pleasant, helpful sort of person, and took several teaching sessions. I remember once he told me that a similar course to this in the US Army would devote considerable time to the problems of drug abuse. I was amazed, then. One of the sessions he took was the two page system of taking orders. Essentially this consisted of writing down the orders for the platoon on the left page, and then opposite it on the right page, writing the orders for the section. We couldn't understand the need for so much duplication. We argued and argued. Eventually he said "I will tell you the reason." And turned and wrote on the blackboard 'CUZASED'. "That's why." We looked at it this way and that. We couldn't get it. Eventually he explained "Cuz Ah Said, that's why."

Having been taught how the Army expected us to teach, we had to each deliver three teaching sessions according to the Book, at weekly intervals. I swotted, delivered mine, and got a 'B'. The second one, the instructor said "What can I say. You are nearly as good as me." And gave me an 'A'. My third one was Lesson One on the General Purpose Machine Gun. Having used one for real in Dhofar, I could have done that in my sleep, so, apart from a cursory glance at the book I didn't do any work on it. The night before, the door crashed open, the DSM marched in, and the Paras went into their usual routine of heel crunching. He came over to me and said"I hope you have prepared well for your teaching session tomorrow." I assured him that I had. "Because the General-in-Command (GOC) of Western Division is visiting tomorrow, and we are going to walk in on your session." "No problem," I reassured him. He looked at me curiously as I leaned against my locker, asked how I was doing, and departed.

The following morning I was well into my lesson when the door burst open and the GOC came in accompanied by the Commanding Officer, the course commander, the Regimental Sergeant Major and the DSM. I ignored them and continued. After a couple of minutes my instructor whispered to me"Stop the lesson". Instead I went into 'end of lesson drills', made the weapons safe, and stood the class to attention, including myself. The General walked from man to man, saying a few words to each, as they do. When he reached me, he said "And how long have you been instructing here Sergeant?" The colonel leaned across, "Actually Sir, he is one of the pupils." "He looked at me – "Very good." Then he saw my name badge. "That's an unusual name. Where is it from?" "German-Jew, Sir." I barked. There was a moment's silence as this was absorbed. I noticed the eyes of the group go very round as they waited for a reaction to this obvious piss-take. "Very good. Very good." He said, and walked out. The instructor let out an audible sigh. "After that, I think we will call it a day. What can I say? It has to be worth an 'A'."

Every Monday morning there was an RSM's parade. All the courses on camp formed up and marched onto the square. The orders for the week were read out, and one at a time, by division, the squad leaders came to attention, and bellowed out the status of their squad – how many men on parade, how many absent/sick etc. On one of these, the leader of the Senior Division took a pace forward, raised his right knee to the horizontal, and as he slammed his foot downwards, the heel caught in the seam of his left trouser-leg. There was a ripping sound, and he fell over. The parade quivered. The RSM screamed something to get us under control – I don't know what – like everyone else, the vision of the event was still searing its way across my mind.

Every now and then there was a weapons inspection. It took place in the hut, and we had to stand by our beds with our rifles dismantled on the bed, for inspection. On one occasion an officer we called 'Porridge', carried out the inspection. When he got to my bed he picked up the gas plug. SLR (Self-Loading Rifle) gas plugs foul very readily, in particular the groove. It has to be kept clean, not only so that it will fit back in the weapon, but also to enable it to continue firing. Experience had taught me that it was only necessary to remove the large particles from the groove – the presence of staining did not seem to make any difference. And so it was then. He screeched "This is absolutely fiiiilthy!" I said "No Sir. SAS gas plugs are Parkerised for tactical reasons." (Parkerising is a kind of paint applied to external metal parts of weapons, largely to prevent rust). "Really?" he said. "How interesting." He must have gone to the Officer's Mess afterwards and recounted this piece of esoteric information, where they would have thrown things at him and laughed him into the ground.

After the first month we started doing more and more work on the Sennybridge ranges. Sennybridge Range is one of the most desolate pieces of real estate in the world. It is mountain moor-land with valleys, streams and clumps of evergreen trees. The wind whistles across it and cuts straight to the bone. In winter it is desperate. We practised section attacks by day and night. We practised patrol work in a variety of scenarios. It was miserably cold, exhausting work, and I really understood, for the first time, why shouting plays such a large part in the Army. It is the only way of getting through to exhausted men, above the deafening racket of battle.

We each took turns to play various roles – Platoon Commander, Section Commander, 2ic (Second-in-Command), runner, whatever. Every one on the course was a Para, apart from someone from an infantry regiment. He was a different kind of animal. Didn't seem motivated, and more to the point, did not drink tea or coffee. In that environment it was tantamount to suicide. On one occasion, when I was Section Commander, we had completed an assault, and I was running round organising arcs of fire for defence. When I came to him he had adopted a hopeless position. I picked him up by his webbing, screeched at him and physically threw him into the correct fire-position. Where I found the strength to do it, I don't know, but that display of decisiveness, strength and aggression won me brownie points. The Paras love that kind of thing. On another occasion, we were having lunch in the field. We queued up with our mess tins for stew, pom (reconstituted potato mash), bread and tea. My mess tins I had captured from the *adoo*. They were ex-British Army, presumably left over from Aden, where lots of the stuff thrown at us in Dhofar came from. The outsides were shiny black from all the wood fires they had been on with the *adoo*, and the insides were deep brown from all the tea which had been brewed in them. When I presented them for filling, there was a shout "For God's sake come and look at these!" All the instructors came over and gazed at them in wonder. "I bet there's been a good few brews in those!" Anybody else would have been shot. SAS – I was bullet proof.

At the end of the course was the 'Defence Exercise'. This was the culmination of all that we had learned during the course. We were to spend four nights out on Sennybridge Ranges, being chased from pillar to post. It was endless. There was to be no rest. The weather, predictably, was atrocious. Freezing rain, sleet, ice. On one of the exercises we were to be inserted by helicopter. Things look different from two hundred feet up at 100 mph, but with my Dhofar experience, I had no difficulty in map reading from it. Porridge was in charge. When we landed I told him that we were in the wrong spot. He disagreed. I insisted. He told me to shut up. When he had orientated himself I could see he was having doubts. He told me to run to a feature five hundred yards away and report back what I saw. I said "I can tell you now what I will see." He wasn't happy, and told me to get on with it. I was right and he stayed unhappy. The following morning we were in a wood. People were suffering, and we were told to go untactical for the duration of breakfast. This was to give people a chance to brew up and cook a hot meal. I had finished mine, and had made a small fire of twigs to warm my hands, when Porridge turned up. "Put out that fire. We are supposed to be tactical" "No, and we are not tactical." "Put it out or I will put you on a charge." He was probably still smarting from the gas plug incident.

One phase of the defence exercise was digging in at night. I had been assigned to the acting Platoon Sergeant. He was a Parachute Regiment 'hard man'. Big Zapata moustache, gruff voice, steely eye. He wouldn't have looked out of place as one of Genghis Khan's horde. He left me to dig our trench. It was to consist of a 'fire bay', for fighting from, well dug in with the spoil concealed under the turfs to the front, and a sleeping bay at right-angles to it. The weather was foul. He spent his time wandering around talking to his friends while I did the work. Every now and then he came back to see how I was getting on. When I had completed the fire bay he came and helpfully informed me that I had completed the fire bay, and told me to start work on the sleeping bay. I had got down about 18" when the order came round to stop digging and get some sleep. Genghis appeared, saw that the fire bay would afford most protection from the weather, and said that he would sleep there, leaving me the shallow sleeping bay. Thank you very much. I spread my KIP sheet over the top, (This was a nylon sheet designed to be covered with earth as overhead protection for a trench) and went to sleep. I woke up some time later with a weight on my chest. I woke up very quickly, because I am not accustomed to having a weight on my chest. I woke up even faster when I realised the weight was caused by about a million gallons of freezing water which had collected in the KIP sheet. This was serious. I could get very wet. Goose-down sleeping bags become useless when wet, and I was in one (my own personal one). I knew I had to get rid of the water quickly. I considered the options. There weren't any. The only way that water could go was over my head and into the fire-bay behind me. I considered it, but not for long. It was either him or me. No choice. Pay back time. I alternately pushed the KIP sheet with my knees and then my hands to get it swilling back and forth. When I was satisfied I gave a last heroic heave with my legs, and pulled the edge down over my head. There was a whoosh, followed quickly by a gasping, drowning sort of sound from Genghis. I made snuffly noises as if I was half asleep. He was drenched. It was first light, and we had to get up anyway. He was medivac'd out with exposure a couple of hours later. One of the things I have noticed is that the hard men, who do well in pub brawls, often do less well in situations over which they have little control, such as adverse weather conditions or being on the receiving end in a fire fight. So be it. The infanteer who wouldn't drink tea went at the same time.

Because the weather was so bad, they had erected an Airborne shelter for the morning briefing. An airborne shelter is a canvas tent shaped like a shoe box about 15 feet by 10. We all went in to take our orders. The air was thick with condensation, and the instructors, looking like Michelin men in all their layers, were stamping their feet and clapping their hands together. Under my uniform I was wearing a complete Helly Hansen fibre-pile suit. I was as warm as toasties. Because of this I could think straight and write quickly. Consequently I finished long before the rest. I got up. "Gosh, it's stuffy in here. I think I'll go out and get some fresh air." The instructors all laughed. This was good roughy-toughy Parachute Regiment humour. Their jaws dropped when I did actually go out and wait in the bitter wind. Good kit helps.

The exercise was to be completed at the end of the following day's assault by a ten mile battle run. Everyone was exhausted. We were told to ensure that we were all carrying our sand-bags in our pouches as there would be an inspection at the end, and anyone found to be without would be RTU'd (Returned To their Unit, having failed). I was gob-smacked when a couple of them held their hands up. They were RTU'd on the spot. Idiots. I didn't discover until after it was all over that the SAS were the only ones to have worn steel helmets. The Paras had all made fibreglass casts of their helmets and worn those instead. A steel helmet covered in canvas, net, and vegetation weighs a ton when wet. Anyway, we set off in the gloom along an undulating narrow tarmac road. I only wanted to survive, but I realised after a while that I was in the leading group. When the end was in sight Wally, a Para I had been trying to persuade to apply for selection, surged ahead. I let him go, and came in second. I had still broken the course record, but he held the new one. Well done him. He did later go to Hereford.

When I got my course result I was pleased to see that out of 28 categories, I had achieved 2 C's, 21 B's and 5 A's, with an overall grading of B. I was told privately that my friend Porridge had been the one who had consistently downgraded me, and but for him would have got an A. I had a final stab at him. At the end-of-course party he came over to the group I was standing with. "I am thinking of coming to Hereford," he said to me. "Don't bother." I replied. "Why?" he said. "Because you won't pass Selection," I said. In spite of all this I was pleased with my report, which was written by the course commander from US 10th Special Forces who had served in Viet Nam. "His leadership qualities and individual skills reflect tremendous potential and I strongly recommend the he be considered for commissioning as an officer. I would have no hesitancy in employing him as a platoon commander in combat." The OC of the school recommended me as a 'suitable candidate for commissioning." In hindsight, having served in Dhofar was both an advantage and a disadvantage for me on the course. The weapons being used against were all the communist ones I was familiar with. This led to frequent disagreements with the directing staff about what was effective at what range, and therefore about my tactics. Probably not what they expected, although I couldn't tell them how I knew.

I had Christmas at home with Maggie and John, and then on the 18th January went to Brunei, where we did the usual green things. Part of the exercise involved our patrol attacking a road bridge in the jungle. We decided to carry wet suits and attack it from the river. They were hot and heavy. The first night we swam two miles upstream and recce'd it, swimming back again. The following day we prepared our charges, and that night swam back upstream, placed them, and swam down again. It was eerie, swimming in the night in the jungle. The noises, the sudden movements in the water around us. We exfiltrated towards the coast. Drinking water was hard to find, so we carried two Jerrycans, which was hard work. John, the patrol commander walked into a group of trees, disturbed some hornets and fled, dropping the Jerrycans. We did likewise, because those hornets have a very nasty sting. Having given them the slip, we paused to get our breath back. John said "Right, we have to go back and pick up the Jerrycans." "Cut the 'we'," was the answer. "You dropped them. You go and get them." With considerable ill-grace, John did so.

We reached the sea, where an assault craft had been cached for us, and set off across Brunei Bay, watching out for Malay gun boats which we knew would be looking for us. At one point the craft lost speed and slowed right down. We had an argument as to why? John, who had been a sailor, said it was because the propeller was fouled, and insisted on jumping over the side to free it. We argued against it. He insisted furiously, not having forgotten the hornet incident. He stood up and jumped in. He remained towering over us. We were on a sandbank. He was up to his ankles, in the middle of Brunei Bay! We screeched. He was known as "Johnny Sandbank" for a long time after.

After the exercise we flew over the area to assess the effectiveness of our attack. The first thing we noticed was the hordes of crocodiles in the river. That was what all the movement in the water had been. We would never have swum to the target if we had known. It was probably because we were wearing wet-suits that they didn't smell us. We had a couple of days off in Brunei, and then on 26th February 1974 we flew to New Zealand.

The aircraft staged at Darwin for refuelling, so we all had to get off. We were incensed that as soon as the doors opened some Aussie erk stepped in and sprayed us with insect spray – they were very sensitive to the risk of imported bugs. When we walked down the steps there was a coach to carry us to the terminal. We refused to board it out of principle, and walked, the coach driving parallel to us as the driver shouted abuse.

When we arrived at Auckland the New Zealand SAS were our hosts, and what wonderful hosts they were! Everything was prepared for us, and we got on very well. They were the supreme sportsmen of the New Zealand Army, and challenged us to every game they could think of. They thrashed us at everything until we challenged them to a long run. We beat the lot of them. Honour restored, after a fashion.

We carried out a beach reconnaissance exercise in Kleppers (Collapsible sea-going canoes). This involved creeping up selected beaches at night having landed from the sea, and assessing their suitability for landing troops and heavy equipment. The first two beaches were no problem. The sea was like a millpond. The third one, around the point, turned out to be different. We hadn't realised that there was a heavy swell, and as we were making our landing the stern went up into the air, the Klepper went like a torpedo to the bottom and collapsed. Tikus and I finished up in a heap. After we had extricated ourselves, we crept up the beach in fine military fashion until Tikus caught his rifle in the handle of his airborne life jacket. It immediately inflated with a hiss like a jet engine, and Tikus was enveloped in dayglo orange life jacket. He was frantically trying to beat it to death with his hands, as I rolled hysterical with laughter on the sand.

We were to use Huey 205 helicopters, so the Kiwis decided to orientate us to them. Although we all knew them from Dhofar, we had to pretend that we didn't know anything about them. When they asked if anyone had any questions there was silence. Being a demolitionist (and therefore a saboteur) I helpfully asked what the best way of sabotaging a group of Hueys was. This wasn't what they had expected and went into a huddle, before producing an answer. They eyed me suspiciously after that.

Some training that we did which really worried me at first was rappelling out of a Huey 205. It is used as a means of insertion into the jungle. You have 200 feet of rope with a weight on the end. Four of you sit in the back of the chopper. One end of the rope is attached to a strong point in the aircraft, and you loop the rope through a karabiner on your waist. When the heli gets near the drop point, the doors are opened, and all four sit on the floor with the feet on the skids, two on each side. The aircraft is still doing about a hundred knots. The Loadmaster then tells you to face the aircraft. This involves standing on the skid, letting go with one hand and foot, and turning to face the heli, the slipstream providing the impetus. Terrifying. He then signs to you lean outwards almost horizontally, and when he is happy, the aircraft goes into the hover, and all four go down together as fast as possible. If the heli has a problem or comes under fire the drill is to drop the rappellers. I was in Grik, in northern Malaya in 1969, when we had a fatality doing this. Tapes were used instead of ropes, and when Nick applied the brakes about half way down, the tape snapped and he fell to his death on the baked earth airstrip. After this accident tapes stopped being used. We did several descents, and I was relieved when it was all over.

The Kiwis organised various tours for us, and I almost considered emigrating there. It is a lovely place, but just a bit too far away from anywhere. The final part of the trip was to go climbing in Arthur's Pass on South Island. We flew down from Auckland in a Bristol Bombay, an old bomber transformed into a freighter. After take off I got into the bomb aimer's position and stayed there for the whole flight. It was a wonderful sight as the whole length of New Zealand passed under me at a height of about three thousand feet. When we got to Arthur's Pass, we were assigned guides from the NZ Mountaineering Federation. We went to the foot of Mount Rolleston (7449 feet). There was a glacier to one side of it, and our guides told us to pair up, get to the top by midday, turn left and walk down. Graham and I went together, and we climbed every pitch we saw. This was a mistake, because the guides had intended that we walked whenever possible, and climb only when we had to. We weren't the only ones to make this mistake. When it became obvious what we had done, we had to climb – nothing was walkable. We reached the summit at about 1600 and started down. We had only come about a thousand feet off the top when we encountered the glacier in failing light. As Graham was the better climber he told me to lead, on the basis that anywhere I went he could follow. I was trying to traverse above the glacier when I got stuck, so Graham lowered me down inside the edge of the glacier, with the intention of completing the traverse and then helping me out. He got stuck too, and asked if I could belay onto anything. There was nothing, so he said he would jump onto the sloping crevasse and I would have to support his weight. He did so, swinging like a pendulum, and I hit the side of the glacier with more force than I would have liked. We both then climbed out of the fissure, found a lump of rock and sat on it. As it had been a short climb on a bright sunny day we had minimal kit (The first and last time I ever went up a mountain with inadequate kit). Trousers, windproof smock, woollen pullover, bar of chocolate and a couple of brews. I sat on the coiled up rope, he sat on the empty water bag, and we told silly stories to each other as it got colder and colder. We could see lights at the bottom of the mountain as search parties looked for us, but we had no means of communicating with them. At least it didn't snow. We stayed awake all night, and at first light found our way off the mountain. We went back to the hut and I slept for 24 hours.

When we returned to the NZ SAS camp at Papakura they laid on a fantastic farewell for us. They accompanied us to the airport, playing guitars, and some of them were crying. I was amazed. Smiler and I were assigned to the baggage party. That is, we had to supervise the loading of the squadron kit onto the VC10. When we had left the UK a Service Corps Air Mover had been assigned to us. We had never needed one before, and he was a pompous ass, who didn't do anything. Everywhere we had landed he had disappeared, only to reappear immediately before take off. He did the same this time. Spotting Smiler and I standing there, he marched up to us and said "Keep an eye on this lads," and disappeared. Smiler and I looked at it. It was his brief case with the red and gold Air Mover's emblem on the side. As soon as he was out of sight we opened it. It was empty apart from a large bar of Cadbury's Fruit and Nut. We ate it, and put the wrapper back in the case. He never said a word. We arrived back in the UK on 2nd April 1974

Chapter Twelve

Operation Storm, fourth trip

On the 15th May 1974 we returned to Dhofar for what was to be my last trip with the regiment. We had staged in Cyprus, and I had bought a demijohn of Cyprus sherry. First night in Umm Al Ghawarif I drank too much of it. The following morning I had such a crashing hangover that I couldn't keep water down, let alone bread. The briefing was a haze of misery, as was the flight to Tawi Atair. On arrival I was horrified to find that the cork had come out of the demijohn, and my kit was soaked with sherry. I never entirely got rid of the smell all through the trip, and every now and then it would ambush me when I least expected it.

As usual I was on the advance party, and I spent a week going out with the resident squadron, getting used to the new situation. On one of these we went out to what we knew as 'Steve Moore's Hill' – where he had been fatally wounded in 1971. There were just the four of us, and we spent our time on the way back winding up 'G'. "Why are you staring at me?" "I'm not. Just wondering how heavy you are." "Why?" "In case we have to carry your body back." Etc. He was really wound up by the time we got back to Tawi.

The previous squadron had kindly built us a waterproof hut to eat and read in. Unfortunately the only materiel available was surplus galvanised iron sheeting from a water tank. When it rained we couldn't hear ourselves speak for the rattling on the roof, and the condensation was awful. When the rest of the troop arrived, Taff, the troop sergeant gave his first briefing in it. At the end of it, Billy, who was new to the troop asked "All through my training I have heard the phrase 'When you come under effective fire you ------. What is effective fire?" Taff said "You know when you are under effective fire when men start falling." We all burst out laughing, but Taff meant it. On another occasion when Taff had been swinging the lead, Jimmy went out and threw a large rock onto the roof. The noise was appalling. We thought it was an incomer and Taff wasn't very amused.

The troop officer was affectionately known as 'Wooly Bear'. He thought it was because he was hairy – it wasn't. It was because he got everywhere (Wooly Bear is a bug which infests stores). He was always trying to lose weight, and then we would catch him eating rice pudding, and rich cake (a favourite from the compo), and eating it with condensed milk. As there were no light-weight stretchers available Jimmy Daubney (The Squadron Quarter Master Sergeant) had made one out of a camp bed, and had spent hours stitching it together. When it arrived, Wooly Bear said "As I am the heaviest here, I will test it". He lay on it, instructed us to lift it, whereupon he started thrashing about until the handles tore off. When Jimmy heard about it he was furious.

Before the monsoon came down, the Royal Engineers came to establish a pump in the Tawi, partially to help the *Jebalis*, but also to give the position its own water supply, because up until then all water was airlifted in 40 gallon plastic burmails. A dirt track was constructed from the top position to the Tawi, and they had the only Land Rover on site. We were already upset with them, because when we went for R&R in UAG we slept in tents, waking up covered in dust, whereas they had air-conditioned huts. And now they had the only wheeled transport on site! Taff enjoyed getting a sun-tan in the afternoons when we weren't doing anything else. His favoured position was close to the Sapper's road. They would drive past him at speed in the late afternoon, covering him with fine red dust which would stick to his suntan oil. He was enraged, and complained several times, to no avail. One afternoon in siesta time we heard the sound of metal on earth and rock. Taff had a pick and shovel. "What are you doing Taff?" "I'm going to teach those f*****g Sappers a lesson". When he had dug one trench 18" wide and 18" deep across the road we thought he would stop. But he didn't – he started on another, six feet further on. When he finished that, we thought he would stop. But he didn't – he started on a third identical on another six feet further on. By this stage we realised that he was serious, and felt it best not to comment any further. When he had finished he went and sat on a rock nearby, and waited. We sat up and watched. At the appointed hour we heard the Sappers driving back up the road towards us. As usual, at breakneck speed, a large plume of dust behind them. The Land Rover itself was a long wheelbase, with the upper body removed – ie nothing above the level of the bonnet, and no doors. It hit the first trench, and they flew into the air, but managed to hold on. It hit the second trench at the same time as they were nearly in their seats. They went into the air again. This time they went further, and by the time of the third trench they were thrown clear of the vehicle. They were scattered over the ground, and the Land Rover came to a halt among the low rocks which littered the position. When they had picked themselves up, dusted themselves down and realised what had happened, they were furious. They didn't come over, because they knew we were better armed than they were. Taff looked at them expressionlessly. "I warned you." He said through gritted teeth in his Welsh accent. Later their officer came over and asked Taff to fill the trenches in. He refused point blank, and they drove a lot more cautiously after that.

Every previous monsoon, the position at Tawi Atair had been withdrawn due to the difficulties of resupply and casevac through the mud and the mist. Wooly Bear had told us we were told to take only what kit we could carry in the event that at the end of trip, we had to walk out. We had a doctor and nurse (male) on the position, and a battery of 25 pounder field guns in addition to our usual establishment. As troop Arabist, my job was to live with the *firks*. They had a separate position 450 metres north of the main position, surrounded by barbed wire. With help from the rest of the troop, I dug a *sangar* twelve feet long by six feet wide, three feet into the ground, with three foot high walls. The walls were made of sand bags, the roof 4"x2" wooden beams covered with corrugated iron and sandbags, and I had a fire slit in the western end for a GPMG. The idea was that I should never be alone down there – the rest of the troop would rotate through, one at a time. So it was designed to sleep two. They didn't like it, and in practise, I was often by myself. The 25 pounder position was only a hundred yards away from me, and the lonely Brit officer there soon made contact with me. He was not a happy man because he had been told that he was coming out to a base job, and on arrival had been sent straight to Tawi for the monsoon. He had all his Mess kit with him, which would be spoiled by the warm dampness which pervaded everything.

One of the main worries was the problem of casevaccing

any injured to Salalah during the monsoon, so a flight of RAF Wessex helicopters came down from Cyprus, and we practised marshalling them in the mist. The squadron leader promised that no matter what the conditions, he would come and take any casevacs. This did wonders for morale.

When the monsoon finally clagged in, everything changed dramatically. Whereas before, you could see for miles, now visibility was about a hundred yards or less. This affected our tactics, because there is no point in picketing hill tops if the pickets themselves cannot see. We therefore tended to patrol in small groups, lie up outside villages in the mist and drizzle, hoping for a close contact, and then after first light, go in and talk to the villagers. The only problem was that sometimes the cloud base would lift a hundred feet, and then suddenly we would feel like beetles on a white ceiling. Visibility would go from a hundred yards to ten miles, the hill tops would be visible, and we would freeze, praying for the mist to drop again. Walking was difficult, because the thick 'black cotton' soil would stick to our boots and build up to a thickness of several inches before being knocked off. Walking around the position I found that putting sand-bags over my boots stopped the mud from adhering. This was unsuitable for patrol work because they wore out quickly.

Everything turned mouldy. I had a paraffin heater in my *sangar*, which I mainly used to heat pudding. One morning, after about a month, I got up to see that the ground had a fine green haze over it, as the first grass broke through. It was absolutely magical after the months of the remains of barren white grass from the previous monsoon. The grass grew thickest under the barbed wire and the edges of the trees, where the mist collected and then dripped onto the ground. I had some ground vibration detectors (Called Osiris) which I placed on the other side of the wire from my *sangar*, because at night the visibility dropped to a few yards, and I didn't want a rude awakening. The only rude awakening I had though, was when I found an adder in my *sangar*. I killed it quickly, and photographed it on the fire slit. I had to kill it, because it had been drawn by the heat of my paraffin heater, and would have come back. Another phenomenon was the ants. I had noticed the ant's nests, and had assumed that they would continue to walk. I was amazed one morning to see them coming out and flying around in clouds. It could be quite claustrophobic, as they all seemed to want to fly up my nose. Fortunately it didn't go on for very long.

On the clear days we took the opportunity to dry our kit, which was always damp and musty. There was a standpipe near my *sangar*, where the children would be sent to collect water for the *firk's* brews. The buckets were too heavy for them to carry, so I used to help them. The only contact I missed took place on one of these clear days. The ground had hardened, so I took the opportunity to go for a run around the circular track which had developed inside the wire. It was about two kilometres long. While I was out, I heard a rattle of gunfire out to the west. The BATT got up and rushed out. By the time I got back to my *sangar* the mist had fallen again, and I was faced with the choice of going out alone into the mist, not knowing where anybody was, or staying put. I decided that discretion was the better part of valour, and stayed where I was. I didn't want to be banjo'd by my own side. They killed several *adoo* in this brief skirmish, including two women. Women often used to fight for the *adoo*. The communist way of life had attractions for them. Freedom, contraception, no household drudgery, to name but a few. They brought some *adoo* kit back with them, including an old British Army 37 pattern small pack. I had been looking for something like that, so I soaked the blood off and used it, to the horror of the *firks*.

At that time SOAF had a De Havilland Beaver. This was a high-winged monoplane, powered by a single big radial engine. It first flew in 1952, and the Americans had used them in Korea and Viet Nam. The pilots loved it because it was a 'proper' aeroplane, that they could fly by 'the seat of their pants'. It had a top speed of about 160mph, and could land on the short bumpy strips so prevalent in Dhofar. I went up in it to carry out a recce to the North West. Getting up was no problem. It was the getting down again that presented difficulties, because by the time we wanted to, the cloud had clagged in again. We spent half an hour stooging about looking for gaps in the cloud, popping down through them so I could try and see where we were, avoiding the hill tops which suddenly appeared, when suddenly we spotted the strip at Tawi, and landed. After this incident it never came back.

The Baluch troops built their *sangars* like blockhouses, above ground, with a double wall of rocks, the space being filled with soil. This was to be their undoing. One night I heard a rumble, followed by two more. What had happened was that the rain water had trickled inside the wall, turned the soil to mud, which had lubricated the rocks enabling them to slip. Three of their blockhouses had collapsed, necessitating urgent rebuilding the following morning.

One evening, the *firks* came and told me that they had received information that we were to be attacked the following day. I got on the field telephone – dead. The cows which roamed between the two positions must have broken the cable. I got on the National (a handheld radio we used) – no answer. I got on the Squadcall – no answer. I knew that all locations were in the habit of turning the volume down at night because the noise of the "squelch" was a nuisance. Only one thing for it. I loaded my M79 grenade launcher. This was a single shot device which fired a 40mm grenade 400 metres and was very effective. I fired three rounds rapid at the top position, knowing that at that range they would all fall short. There was a pause, and then the whole position opened up; GPMGs on fixed lines, 81mm mortars, 60mm mortars, 25 pounders, all on X rays (Pre-determined targets). The airwaves were a babble of noise, as Brits, Arabs and Baluchis were all trying to find out what was going on. When about half a million pounds worth of ammunition had been expended, someone remembered me. "Hello Tiger Two Three Lima this is Tiger Two Three. Did you see where those came from, over?" "Yes. My location. I fired them. Over." They went completely apeshit, until I suggested that if they had bothered to keep their radios open I would not have had to resort to that method of communication.

I made a particular friend of one of the *firks* called Ali Said Aateyq. His tribal area was on the plain below the ridge, but he had joined the FAU until a *firqat* of his own tribe could be established near Sudh. He wanted to learn English. I agreed to teach him, provided he taught me Arabic script. It was a perfect arrangement, and we both benefited. Near my *sangar* was a breezeblock building to be used as a school. It was closed during the monsoon, so I borrowed some of the books to help me.

In October we were told that a SAF convoy, comprising the Frontier Force (FF) and armoured cars, was going to open the Taqa-Mirbat road. Our offer to picket was refused. We listened in fascination when they were ambushed in the bottom of the Wadi Hinna. It wouldn't have been such an issue, if the Saladin's main armament hadn't been chained down, and therefore unusable. Apparently they had done this to prevent damage to the gun's bearing when negotiating broken ground. It didn't take the *adoo* long to realise their predicament. They had trapped a Saladin, kept FF away, and had sent for their RPG anti-tank launchers, and were taunting the crew about their inevitable fate. The 25 pounders at Tawi were called into action, but the FF force commander insisted on adjusting fire himself, having been quite rude to our Fire Observation Officer, whose job it properly was. It was only after he had got his fire orders mixed up, (He confused the Observer/Target and Gun/Target direction) and peppered his own troops with shrapnel, that he agreed to let the FOO take over, and the convoy got through.

Towards the end of the trip, Wooly Bear decided to go to UAG for some R&R. Nobody else had risked this due to the cloud problems preventing aircraft from getting back to Tawi. He got stuck, decided that he was not going to return because the trip was almost over, and asked us to send his kit down on the next available aircraft. Remembering that he had told us only to bring a Bergen load of kit, whereas he had brought tons of the stuff, enabling him to live in relative luxury, we packed a single Bergen load for him. The squadron OC picked up what was going on, and when we returned to the UK, made him stay behind to return to Tawi to collect his own kit.

Chapter Thirteen

Between armies

Following the recommendation that I be commissioned I was told to apply to the Regular Commissions Board (RCB). I said I didn't want to, and was told that I would not be promoted any further if I didn't because it would be a waste of a promotion because I should be an officer. Reluctantly I did so. While I was waiting to be given a date, my OC told me that if it was in the first part of that tour, I would not go on Storm. If it was during the latter part of the trip, then I would go on Storm, but would come back early to attend it. Needless to say it didn't come through. My OC tried hard on my behalf, sending signals back to the UK which were ignored. Eventually, at the end of the trip, a signal came saying that my RCB would take place during my end of trip leave. I was furious. That had obviously been some clown in Hereford's plan all along, and I was going to have to pay for it by missing some of my leave. I paid a visit to the CO of Firqat Forces in Salalah. He said that he could not possibly be seen to try to poach a serving soldier, but were I a civilian he would welcome me with open arms. On my return to the UK I purchased my discharge. Before I was allowed to do so I was summoned by the Adjutant who wanted to know why I was leaving. On the basis that an argument is unassailable if it is not known, I gave a different reason. Naturally, he was unable to dissuade me, and I left. Taweel, who by that stage was the CO, told me that he would put a six month block on my return to Oman in order to discourage any others who had similar ideas. The intention was to starve me back in. This made me more determined.

I went to 21 SAS in London. Rocky, who ran the Motor Transport Section, offered me a job as a Vehicle Mechanic Grade 2. I told him I knew nothing about engines. He said I didn't have to on the basis that my main job would be to drive 4-ton Bedford RLs from the Duke of York's Barracks to Chelsea Barracks to fill them up with petrol. He told me where to go, how to apply, what to put on the application form – a fine example of creative writing, and I got the job.

On my first day, Rocky duly told me to take a 4-ton Bedford RL to Chelsea Barracks and fill it up. I said I didn't have an HGV licence. He told me not to worry. I said "What if I have an accident?" He said "Don't have one." After two months of driving through the ferocious traffic of King's Road and Sloane Square, he had a word with the unit tester. They agreed that if I could do that, I could drive. He gave me my test slip, told me where to take it for processing, and I was given my HGV licence.

Due to the risk of IRA bombs at the time, all vehicles had to be parked under cover at night. One day, I was last in, and there was one space left for me. It was a tight squeeze, and after parking I had to climb across the roofs of the other vehicles. I reversed into the gloom. I was about half way in when I heard a horrible squealing sound. I stopped immediately and pulled forward. On the back of a Bedford there is a rectangular piece of angle iron on each side to protect the brake lights. The nearside one had scored a groove down three panels of the Brigadier's car, from the front wheel to the back door. In misery I realigned the Bedford, parked it properly, and went home. The next morning I went to see Rocky. "Rocky, I have a confession to make." "No you haven't." "Rocky, I have." "No you haven't. Start again." "Rocky, I have something to tell you." "That's better." I told him. "Did you check the Brigadier's car before you reversed in?" "No, I didn't." "In that case how do you know that you did it?" I said I must have done. "Rubbish," he said. At that moment the Brigadier's driver came in, screaming blue murder, accusing me of scraping the car. Rocky gave him a huge bollocking, told him that he knew that he was partial to a drink when on duty, that he had probably done it whilst pissed, and if he didn't shut up he would report him.

I had only been there a month when the 2ic called me in. He told me that a millionaire had been threatened, and asked me if I wanted a job as a bodyguard for a while. I went down to Bath, and discussed it further with the man's general factotum, a blimp-like retired army major. It seemed that the millionaire's driver was a leading member of the local criminal fraternity, and had used his Rolls Royce as a means of ferrying stolen goods, secure in the knowledge that the Police knew the car and would not stop it. He had also compromised the management of the company by giving them money, saying that it was the winnings of a bet he had placed for them. He had done this time and time again. When caught, he had been released on bail, but had threatened the safety of the millionaire's two small children, so he was selling up and leaving the country. My job was to live in the house with the family, and watch the children. The pay was reasonable, the risk minimal, and the surroundings luxurious, so I agreed. I couldn't understand why someone with as much money as he had was doing a runner – why didn't he pay someone to do something a bit forceful? Anyway, I could see why he was a millionaire. Apparently he had started off with an ice cream van. He worked non-stop. He ate his breakfast standing up in the kitchen. Didn't get back until late, ate his supper quickly and then went upstairs to continue work. He would come down at nine o'clock to watch the News, standing behind the settee, then go back upstairs again. He gave himself two, two week holidays a year. As it happened, the hood never turned up. A month after I had started when the final day came; I drove the family to Bristol airport in their top-of-the-range Mercedes, saw them onto the plane, drove the car back to the house, put the keys through the front door, and went home. I never heard of him again.

I returned to London and contacted one of the civil engineering companies which had a contract in Oman. When I told them of my background they offered me a job immediately as head of security at Midway airfield, dependent on their obtaining for me a 'non-objection certificate' (a kind of visa from the Oman government). I went back to the Duke of York's, resigned, telling them that I had landed a huge job in Oman, squillions a year, palace etc. I hired a camper van and Maggie and John and I went on a tour of England. When we returned ten days later, there were three telegrams for me. Two from the engineering company, and one from the Sultan's agents in London confirming that I had been granted a commission in SAF with the rank of captain. I contacted the engineering company and told them I would not be joining them, and then strolled down to the Duke of York's. They already knew. Brummy said "You are a very small wheel in a big machine. Don't forget that." Somebody high up had obviously made the decision that it was better to keep me in Firqat, than lose me altogether to a civilian company.

Chapter Fourteen

Firqat Force

On the 8th December 1974 I was granted a commission in the Sultan's Armed Forces in the rank of captain. I was to serve with *Firqat* Forces. I flew out to Muscat in January 1975 and went straight to the SAF HQ at Bait al Falaj. It was very quiet. On my first night in the Mess I noticed three other new boys, some of whom had been on the same flight. We drifted together and sat around a coffee table. They were all young regular officers, and were sniffing round each other. Regiment? Date of commission? Etc. I didn't say a word. After a while they turned to me and asked which regiment I was from. I said "22 SAS Regiment". There was a silence, because I didn't say any more, and they were back on their collective heels. Then one said "Tell me something. I hear that the men there can be a bit difficult at times". I said "Before we go on I had better inform you that I was one of the men". There was another long silence, and then one of them said "Oh jolly well done!" I said "Why?" and got up and left them. I never saw them again. Obviously rear echelon.

After a couple of days of administration I flew down to Salalah in a SOAF BAC 111. I reported to CO *Firqat* at *Firqat*

HQ in Salalah. He was a very pleasant, ascetic sort of man who later became a priest. Accommodation was arranged for me in the Plains Battalion HQ at Umm al Ghawarif a few miles to the east. This was in short supply, and I had to "hot bed" for a while. Shortly after this Harry Woolley, who was the 2ic/QM for *Firqat* Forces kindly let me use his accommodation while he went on leave. Harry had been in Oman for some time, and understood how to deal with *jebalis*. When one of them came storming into his office, demanding something or other, Harry would quietly search for his pipe. Having found it, he would carefully tap out the old tobacco, examine it, and then ream it out with an old knife. Meanwhile the *jebali* would carry on with his rant. Harry would then search through his pockets for his tobacco pouch, and, having found it, carefully and slowly fill the bowl. He would then tamp it down, examine it, and then start a search for his matches. Having located his matches he would proceed to light his pipe, and, when it was lit to his satisfaction look up and quietly ask if he could help. The *jebali*, having let off steam, was by now in a far more amenable mood.

I was assigned to the Firqat Salahadin (FSD), which was comprised of tribesmen from the Bait al Kathir. The three sub tribes were the Bait Ali bin Badr, the Bait Amr bin Mohammed and the Bait Mohammed bin Ahmed. The Bait Ali bin Badr group was based at Hedgehog Delta, and the other two at Hedgehog Bravo, and were rivals with each other in the firqat, which led to much squabbling. The firqat leader was Mulaazim (Lieutenant) Masaud Ahmed Said, of the Bait Ali bin Badr. My role was to administer them – rations/health care/anything they wanted. On the military side, I liaised between them and the Plains Battalion, which at this stage was the Jebel Regiment (JR) commanded by Ted Ashley, an affable Staffordshire man. Being an avid fan of "Lord of the

Rings" I selected "Ranger" as my radio callsign.

At this stage, SAF (Sultans' Armed Forces) had established positions known as "Dianas" on the lip of the jebel scarp, to prevent the *adoo* from firing Katyushka 122mm rockets at RAF Salalah. These were numbered from 1 to 4, from East to West. The *firks* wanted bases more central to their tribal areas, such as had been established by the Bait al Maasheni at White City, and the Bait al Umri at Tawi Atair. I discussed this with John Akehurst, the CO of Southern Oman Brigade. He was happy for them to go ahead, provided they could be supplied by land. He did not want SOAF to be stretched still further with resupply tasks. I quickly moved myself up to Diana 3, partly to get away from the squabbling, but also to carry out a more military role. I patrolled out with the *firks*, partly to dominate the area, because SAF in Diana 3 were reluctant to do so, but also because I wanted to get to know it.

A lot of these patrols degenerated into hunting trips. The wadis were full of Hyrax, relatives of the elephant, but looking more like big guinea pigs. The local word for them was *thifn*. We would set out before dawn. About ten of us, armed with rifles, a Bren gun and a tea pot. We would lie in ambush until the sun was well up, and then descend into the wadi bottom to shoot hyrax. The *firks* were phenomenal shots, and rarely missed. We would have some tea and dates, and then walk slowly back up out of the wadi to Diana 3, where the hyrax would be prepared for the pot. Occasionally we recovered land mines or ammunition, which had probably been hidden by the *firks* before they came over onto the Sultan's side.

On the 14th January I went out with Masaud and 7 *firks* to recce a new position north of Diana 3. We moved out at 0400, and on arrival at the suggested new location, lay down to wait for sunup. I froze – it was bitterly cold. The location was ideal, except that it lacked water. However, looking at the map, it appeared that a road could be put in from the north. I tried to raise Cracker battery (Artillery) and Foxhounds (Infantry) on the radio – no reply. They were all asleep, which made me furious. I was all the more annoyed because the Cracker Battery officer, a Brit, had previously asked me to remove a huge boulder over which his *sangar* had been built, and which cramped his living accommodation. I had done so using plastic explosive in a sufficiently small quantity not to damage his *sangar.*

At this stage I was joined by Chris Dry, a former member of BATT, because it was policy at that time that Brits should not work alone if possible. On the 8th February we went out with 14 *firks* and a section from JR to mount an ambush on reported *adoo* movement. There was no contact, but it served as a useful further recce of the proposed new position to be known as Diana 5.

15th to 17th February was Op Ta'aawan. This was to be a search of the Wadis Gheylal and Jizzi. Troops involved were 2 companies from JR, one company from the Desert Regiment (DR), 34 members of BATT, 53 Nomads (*Firks*), 4 armoured cars (Saladins), 3 Land Rovers, (2 carrying .50 Browning machine guns and one carrying a 106mm recoilless rifle), and supported by three 25 pounder field guns. The forces were deployed from Salalah to Diana 1 and Diana 2 by helicopter on the 15th, and at midnight we moved to picket positions above Wadi Gheylal. Some *adoo* were sighted, but no contact was made. We carried out a wadi search, and found a variety of military supplies, from ammunition to mortar rounds to medical kits. These were carried out of the wadi and airlifted to Salalah. We carried on in this fashion for the next two days, doing the same in Wadi Jizzi, and finished by walking out down the Wadi Nahiz to transport waiting in the wadi mouth. My conclusions at the time were that the *adoo* had probably been weakened by operations in the West, and were hiding in the Wadi Rishm to the north.

On the 24th February Chris, myself and 14 *firks* carried out a search of the Wadi Theat, to the East of the proposed Diana 5. We spotted one *adoo* running away, and found an *adoo* camp. There were numerous sleeping bays and camp fires. It was strewn with discarded clothing and military equipment. It took only 5 hours, but it was most useful. The following day I took 9 *firks* and searched the Wadi Sheikh, close to Diana 3. We found two Russian jumping mines, and roasted a *thifn (Hyrax)* we had shot, before returning to base. I blew one of the mines at Diana 3, and sent the other one down to Brigade HQ for identification. When I went down several weeks later, I found it in use as a door stop in the Brigade Major's office. When I told him it was live he seemed quite concerned.

I gained permission to establish the new Diana 5. The operation to install it was called Operation Husn. The other aims of the operation were to search the major wadi systems in the area, and to kill the enemy. It was at the briefing for this that I told the officers of JR that if they could see the enemy they were *firks*, and if they couldn't, they were *adoo*.

Friendly forces were 50 Firqat Salahadin (FSD), 15 Firqat al Rubha (FAR), 34 BATT, three companies of Jebel Regiment (JR), one company of KJ (Kateebat al Janoobia), one company of FF (Frontier Force), one company of DR (Desert Regiment), 91 Battalion Jordanian Special Forces, armoured cars, artillery, SOAF, Z Company (Land Rovers with .50 Brownings and 106mm recoilless rifles). Two days before the op, on the 9th March at 1250 a JR company commander and his 2ic (Second in command) hijacked a SOAF 206 helicopter to recce the area. It was shot down, killing all on board (The pilot, Peter Davies, Nigel Marshall and Mike Shipley). Troops were lifted in by helicopter to recover the bodies, so the op was probably compromised before it even started. On 28th April the *firks* told me that the men who had shot it down were Mohammed Obaid Bait Gidad, Said Adenan Anobi and Amr al Kimer al Haman.

The operation started on 11th March from several start points around the area. I walked out with Chris and the 50 FSD from Diana 3 with two companies of JR and reached Diana 5 at midnight. Having secured the position, and set out ambushes, the rest of the group went to bed. The whole position stood to at 0200, when terrible howls were heard, and a giant green caterpillar was seen to be thrashing around in the long bleached grass. It turned out to be one of JR's officers who had awoken to find a rat in his sleeping bag. They had taken a mutual dislike to each other, and both were trying to leave the bag simultaneously.

When the sun rose, I discovered that I realised that I had placed the location a 1,000 yards out. This did not endear me to the mortars or guns, who had to rewrite their plotter boards. The problem was that the new location was exactly on the joint of two maps. Not just any old two maps, but ones where the lines of longitude converged. There must be other places in the world which have this anomaly, but I have not heard of them.

Every body sat tight and waited for a reaction from the *adoo*. It was not long coming, and there were numerous contacts, both at our location, and several others. During a pause in the fighting, Chris and I left with the *firks* and headed for Wadi Ashoq, to the North West. The plan was that JR would picket the top of the ridge, a group of BATT would walk north east in the wadi bottom, and we and the *firks* would contour along the sides just above the BATT patrol. I was amused to note that they moved as if they were patrolling a street in Belfast. I could hear them plainly chuntering "F*****g

Sibley should be down here." They were clearly unhappy, and unaware that I was just above them. I could have taken the lot out. Then the troop sergeant restored discipline, and they continued to advance in silence. We moved on ahead of them, and spotted a group of *adoo* in the wadi bottom, heading towards BATT. I radioed their location, expecting them to go to ground for an immediate ambush. Instead they doubled forward, spotted one of the *adoo*, opened up, missed, and then went to ground. Me, Masaud, Chris and two firks ran after the *adoo*. It was exhilarating. I felt as if I was flying. We caught up with them at a bend and opened up. I fired off half a magazine, as the *adoo* returned fire and disappeared out of sight. We ran on, and saw them again at the second bend, about 200 yards away. I bowled one over, and saw him pulled away behind a rock. We dropped down into the wadi bottom to follow up. There was a heavy blood trail, then we found discarded bloody dressings, and the blood trail moved to one side of the path. He was clearly being carried. At this point we were a kilometre ahead of our own forces. JR on high had seen the movement in the wadi bottom and called in a jet strike on us. As they started their run in, one of JR's officers (Andrew Booth) recognised my *shemagh*, which had had the green dye bleached to a dirty red on the crown, and called them off. That was the second time SOAF had had a go at me. At this stage the *firks* lost interest, and refused to chase them any more. Their reason was that the *adoo* had clearly taken a pasting. The real reason was that they had probably recognised them as members of their own tribe.

We continued heading north east along the wadi bottom, following the blood trail for another three kilometres until it disappeared. We found a food cache of about 400lbs of grain. In the late afternoon our kit was heli'd down to us in the wadi bottom. The *firks* had selected our sleeping place. It was under a huge slab of rock which had slipped off the mountain, and was propped up against the wadi side. It was about thirty yards long, and there was room for all of us. The following morning we continued to search the wadis, and found a variety of weapons and ammunition, including the .30 Browning machine gun taken from Mike Campbell's Commando Carrier, when he was killed in 1972. That afternoon we found an *adoo* sleeping area, with a blood soaked shirt, still burning. That evening we moved out of the wadi bottom to a pimple half way up the side, where the *firks* killed a cow for supper. We continued our searches the following day, before being lifted out by heli to Hajeef to prepare for the next phase.

We walked out at 0430 on the 15th and went down the Wadi Risham, where we expected to make further contact with the *adoo*. As it happened, although we continued to make considerable arms finds, they did not engage us, although we spotted them from time to time. The local civilians were clearly informing them of our movements.

On the 17th the *firks* got a sad on, and refused to cooperate. SAF did not want to go down the Wadi Firm without somebody else going point. I tried to shame the *firks* into cooperation by saying I would do it alone. Fat chance! I set off, going point in front of a company of shuffling, clanking, coughing infantry, through thick scrub in the wadi bottom. I was convinced that the first I would know of the *adoo* was a burst in the guts. I was quickly joined by a Marine officer known as "Half Brick". He was carrying a pump-action shot gun, and stayed by my right shoulder, since I was tracking the *adoo*. There were traces of them everywhere. Again, they avoided contact, but one of them must have had a sense of humour, because I found a fresh human turd right on the track! We continued until after mid day, when we reached the far side of the Wadi Naheez. As I walked up out, I saw what I thought were American troops. Tall, fair and red haired men in US uniforms. As it turned out they were the Jordanian Special Forces, who had been deployed to picket our route out. I was to get to know them better later. I felt that the whole operation had been far too ponderous. The *adoo* were close to us throughout, sometimes within minutes. We could have had a greater return for our casualties of four killed in action and five seriously wounded.

I returned to Diana 5, or Ghadaw, as it was known locally, and continued to patrol the area with the *firks*. By this time, Chris had had enough of them, and had left to join the Frontier Force. Living with the *firks* was interesting. Masaud insisted that I have my own tent, to signify my status, with him sharing it, to confirm his own. I had an aluminium trunk (*Jundi* box) to keep my belongings in. Masaud insisted that I lock it. I said I didn't think that anyone would steal from me. He said there was no chance of that, but in their culture, anything not locked was common property, and I could lose things. We generally started the day with a cup of sweet tea, made with condensed milk, which formed a skin on the top, and a freshly made *chappati*. After that, meals were a bit haphazard. They could cook at any time. The food generally was based on boiled rice served up on a large aluminium tray, with a knob of *saman* on top. *Saman* is butter, which, not being refrigerated is always rancid. I acquired the taste quickly – there was no option. The idea was that you knelt in a group around the tray, and using your right hand, take a handful of rice, squeeze the surplus *saman* out of it and flick it into your mouth with your thumb. Sometimes they killed a goat. They were always halalled, ie. had their throats cut according to Muslim law. Nothing was wasted. The meat was usually boiled, and finished up very chewy. Their idea of a barbecue was to light a fire, and when it was well established, pile stones on it, which would heat up. In the meantime, the intestines of the slaughtered goat would have their contents squeezed out, then without being washed, the mesentery would be stuffed into them. They would then be placed on the hot rocks, where they would be left for ten minutes or so. One side would be burnt, the other raw. They would cut them into chunks and share them out. That was the only item on the menu I managed to always avoid. A favourite in winter was broad beans, boiled and served alone, to be eaten like popcorn. On patrol and on operations I always carried a green waterproof bag with some dried dates. This gave me a ready source of energy which would keep, and not make me too thirsty. For tea and main meals I relied on the *firks*, as usual.

On 5th April I went north to Ayun, to recce a road route to Diana 5. The position commander was a seconded officer called Mike. He was interested in establishing a position on the jebel west of Diana 5, so we pooled our resources and found a route which would serve both locations. I later confirmed its feasibility from the D5 end, and submitted my plans to Brigade HQ. They were accepted, and on the 19th April Op Tashaabuk commenced. There were two companies of JR, three armoured cars, Recce platoon, FSD, and one D6 bulldozer.

The armoured cars, Recce platoon, bulldozer and JR left Ayun and headed south to the tree line. I and the FSD went North West from Diana 5 to meet them. When we could see the other force on a ridge a thousand yards away across a shallow scrubby basin, the *firks* suddenly stopped, and refused to go any further. They said they had come to the edge of their tribal area and could go no further. Frustration again. No matter what I said about their best interests, one country etc, they wouldn't budge. SAF wouldn't move into the tree line without the *firks*, and the *firks* wouldn't go to SAF. Trying to embarrass them again, I set off, this time alone, into the scrub. They didn't follow. Fortunately, there were no *adoo*, and when I popped up by the armoured cars at the other side, Ted Ashley was surprised to see me. I explained the situation. The armoured cars didn't want to go into the scrub without infantry support, so I went point again, closely followed by the bull dozer with Half Brick sitting on the engine with his shotgun. The road was duly established and that was that. It was after this that CO JR (Ted Ashley) asked me if I would like a position as a company commander in JR. I did, but my request to transfer was rejected from on high.

With the monsoon approaching it was imperative that I built weatherproof accommodation for myself at Ghadaw (Diana 5). The *firks* had built for themselves a stone blockhouse on the highest point at their end of the position. I scrounged corrugated iron and sandbags, and set about building a bunker near them. I don't know how many sand bags it took, but it was a lot. It was only visible from the wire on one side, so I built an extra blast wall there as a defence against RPG rockets. When I had completed it I returned to the UK for some leave. On my return to Dhofar, I was told that I was to be reassigned to Makinat Shihan as Officer Commanding, for the duration of the monsoon, and that I should see the Brigade Major (BM) as soon as possible. Makinat Shihan was a position about half way up the Omani/Yemeni border, on the edge of the Empty Quarter. When I saw the BM, he just told me to make my way to Midway, and pick up a convoy to Makinat Shihan, and that was it. When I asked him for a proper briefing, he asked me what I wanted to know! I was gobsmacked. I said I wanted a full briefing. He said I would have to see the Brigadier. When I duly did so, I felt that he was holding something back. When I asked him what my rules of engagement were/ aggressive patrolling/strike fighter support etc, he blanched. He said that as no one knew exactly where the border was, I was to ensure that in the event of a contact I was in Omani territory before calling down a strike. If he had told me what he really wanted, namely that he wanted me to defend the position against Yemeni aggression, and not open a second front in the Empty Quarter, I would have understood. They were concerned that the Yemenis could have struck the airbase at Midway in a night attack across the border, and Midway was a vital aircraft base and storage area. But no one told me that. Instead, when I arrived at Makinat Shihan, I discovered that all my wheeled transport had been pulled out, thus making any form of patrolling impossible.

The position at Makinat Shihan consisted of a low horseshoe shaped ridge sticking up above the sand and gravel plain. In the middle of the horseshoe was a well-head. Defending it were a company of Oman Gendarmerie, a hundred *firks*, and an Iranian anti aircraft detachment (The place had been bombed previously). My accommodation was a wooden hut. Electricity was supplied by a generator, which was switched off at dusk, to ensure that no lights gave the position away. I took over from Jim, the outgoing OC, who left on the same convoy I had come in on. It was incredibly hot and as sleeping in the hut was impossible, I quickly moved out onto the veranda. Everybody was very friendly, and my sole source of pleasure was the tinned fruit, which the Iranians had in vast quantities. I ate them first thing in the morning, when they were still cold from the night. After that, everything was warm and vile.

To stop myself from going mad, I made a point of visiting every position every day. Since this comprised several hundred acres, it took some time, and amongst the people I met were Salem bin Ghabaisha and Salim bin Kabina, who had been Wilfred Thesiger's guides during his epic crossing of the Empty

Quarter. They were concerned about refugees crossing the border, and said they needed assistance. When I queried this, they produced a battered civilian Land Rover, and we went to visit them. We travelled west for two hours. When I said that I reckoned we were about fifty miles inside Yemen, they laughed, and asked where the border was. I hoped not to have a contact – it would have caused a diplomatic incident. We visited several Bedu encampments, and what a fine, generous, healthy lot they were. I quickly realised that they were not refugees at all – they were *firqat* families who roamed the area all the time. They ruled the territory – there was no chance that Yemeni forces could have appeared unbeknown to them. The reason the *firks* had brought me was that they had heard about the government assistance the *firks* on the jebel were getting, and they wanted their share. Another frequent visitor was Barakat. He was the leader of the Firqat Southern Mahra, and their tribal area was north of the jebel, in the Negd and straddled the border with Yemen. He was a small unobtrusive sort of a man, and when he wore military uniform his jacket buttons were always out of sequence. I am sure he did it on purpose. Because the Army was afraid that he would stir up trouble with the Yemenis, he was told to move his base to Fasad, a long way from the border. He hadn't been there a day when he signalled to say that the water was undrinkable. When it was tested it was found to be polluted with diesel oil, undoubtedly poured in by Barakat.

I had a lot of spare time at Makinat Shihan. Fortunately, nearby were fields of geodes. A geode is a spherical lump of rock, hollow inside, the inner surface being lined with crystals. They vary in size from about 1" in diameter to 6", and the colour of the crystals varied from white to blue to brown. They were revealed as the sands shifted. Most days, I would go out with a Sharps Toffee hammer, and crack them open. The nice ones I took. We were allowed to use the British Forces Post Office (BFPO) post, which meant that I could send ten kilos for one pound sterling. I duly filled up old Compo ration boxes with the things, and sent them back to Maggie. I later found out that the boxes arrived back in the UK in the most terrible condition. When Maggie phoned the Mount Vernon Sorting Office to complain, it transpired that no one there thought that somebody would send back boxes of rocks – they were convinced that I was smuggling something, and had even gone to the extent of splitting the corrugated cardboard! They offered her their sympathies, and after that, the boxes arrived intact.

After several weeks of this I wrote to my colonel and asked to be moved. My justification was that I was doing nothing, not from my own choice. At this time, the Jordanian 91st Special Forces Battalion on the Midway Road were in difficulties. They had fought against the Palestinians in the Black September rising in 1970, in Jordan. Their minimum response in a contact was to fire off everything they had. As a consequence their heavy weapons had been taken away from them in order to limit the damage they would otherwise have done. They had no sympathy with the *jebalis*, and were rough with civilians. This had led to them falling out with the *firks* in a big way. It culminated in the crew of a Jordanian Land Rover being found dead from gunshot wounds on the road. They had been shot from within the vehicle, and no items of equipment were missing. As they only stopped for people they knew, the Jordanians suspected the *firks*. A couple of nights later, a shot was heard from the *firqat* position adjoining the Jordanian HQ at Jasmine 2. They investigated, and found a dead *firqat* sentry in a *sangar*. Of his companion there was no trace. A search of the camp at first light revealed the missing man in a nearby *sangar*. He was a friend of the dead man, and refused to come out. The Jordanians opened up on him, but didn't hit him. There was no way they were going to get him out without sustaining casualties themselves. They brought up a Saladin armoured car, which fired its' main armament, a 76mm shell. It didn't explode at such close range, and careened off into the Wadi Nahiz below. At this stage Chris Dry arrived. He had been assigned as the Liaison Officer to the Jordanians. He tried to negotiate, and eventually the *firk* agreed to come out if Chris would take his surrender. Chris agreed. As the man came out of his sangar, the Jordanians rushed past Chris, knocked him to the ground, and emptied the magazines of their Armalites into him. Chris had never got on with Major Tahsin, the excessively macho Jordanian commander, and this was the final straw. Chris was reassigned, and I took over.

Tahsin was a very powerfully built man. He specialised in one-arm press-ups, and whilst driving, he would carry his Armalite in the crook of his arm, and take pot shots without stopping, at anything which attracted his attention. I was given a tent on Jasmine 2 close to Tahsin. The monsoon conditions were atrocious – non-stop rain and drizzle, mud up to two feet deep, everything damp and mouldy. In these conditions patrolling was kept to the minimum, especially as there was more risk that there would be a contact with the *firks* than with the *adoo*. They patrolled the road in vehicles, and that was it. I got on well with Tahsin as there was nothing happening which could provoke an argument. I didn't see his macho posturing as a challenge, as Chris had, and most importantly, we discovered early on a mutual love of Backgammon. They called it "TricTrac" after the sound of the pieces being moved around the wooden board, at speed. The Jordanians played the game very fast, moving almost without thinking, whereas I played slowly and thoughtfully. It was a contrast in national characters. I wondered if relationships on the Midway Road would have been different if they thought things through first. We mainly played at night, when it was cooler. Tahsin was extremely autocratic; if he wanted to eat at 2 o'clock in the morning, he would shout to get a cook out of bed so he could cook us a meal. If he didn't like the way a soldier walked past his tent he would shout at him to do twenty press ups in the mud on the spot. I was only there for a month, when it was decided to withdraw the Jordanians and return them to Jordan. I gave Tahsin a Zippo lighter with a SAF crest on it, and he gave me a Jordanian *khanjar*. He said he would send me an inlaid backgammon board from Jordan, via the Jordanian engineers who were to remain. I have no doubt that he sent it, but it never reached me.

I then became liaison officer for the *firks* who lived along side the Midway Road. Brigade rules were that all vehicles had to travel in convoy because of the risk of ambush. If I had abided by that I would never have got anywhere, and also it would have inhibited the conversations I had with the locals. These were invaluable because I learned so much from them. I would always stop and give them a lift. My main worry was that my weapon was a 7.62 FN rifle. I really needed something more compact for use in a vehicle, even if it was an open Land Rover with no windscreen. I managed to get my hands on a 1½" Verey pistol (Flare pistol) which I kept in the dash. I was driving up the Midway Road one day during the monsoon. I had just gone past Jasmine 1, when I saw a figure running through the mist about 30 yards to my right. He was dressed in the purple *Sbeaka*, a kind of kilt the *jebalis* wore especially during the monsoon; he had communist belt kit, and was carrying an AK 47. He was shouting at me to stop. I decided that if he was *adoo* he would be able to kill me from where he was, so I decided to stop, and have it out at close range. I cocked the Verey pistol and leaned across the passenger seat. He ran up to the door and looked straight down the Mersey Tunnel. He said "Don't shoot." I didn't say a word. He threw the magazine off his AK into the foot well. I still didn't say anything. He said "I am a friend," and showed me his *firqat* ID card. I eased the spring on the Verey pistol and told him to get in. We drove on in silence – very unusual for a *jebali*. He suddenly said "If you thought I was an *adoo*, why did you threaten me with a flare pistol when you had an FN?" I said "It is difficult to use an FN in a Land Rover, and in any case, if you get hit by one of these you die in agony after three days." He asked to get out and ran off towards Qairoon Harritti. Several days later I bumped into Hilal Fadhlullah at the Firqat HQ. He was a tall, thin serious man who moved a bit like a marionette. "I hear you gave my brother Ali a lift the other day." "That is correct." He says you threatened him with a flare pistol." I said "That is true." He burst out laughing, slapped me on the back and said "He was terrified. He hasn't stopped talking about it since."

The *adoo* were still all over the place, and from time to time I came into contact with them. Not in a military sense, but by accident. On two occasions I was invited into *baits* by the owners to see *jebalis* who I did not recognise sitting by the fire. They were hyper-alert, and had the thin, hunted faces of men on the run. They had their Kalashnikovs close to hand, and eyed me with distrust. They never said much. Nothing ever happened of significance, presumably because it wasn't in the best interests of the tribe to allow it, but I had no doubt that had I bumped into them on the jebel it would have been very different. On one particular occasion, later, when I was worked for the Civil Aid Department, I was driving in my Land Rover pick-up with Gareth, the Engineering Officer from Dhofar Brigade HQ. I spotted a *jebali* obviously wanting a lift.

I stopped. He said he wanted to go to Said bin Ghia's house in Salalah. He had *adoo* stamped all over him. He didn't appear to be armed. I said to Gareth "Watch him. He is *adoo*". Gareth was clearly perturbed, and watched the reflection in the mirror carefully. I wasn't particularly concerned – I deliberately drove fast, and if he had pulled a gun and shot us he would have died as well. When we approached Said's house he tapped on the rear window and asked to be let out, and he disappeared into the night. A week later we heard that the Treasurer for the Central Area had surrendered. Presumably the money had been cached on the jebel before he came down.

Hilal's brother Mohammed was the *Mindoob* (Government Representative) for the Bait Tabawk. We always got on very well, but one of the things which worried me was that if we were arguing about some aspect of government aid, he would start jostling me, and when I resisted he would whip out his *khanjar* and threaten me with it. It was all in fun, of course, but it worried me that one day it could get out of hand. Then the solution came to me. There was to be a fancy dress party at the FF Mess. I decided to go as a *jebali*. I had all the kit except for a *khanjar*. The next time Mohammed threatened me with his, I said "That is a very fine knife. Can I have it?" The rules of Arab generosity and hospitality demanded that he give it to me, which he did straight away, and without complaint. I felt sorry for him, but it was the best solution: he could no longer threaten me with it, and I had the final part of my costume. At that time I had a very fine Smith and Wesson hunting knife. The next time I saw him I showed it to him, and asked him what he thought of it. He agreed that it was very nice. I immediately gave it to him. It salved my conscience, but I noticed that he didn't get a decent-looking *khanjar* for some time. When he did, he never threatened me with it. When I eventually left Dhofar I gave him my Smith and Wesson .38 Special revolver, which he was very pleased with.

By this time, the CO Firqat had been replaced by Ken Wilson. He was a small aggressive Jock from the Royal Scots (Pontius Pilate's Bodyguard) with an impressive Korean War record. He had lately been OC Dhofar Company of the Trucial Oman Scouts, and so well understood the *jebali* mentality. He used to hold court in his office in the mornings, as queues of *firks* waited to see him with their requests, which he skilfully dealt with. The problem was, that he enjoyed doing it, and he liked having an audience when he did so, which kept me waiting. At this time I was always in a hurry, so couldn't afford the luxury. I solved the problem by taking a paperback book with a particularly garish cover into his office. Having saluted and greeted him I sat down and ostentatiously started reading it while he duelled with a *firk*. I was aware of him looking at me with mounting irritation. Suddenly he asked me what I wanted. I told him, and got it. I never had to wait again.

There wasn't a lot of activity in the Central Area after the monsoon, as there were major operations going on in the Western Area. At one point there was a plan for a last major operation in the West. SAF was going to concentrate its' forces, and Central and Eastern Area Firqats had been persuaded to fight outside their tribal areas in the West. There was a lot of tension in the air. Salem Khuwaidham Ahmed, from the FSD, who had been wounded several times and awarded the WKhMB (VC equivalent), insisted that he would come along as my bodyguard. As it happened, it all came to nothing.

I had become friendly with the Hunter and Jaguar pilots based at Midway (Thumrait). They had seen a waterhole from air, and wanted to visit it. I identified it as Ayn Andhur. Although clearly visible from above, it was difficult to find on the ground. They said that if I took them there, they would supply all the refreshments. On the appointed day we set off. I found it without difficulty and we had a barbecue and drank cold lager long into the night. The following morning I woke up and looked for some fresh water. They hadn't brought any! I couldn't believe it. They said that they had been relying on the water hole, but it was only fit for animals. The drive back was torture. When you are really thirsty, cold beer tastes like treacle. We were desperate by the time we returned to Midway. My only consolation was that if we had had an accident, we had radio contact, and could have been rescued, but that wasn't the point.

The social life increased as the war drew to a close, and a fine time was had by all. A particular friend was Martin Ward-Harrison, in the Jebel Regiment. He was an extrovert character with large mutton-chop whiskers and sported a fly whisk and a moth-eaten Panama. His father was a general, and frequently sent him hampers from Fortnum and Mason. We used to go to the beach where the Holiday Inn now stands near Salalah, and eat our way through them. Anything we didn't like was fed to the *pi* dogs which were always hanging around – expensive dog food. On one occasion, it was decided to hold a party at Ayun Pool, just south of the position at Ayun. We loaded the Mess furniture onto the back of an open three tonner, the chairs arranged around the edge, and a coffee table complete with copies of Horse and Hound. The officers of the Jebel Regiment climbed aboard, and off we went. Martin looked around, and said, languorously "The whole thing is an absolute disgrace." We all laughed joyously, and it became the in-saying, often reduced to,"The whole thing.....," to describe anything we were enjoying. Martin sadly died on the 11th February 1976, four days after suffering massive head injuries when the Land Rover in which he had been travelling as a passenger hit the town gates at night. For some reason best known to themselves the *askars* guarding them had chosen to close them. In the absence of street lights the driver simply could not see them.

An operation was planned to search the wadis of the Central Area. I didn't expect any opposition by this stage of the war, so when two of the pilots asked to accompany me, I agreed. The plan was to move out of Hajeef, west of the Midway Road, at dawn on the 20th March. I had spent the previous night at Midway, so we set off at about 0300. We had been travelling for half an hour when I noticed a bright light in the sky to the east. I said it looked like an aircraft landing light. The pilots agreed, but then said that aircraft did not land at Midway at night. We stared at it, nonplussed. When we reached Hajeef, there were hundreds of soldiers lying out on the ground also staring at it. When it became light, it disappeared, and we set off on the op. It was only later that I discovered that it was the Comet West, one of the brightest comets of recent years. Op Sahara lasted until the 24th March. Friendly forces comprised the Desert Regiment, and the *firks*. We searched the deep wadis, including Wadi Rishm, W. Firm, W. Geti and W. Ageyti. There were no contacts, and we recovered a considerable amount of equipment and food. It was almost surreal, because these were the deep wadis which only a year previously would have taken enormous numbers of troops to enter, at a considerable cost. This was my last operation with Firqat Force.

In retrospect, the Dhofar War changed my attitude to life. In spite of all the years of training, nothing can prepare you for the first angry bullet. The sudden realisation that the people firing at you intend to kill you, and, if you don't do something about it, they most surely will. What the training does succeed in doing though, is in teaching you how to react. How many times, after the initial shock of a contact, did the phrase 'Win the fire-fight' jump into my mind? When the mind has been drained of all sensible thought, it is the repetitious training which takes over and carries you through until you can adapt it to the specific situation in hand. I have never forgotten an incident in UAG when people suddenly started milling around without a clear idea of what to do. A Senior NCO bellowed "Stop! If there is going to be a panic, let's organise it!" Dhofar taught me how to recognise what is truly important and what is not.

Looking back on the whole thing, having survived the war relatively unscathed, it is easy to forget, that when we first went there, the result was not a foregone conclusion. The *adoo* had control of the whole of the jebel, and all but three towns (Salalah, Taqa, Mirbat). They were locals, who knew the ground like the backs of their hands, whereas for us, the mapping was very poor. They were being trained and supplied by the communists (South Yemen, Russia, China, and East Germany). They were aggressive in action, and their combat skills were of a very high order. Initially we were outnumbered. Initially their personal weapons were better than SAF's (AK47s, RPDs, 60mm mortars, against .303 rifles, Brens and 3" mortars). If the *firqat* had defected *en masse* at any stage, the war would have been over. As it was, several did defect, in one case killing a Brit officer (Eddie Vutirakis) on the way. The attitude of the *firks* was often ambivalent. As it developed effectively into a civil war as families and individual members of families changed sides, there was often a reluctance to kill the enemy when they had the opportunity. Many ambushes failed because if a *firk* recognised a member of his family in the killing zone he would stand up and shout for him to surrender. They never did – the result would be a hail of AK fire, and the total failure of the ambush, much to the frustration of all involved. As the war progressed and the *jebalis* saw that they were being given the development that they originally went to war to obtain, more and more came over. It became a lost cause. Consequently the pressure increased on the remaining *adoo* – difficulty of supply/increased risk of a contact on unfavourable terms/casualty evacuation etc. The final straw was the closure of the supply route from South Yemen. With that the war was declared over, although some refused to surrender, and were supported by their families. Attacks by them on government forces decreased largely because the tribes resented the disruption to their way of life caused by SAF operations following an incident, and because they also ran the risk of being declared common criminals, and treated accordingly when caught.

On the first National Day (18th November) after the end of the war it was decided to have a fire power demonstration. It would take place north of Salalah on the plain below the jebel. This was the area where the camel people usually gathered at this time of year. They would have to be informed. The word was put out, but they showed no sign of moving. I was given the job of telling them. A couple of days before, I boarded a helicopter at dawn, and we searched for their camps. When we spotted one, the heli landed about a quarter of a mile away, to avoid frightening the camels, and I would run into the camp. I quickly found that my running into a camp alarmed them, so I slowed to a walk for the last hundred yards. It is impossible to go into a *jebali* camp, tell them something and walk away. It would have been rude. So I had to go through the usual greetings, sit down, and have some refreshment. In this case it was fresh camel's milk, with the froth still on it, out of a *gaalo* (milking bowl). Camel's milk is very heavy, and to run, drink a pint of it, and then run back to the waiting heli, was arduous. To do it four or five times in an hour, heroic. The weight of it built up in my belly. How I was never sick, I don't know. As it turned out, I performed this function every year until I left Dhofar. For the demonstration, a large fort made of empty oil drums was erected under the jebel on the edge of Salalah Plain, and the various branches of the armed forces attacked it in turn. I was in charge of ten *firks* armed with RPGs, a favourite *adoo* weapon. A fortnight previously when I had taken them into the Negd to practise on an old Saracen Armoured Personnel Carrier, they had been hopeless, and I was worried, but I needn't have been. They had only been taking the Mickey. Our targets were only two hundred yards away and on the day, they were spot on. I was glad to be behind them and not on the receiving end. In the line up was a 5.5" field gun. These things have a range of about 18 miles, so to use one at a target a thousand yards away seemed a bit difficult, and so it turned out. They had the most senior NCOs in the Oman Artillery manning it, under the command of their colonel. I was lying down on the ground fifty yards to its right when it fired. I saw the shell leave the muzzle, and it crested about a hundred yards in front. I saw it in slow motion and I buried my head in the dirt. There was a huge explosion, but the only damage done was to a Bedford truck, which was peppered. The problem was that artillery guns usually fire a trajectory. With the target so close it was line of sight. Nobody had thought to check a rise in the ground in front.

There were also crazy car races. Anybody could enter, and there were no rules. There was a water bowser which dropped several hundred gallons of water on one of the bends, a Land Rover chassis with batteries of smoke grenades on the back, a Bedford truck which dropped loads of empty oil barrels on the track and anything else anybody could think of. SOAF cheated by underslinging their entry from a Huey helicopter and flying it around the course at an altitude of about ten feet. The SOAF Hunters flew so low, inverted, that the spectators on a rise appeared to part like cilia as they approached.

As the war had effectively ended, I foresaw that the exciting times were over, and my time would be spent administering the argumentative *firks*. I was approached by Martin, a former Ghurka officer who had also served in the Muscat Regiment, and who was now in charge of the Civil Aid Department (CAD). Would I be interested in joining CAD, and replacing Trevor, who I already knew? I would still be working with the Jebalis, but I would be able to bring Maggie and John out to Oman. That was the clincher, and I agreed immediately.

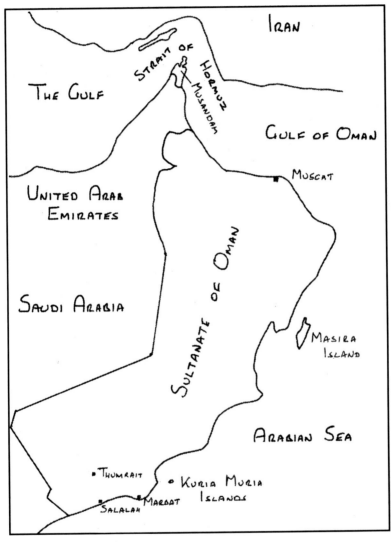

Sultanate of Oman

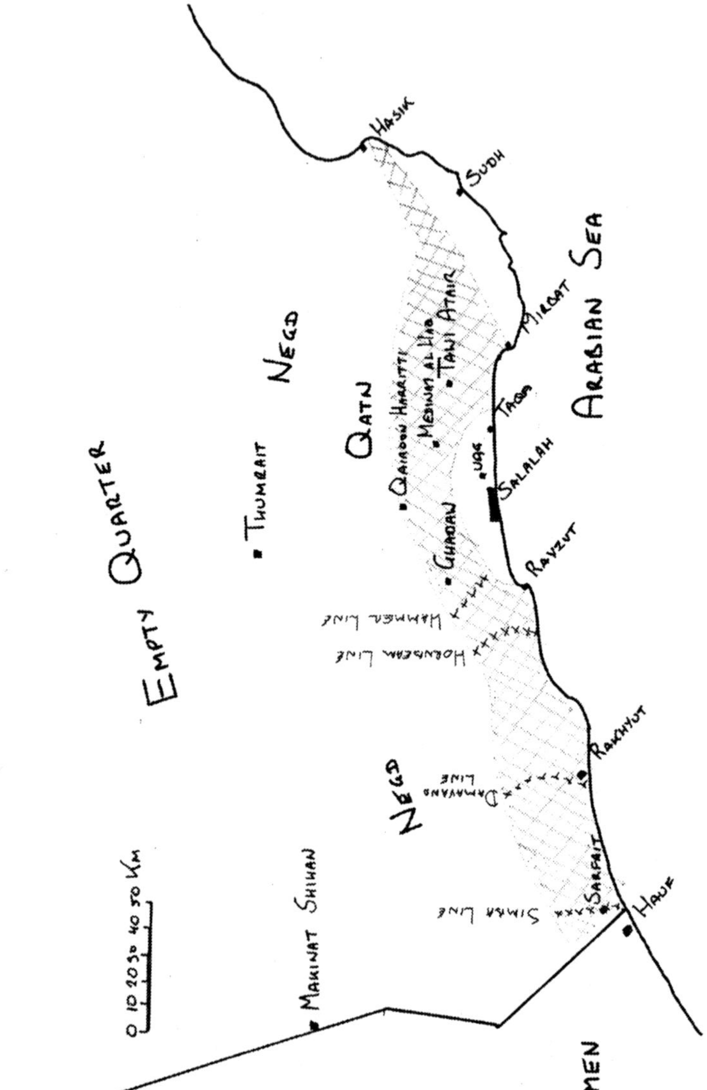

Empty Quarter

Negd

Thumrait

Qatn

Hasik

Sudh

Arabian Sea

Qairoon Hairatti
Mekun al Har
Tawi Atair

Mirbat

Taqa

Rugs

Salalah

Raysut

Ghadan

Hornbeam Line

Hammer Line

Rakhyut

Damavand Line

Negd

Sarfait

Simba Line

Hauf

Makinat Shihan

0 10 20 30 40 50 Km

Yemen

Dhofar

190

Taqa BATT House showing shell damage

Taqa Fort. Note repaired shell–hole in top parapet

Sumhuram 1971

Umm al Ghawarif 1973

Author with Strikemaster

Tawi Ateer 1973

Patrol west of Tawi Ateer, 1973

Ahmed Muhammed Salem al Umri (Kartoob)

Wadi Jenin. Op Husn

Firks pulling out near Qairoon Harritti

Firks with captured arms

Masoud during cave search in Wadi Ayb

John, on wrecked Commando Carrier in Wadi Jarduum

Camel People in Wadi Darbat

197

Chapter Fifteen

Civil Aid Department

On the 1st April 1976 I was transferred by order of The Palace to the Civil Aid Department of the Wali's Office (Governor's Office), with the nominal rank of major. The function of CAD was civil assistance in the areas affected by the war. Organisationally it was split into three areas: - The Negd (gravel plain on the edge of the Empty Quarter), the Coast, and the Jebel. The intention was to develop government centres in each tribal area. A government centre consisted of a shop, a mosque, a school, a clinic, and water bore hole and distribution system. On the coast the existing villages were rebuilt along the same lines. The Negd was fairly quiet, and was run by an Omani called Salem. The coastal development involved the reconstruction of the villages of Dhalqut, Rakyut, and Mughsayl, in the West, and Hasik, Shwaymia, Sharbitat and the Kuria Muria islands in the east. Mohammed Said was responsible for the Western Area, whilst Ali Awadh Mubarak Al Shanfari looked after the East. The jebel area had been the responsibility of Trevor (ex- SAS), who was moving to the Oman Research Department (Intelligence).

While I had been in Firqat Force in 1975 I had run from

Qairoon Harritti on the jebel to Umm al Ghawarif, on the Plain, a distance of 32 kilometres. I did this several times, initially being escorted by Lofty, a former SAS man then in Firqat. It was an interesting run, because the first half was in the mountains, and so fairly cool, but when the Plain was reached it was hot, and the road stretched for ever in a long shimmering curve of heat haze, which never seemed to end. At about this time three SAS soldiers had become paraplegic, one by gunshot, and two in an accident. BATT at UAG decided to raise money for them by doing a charity run. They chose the route I had pioneered. They organised it, and I provided the T-shirts for the runners to wear, as my contribution. The race was held on the 9th April, and there were about seventy-six runners, British and Omani, military and civilian. I had a problem with one of my running shoes, and didn't do as well as I had hoped (I came in fifth, which galled me). However the money was raised, and the following day I flew to Muscat to receive Maggie and John, my legs stiffening all the while.

The SAF Training Regiment Sergeant's Mess had offered me accommodation, and that night at dinner one of them observed that I had difficulty walking. He said he was a Physiotherapist, and offered me heat treatment and massage in his office. I looked at him with grave suspicion, but he assured me it was above board, and so, putting my misgivings to one side, we went to his office after dinner. The treatment was agony. I am sure I could smell my flesh burning under the heat lamp, and when he started to untangle my knotted muscles I almost went out of my mind. Anyway, after about an hour, he stopped, and said if I had any more problems to come back and see him. I hopped off the table like a two year-old, completely pain-free, and went back to my *bait* (Accommodation) for the night. The following morning I jumped out of bed, and nearly broke my neck – my legs had seized up again overnight. I didn't go back for any more massage, and spent the day lying by the pool, waiting for God to effect a remedy. The following day Maggie and John arrived, and we flew down to Salalah.

Trevor had lived in a bungalow on the beach in an area called Hayy al Shatti, near the palace, and this was to be our new home. It was in a magnificent location, right on the beach on the edge of the Indian Ocean. This beach was 90 kilometres long, and ran from Taqa in the east to Rayzut in the west. We could see whales from our sitting room window, and we awoke every day to the sound of waves lapping on the beach. During the annual migration the cormorants flew in a non-stop line out to sea for days. One of our favourite pastimes was to comb the beach. The variety of sea-life was incredible, and we collected shells galore. In September 1976 a red tide of algae developed. This caused havoc to the marine life, and the beach was covered with rotting bodies. This was a great shame, but it enabled us to see all sorts of fish which normally we wouldn't have known existed there, including the little Box Fish, which we dried and bought home. Turtles used to lay their eggs on this beach, and we regularly saw where they had dragged themselves up, laid their eggs, and returned to the sea. Sometimes they died, and their remains were eaten by the ubiquitous ghost crabs. When the young turtles hatched, their instinct was to head for the reflection of the stars on the sea. Because the villas were so close to the beach, many were distracted by the lights, and would head inland instead. We often found them in our garden, from where we would take them to the sea.

The first thing John did on his arrival was to scale the formica-covered wardrobe in his bedroom. He fell, and caught his arm on the edge of the formica, causing a deep laceration. I was on the jebel at the time, and Maggie was kindly helped by a neighbour to take John to the Field Surgical Team (FST) at RAF Salalah. He fought silently and determinedly while he was sutured. A week later the stitches were taken out, and I was surprised to receive a bill for 60 Riyals (about £120). I wasn't expecting to be charged, as it was a British military unit loaned to Oman. However, I recognised that now that I was a civilian I was no longer exempt from being charged. I was told to make my cheque out to the RAF Masirah account, and duly did so. It was several years later, when the FST left that I was told that that account was held in Salalah, and that the money was distributed locally.

One evening we heard a crash from John's bedroom, as if a wardrobe had fallen over. When we investigated, we found nothing. This happened several times, and we couldn't account for it, because the house was of reinforced concrete construction, on a concrete base. I mentioned it to Trevor, and he told us that the house was haunted. He had previously used John's bedroom, and one night he had woken up to see an Omani fisherman come through the wall in front of him, walk past his bed, and out through the wall behind him. Enquiries with locals had revealed that some years previously a fishing boat had sunk in the bay opposite, and all the crew drowned. They had recovered all of the bodies except one. This fisherman was wandering around looking for his body. In order to try to lay the ghost, they had built a shrine behind the houses, but to no avail. We never saw him, but we continued to hear him until we left.

By the front door I planted a couple of banana palms, and they flourished. The first thing John did on going out in the morning was to push two bananas into his swimming trunks, like pistols. When he had finished shooting people with them, he ate them. In their shade I planted mint, which also did very well. We got through a lot mint, as a vital component of Pimms.

My job involved liaising between the tribes and the

Wali's Office. Although the tribes had their own hierarchy of sheikhs, each tribal area had a government–appointed representative called a *Mindoob*. The Jebalis were just as demanding as usual, and habitually bypassed the *Mindoob*. They all wanted a tribal centre, consisting of a water bore-hole, shop, school, clinic and a mosque. They also wanted a road to connect their tribal centre to Salalah. They wanted it now. They also wanted government assistance in the form of tents, blankets and food before each monsoon. In 1976 the only roads were untarmacced, and ran from Mirbat to Taqa to Salalah to Rayzut on the plain, and from Salalah to Midway (Thumrait) to Muscat through the Negd. There were roads which ran from Midway to the western area. On the jebel itself there were very few tracks. I quickly realised that if I stayed in the office I was a sitting duck for any *jebali* who had an axe to grind, and there were many. Also I didn't know if what they were saying was true. If I was to be effective, I had to know the boundaries of the tribal areas, where the centres of population were, how many people, where they got their water, how many cows, goats, camels each had, and where they moved to with the various seasons. In my time with CAD I walked along every ridge and every wadi in Dhofar. I visited every village, not once, but several times. I made a point of giving anybody a lift who wanted one. This gave me the opportunity to quiz them about local names, features, who lived where, where they moved to at different times of the year etc. It was interesting getting them to impart information, because the *jebalis* are a naturally suspicious lot. One of my techniques was to comment that a given village was inhabited by such and such a tribe, knowing it to be incorrect. My companion would furiously deny it, and prove it by saying exactly who lived there, which family and how many. I would store this information away, and when I met someone from the same tribe, I would repeat it back, and they would either confirm or deny it, giving me still more information. On the jebel, unless I was showing somebody around I always worked alone. This was because I found the presence of other Brits distracting – they wanted to talk to me, whereas I wanted to talk to any *jebalis* I picked up. For my protection I carried a 9mm pistol initially, but later managed to get hold of an M58 automatic rifle. In the early days particularly, Brits were warned against travelling on the jebel alone, and the *jebalis* were always surprised to see me popping up in the middle of nowhere. They would look hard to see if anyone else was with me before inviting me into their *baits* (Houses). The *jebalis* had two kinds of *bait;* the permanent winter ones, which resembled bee-hives, consisting of a circular stone wall surmounted by a straw roof, called a *strit,* and the temporary summer ones made from sticks and covered with straw and old clothes, called *mutha.* It was always an experience entering a *strit,* because you would go from bright light into gloom. The air inside would be heavy with smoke and perfume, and as your eyes became accustomed to the gloom, you would make out the open fireplace, surrounded by cooking pots, and the sleeping mats around the edge.

Sometimes I took John with me, and he was a great icebreaker; not only because of his charm, but because many *jebalis* had never seen a European child before, and the fact that I brought him with me demonstrated my trust in them. John could walk for miles at my speed – largely because I told him that there were wolves around. When he became too tired I carried him on my shoulders. On the way back in the Landrover he would be exhausted. The tracks were too bumpy for him to sleep on the back seat, so he became adept in sleeping standing up with his arms through the handles on the backs of the seats. On one occasion near Jib Jat, when I was going off on one of my long walks he opted to stay behind with the *firks*. When I returned several hours later I found him taking part in the butchering of a camel, thoroughly enjoying himself. I collated all this information, and continually updated it (I later gave it to Durham University). A map of the Southern Region covered one wall of my office. I used coloured marker pins to show the distribution of the villages and tribes. John noticed this, and made a map of his own, at his level, just above the skirting board, and similarly covered it with pins. When I was asked to return to Dhofar in 1982 to help sort out a drilling problem, I returned to my old office. I was gratified to see that my map was still there, as was John's!

John and I spent a lot of time together, and this was nearly his undoing. Next to Dhofar Brigade HQ was an Intelligence cell, and part of it was devoted to captured *adoo* equipment, which was arranged as a museum so that people could learn to identify the different types. I visited the HQ on a weekly basis to find out what the military were up to. John found this very boring, so I would leave him in the museum, where he played with the various pieces of equipment. He was especially fond of an anti-aircraft gun which he could swivel round. One day the Intelligence clerk looked in horror to see John in the process of dropping a 60mm mortar bomb down the tube. He managed to reach him in time to stop him. Everything there was live. Had he succeeded, he would have killed himself and destroyed the building.

On one of my trips to the jebel, I was travelling back alone from the Western Area. I was on a graded road on top of a razor-backed ridge. The road had become corrugated by all the tyres which had passed along it, so I was driving at about fifty five mph to fly over the bumps and reduce vibration. Suddenly I noticed a wheel shoot in front of me, cross the mound of spoil at the side of the road and disappear into the wadi bottom five hundred feet below. It didn't take me long to realise that it was my front near-side wheel and that the half-shaft had broken. I struggled to keep the Land Rover straight, and it finished up straddling the road-side spoil where it ground to a halt, partially due to me breaking, and partially due to the sump ploughing along the spoil. I climbed out and looked down into the wadi-bottom where I had so nearly finished up. It was several hours before some passing *Bedu* found me and took me to Thumrait.

In March 1976, in order to show their loyalty to the Sultan, it was agreed that two thousand of the Firqat should visit Muscat. That was given as the reason; however, it was widely thought that it was a political demonstration by the Sultan to show his subjects in the north that he had a force in the south which could be mobilised against them if necessary. In any case it turned out to be a huge logistical exercise, involving both the armed forces, who supplied air transport, and civilian companies, who were only too pleased to rent out their big Mercedes wagons to be used for transport. For me, this meant a quiet couple of months, as most of the people whose main aim in life was harassing me, were away, and there was very little transport available to move things. The impact of two thousand wild and woollies on the north was considerable, and on their return we were regaled with stories about their antics. One of my favourites involved a group of *firks* who visited a road-side café where they were refused service. A group of them kept the café staff occupied at the front, while the rest went around the back and removed everything not nailed down.

At the beginning of June, 1976, most of the grass on the jebel had dried up, and the new shoots on the trees had been eaten. The tribes on the jebel agreed that the fairest solution would be to combine their camel herds into one huge herd, which would start in the east, and work its way west eating all available fodder. I was keeping an eye on it, and one day at Taytum in the Central Area I was having a chat with the drovers when I noticed a little bundle lying in the dust about fifty yards away. It was difficult to make out in the blinding glare, so I went and had a look. It was a new-born camel (*Jowood*). I went back and told them, but they weren't in the least bit interested. I told them that if they left it there it would die. They agreed. When I remonstrated with them, they said that with the herd on the move, there was no way it could keep up, and they weren't about to carry it. I persisted. They said "Look, if you are so concerned, take it". So I did, and put it in the back of my Land Rover and returned to Salalah. We called him Andrew, and straight away had the problem of feeding him. I went to the *Suq* (Market) and bought some baby's feeding bottles, together with teats and large can of Nido, the locally available dried milk. Maggie made up the feed, and we started, having enlarged the hole in the teats with a hot needle to enable Andrew to drink at the rate he wanted.

Andrew was a beautiful creature with a soft woolly coat and huge long eye-lashes. We kept him on the patio, and he quickly worked out that our bedroom was on the other side of the air-conditioner which projected into the patio. He needed feeding during the night, and when he was hungry he would bellow through the air-conditioner to attract our attention. It was amazing how much he drank, and we soon became used to producing huge quantities of feed. He didn't have a mother to lick him clean, so I suggested to Maggie that she should fulfil this role. Not unnaturally she declined, but found that baby shampoo was a good alternative. He became very affectionate, and in the evenings would rest his head on our laps so that we could stroke him. When we went out he would become distraught, and run along the garden fence, crying. The problem with baby bull camels is that they grow into adult bull camels, and adult bull camels are vicious. I once saw one bite a man's bicep off in Taqa. Also we didn't have anywhere to keep a full-grown camel. Sheikh Mubarak Ruwaas, who I worked with, agreed to take him. I have no idea what became of him, and didn't like to ask. We missed him, but at least he had a few months of happy life instead of being left to the mercies of the hyenas on the jebel.

We had a variety of animals during our time in Salalah. On arrival, we had inherited a pair of cats, imaginatively called Tabby and Ginger. They were very affectionate and regularly hunted on the beach in front of the house. Unfortunately, this was to be their undoing, because, when we first arrived the road in front of the house was a gravel track. When the Sultan decided to 'do up' the area, this was tarmacced. Consequently, cars drove very much faster, and they were both killed within a few days of each other.

Ken Wilson (The commander of Firqat Forces) had been given a fox cub by a *jebali*. He didn't want it, so he gave it to us. It was too small to be released, and loved to be cuddled, but we realised that we would not be able to keep it as a pet. He was a wild animal, and would have to be returned to the wild. We kept it in a cage on the patio, and deliberately minimised contact with it, to keep it wild. We fed it, and kept the cage clean, but had no other contact with it. We watched it grow, while we decided where we should release it. We decided that Rayzut Harbour would be a good place, because there was a large fox population there. They lived by scavenging for rotting fish on the beach, so we adjusted our fox cub's diet accordingly. When the day came, remembering how tame he had been, I strolled into his cage and picked him up. This was a mistake, because he was wild. With lighting speed he bit all the fingers on my left hand, so I cleverly changed hands. He took me up on the offer, and bit all the fingers on my right hand. I retreated in disorder to wash my wounds, and returned with leather welding gloves and a plastic dustbin, with lid. We took him to Rayzut, and released him. Pleading the need to take pictures, I persuaded Maggie to hold the bin and lift the lid. He looked out for a moment, and then sped off into the rocks. We spotted him a couple of times in the ensuing months, and he seemed healthy, so I hope he made the transition.

Similarly, Ken gave us a young jebel hare. It was incredibly delicate and beautiful, with great big ears and fine whiskers. We called him 'Inspector Bun' after the chief of police in Salalah – Inspector Nunn. Lovely though Inspector Bun was, we decided that he too would have to be returned to the wild. We kept him until he was big enough, and decided to release him at the spring at Ayn Arzat towards the end of the monsoon, when the vegetation would be at its most lush. With heavy hearts we took him there, and I carried him in his hutch over the stream, opened the door, and then retreated back across the stream. Inspector Bun came out and started nibbling contentedly while we watched. I took some photographs, and then started to go back to the car. Inspector Bun suddenly looked around, realised that we were going, and ran after us, falling in the stream in the process. We realised that he was too tame to be released, and he sat in Maggie's lap all the way home. We kept him for some time, but he was eventually stolen from us by the children of the Palace slaves, who lived nearby in Hayy al Shatti.

Our neighbours, David and Gwen, were adopted by a stray cat, who they called Mabel. She was the most unprepossessing cat I have ever seen. She was mangy, had a hump back, one eye, one tooth, and limped. She clearly had had a hard life, but she came to them for food every day, before disappearing back outside. She wouldn't come anywhere near us or anybody else. When David and Gwen left, we didn't see her for a while, and then one day, she appeared on our doorstep, looking very distressed. We fed her, but she wouldn't let us do anything else. She went away, and came back shortly after with a single kitten, also distressed. She was obviously desperate, and had come to us as a last resort. She came for a few days with the kitten, and then one day came alone. A few days after that, I found her dead in the dust at the back of the house. I never found the kitten.

During the annual migration, the beach in front of the house would be covered with exhausted birds, gathering their strength for the next leg of their journey. Those that were injured, or too exhausted to move, we brought in and fed until they were well enough to fly away. Some, it was kinder to put down, but we rescued scores in this way. One day we found an Aden Gull with a badly broken wing. He had such an intelligent little face that I couldn't put him down, so I amputated the wing, applied a bandage, and kept him in the garden, where he had his own pond. He enjoyed sardines, which were plentiful. They were bigger than the tinned ones, and we kept a supply in the fridge. At feeding time we would throw him one. He would catch it side on, and then throw it up into the air and catch it head on so that he could swallow it. His whole neck would bend to the shape of the fish, and he would jump up and down to shake it into his gullet. He would watch the other gulls flying overhead, and would run up and down the garden trying to take off, but of course, he never could. We called him Fred, or the Spiv, because with his colouration and attitude he looked like an East End wide-boy. He was lovely, and always greeted us when we came into the garden, begging for more sardines.

We also had a Snake-Eagle, who we called Hengist. He had been shot by a *jebali*, and left for dead. Someone found him and brought him to us. He was alive, but his wing had been shattered by the Kalashnikov bullet. With the assistance of an anaesthetist from the FST, I removed the rest of wing on the dining-room table, and treated him with antibiotics. I made a perch for him out of a branch on the patio. His diet was a bit of a problem, because in the wild they eat snakes. While snakes were also plentiful, I did not intend to spend the rest of my days risking being bitten by his intended dinners. Instead, I cut beef into strips, and jiggled them in front of him, several times a day. Not knowing much about eagles, I wrote to the RSPB for advice. Instead, of advice, I received a haughty reply along the lines of "We do not approve of wild birds being kept". I expect they would rather I had killed him. He was a beautiful creature, and became quite tame. I decided to treat him like a giant chicken, so far as care was concerned, and this seemed to be successful. We had him for a couple of years, until he died from pneumonia one monsoon. A few days after his death, a book I had ordered called "Veterinary Aspects of Birds of Prey in Captivity" arrived. My only consolation was that I had been treating his chest infection properly.

We were also given a *Dhob* by Ken. A *Dhob* is a kind of lizard which lives in the Negd. They are about twenty inches long, and are characterised by having a thick spiky tail, which accounts for about half of the length of the creature. They use their tails as defensive weapons, and are much coveted by the *Bedu* on account of the tail, which is said to be delicious, and taste like chicken. He also lived in the garden. One day he escaped, and we only realised it, when the brigadier's wife banged on our door. Maggie answered it "My dear, do you know your dinosaur is on the beach?" We returned him successfully to the wild.

One day, driving on the Midway Road, I found a dead hyena. It was a fine-looking creature, and had clearly been hit by a lorry. I put it in the back of my Land Rover, and took it to a Brigade picnic near Sumhuram which we were attending that afternoon. Maggie was appalled, but it was the centre of attention. Afterwards I pushed the body onto a ledge on the cliff overlooking the sea. I returned to it every now and then to check on the state of decomposition. When enough had gone, I removed the skull, and cleaned it properly, and we still have it in the sitting room.

On the 30th June 1976 I was returning from Hasik on the East coast on the flying doctor run. It was the beginning of the monsoon, and the clouds were hanging over the jebel. The pilot, who was new to the country, was called Ian. I was in the co-pilot's seat, of Huey 205 number 717, and in the back was Khalfan, the Load master, the doctor and several civilians hitching a lift. The war had been declared over, but there were still plenty of baddies running around who had not surrendered, and would attack opportunity targets. I noticed that the flight route was a direct line from Hasik to Salalah, which would take us over the bad-lands east of Tawi Atair. I didn't say anything, because pilots can be very precious about their status, and I didn't know this one.

When we hit the cloud on the edge of the Eastern Area, he chose to fly under it, and we were forced down to about fifty feet. Knowing the area well from the number of contacts we had had there over the years I broke my silence and said "Do you know we are in injun country?" He looked worried and immediately turned to port to fly south to the coast. This didn't solve very much because it would take us straight through the Wadi Hinna, also well known to me. I didn't have time to say anything because at that moment there was a tremendous burst of fire. It sounded like hailstones hitting the heli, and for a split second I thought that was what it was. Directly below me and to the front was an *adoo* firing his AK47 at us. A hobbled camel was trying to lurch to its feet, and a couple of women were running for shelter. On my left, and level with us, on a feature we knew as "Twin Tits" for obvious reasons, was an RPD machine gun firing a long burst of tracer. To our low right were two more *adoo* firing AKs.

Khalfan screamed as he was hit in the arm, and I was sure we were going to crash. I was equally convinced that I would survive the crash, and was worried that I might be trapped in the wreckage, and shot by the *adoo*. Ian put the heli into a dive to gain speed, and I was suddenly aware of blood trickling down my face from a shrapnel-wound to my scalp. There was pandemonium in the back. The doctor asked for my knife to cut the clothing off the wounded Loadmaster. We flew through the Wadi Hinna and immediately landed on the beach. I asked Ian what he was doing, and he said he was checking the aircraft for damage because it was no longer airworthy. I told him that we were still in injun country, that the *adoo* knew that we had landed, and would be joining us shortly. I told him that if we stayed there we would all be killed. He agreed to fly it, but asked me to watch the dials and inform him if anything started moving quickly. When we were airborne I asked him if he had put out a contact report. He didn't answer. When we flew past Taqa I asked him again. This time he complied, but it wasn't until we were flying over the perimeter wire of RAF Salalah that he got through. We were directed to the Landing Pad by the FST. It almost fell out of the sky on to the pad, and I jumped out immediately as the men in the silver suits covered the known universe with foam. I went over to the HQ to tell them where the *adoo* were and say what had happened. A jet strike was put in immediately, but the *adoo* would have gone. Ian left SOAF, and Khalfan's wounds healed eventually. My head healed, although I was able to comb more pieces of airframe out of my hair when I got home. A friend from the Regiment who had become a helicopter pilot was there at the time. He subsequently told me that they had been amazed that Heli 717 had continued to fly with the amount of damage it had sustained to its engine, airframe and blades.

To reach the villages on the eastern coast, and in the Negd, CAD made extensive use of the SOAF's Britten Norman Defenders. These were the military version of the Islander, and could carry about six passengers. On the 3rd of August one of them suffered engine failure and crashed into the sea near a village called Sharbitat. Only Miranda, a friend of ours, and the pilot managed to swim ashore in the heavy monsoon seas, the other five on board all drowned. One of the bodies was washed up later, and I was asked to identify him, but it was difficult after he had been in the sea a while. On another occasion in the Negd, the aircraft was so overcrowded that we were one seat too short. As I was the smallest, the pilot asked me if I would travel in the freight bay in the rear. With some misgivings I allowed myself to be shut in, and we bumped our way through the turbulence to Salalah.

Later that year Foot and Mouth disease was identified on the jebel. This caused a huge panic, until it was realised that the disease was endemic – this was the main reason why the cows' milk production was so poor – that and their poor diet. It was suggested that the entire jebel herd be slaughtered, but the financial and political situation precluded that. The *jebalis*, having lived with the disease, would have considered it an excuse to destroy their financial power base, and would have gone back to war.

In October 1976 Professor Walter Dostal visited Dhofar. Several years earlier he had written a book about Dhofar without actually having been there because of Said bin Taimur's restrictions. He had had to rely on descriptions given to him by Dhofaris he had met in the Gulf. On the 12th October I took him up onto the jebel to meet the *jebalis* in the wild, and he realised that there was much more to the place than he had been told. The following year Professor Fred Scholz and Jörg Janzen visited Dhofar. Jörg had come to write his thesis on the *jebalis*, and Fred was his mentor. I introduced Jörg to the *jebalis* and showed him around. Jörg was a big man, and when he first came to the house, our son John answered the door. He came running into the bedroom saying "There is a GIANT at the door!" Jörg and I got on very well and I gave him a lot of information. At one stage a group of *jebalis* took me to one side and asked if they should tell him the truth, or lie. When Fred returned to Germany he wrote to me several times. Obviously his secretary could not believe that he could be writing to a complete unknown like me because the letters were invariably addressed to "Herr Professor Doktor P Sibley." Jörg came back again in 1978 to continue preparing his thesis. He had been collecting Dhofari silver jewellery as part of his studies. This traditional jewellery was going out of fashion because the *jebalis* had become richer, and they were buying gold instead. A lot of Europeans, me included, bought it. When he showed it to a member of the Ministry of National Heritage and Culture who had apparently befriended him, it was confiscated. Jörg was all the more upset, because he had invited him into his house for a beer when it happened.

There was much interest in the flora and fauna of Dhofar, because no European had had access in modern times. Mike Gallagher, a conservationist who worked for the government was keen to collect information on anything that we could find. We became keen bird spotters – it was possible to get very close, especially in a Land Rover, and I was the first to identify Abdim's Stork in Salalah in 1978. In September 1976 Mike came and had dinner with us and told us about his interest. The following day one of our neighbours came to Maggie in hysterics saying that there was a dead mouse in her swimming pool; would she come and remove it. Maggie did so, and remembering Mike's words, attached a label to the poor thing's neck "One drowned mouse. Didn't have a life-jacket" and left it by his door. Mike was very pleased, and wrote later saying that it had been identified as a Gallagher's Gerbil, the first one identified in Dhofar. We had already named it 'Maggie's Gerbil', in her honour.

Mike was keen to enter the Wadi Darbat and see what was there. Because of the risks I liaised with the Kateebat al Janoobia (KJ), the infantry battalion in whose area it was. They agreed to picket the wadi on the 6th October 1976, so that we could enter safely. When we were in the wadi bottom, Mike and I became separated from the main body. We were in a dried out palm plantation owned by the Sultan's mother, when I saw a snake in a tree directly above him. I called a warning, and he jumped back and looked up. He was excited "It's a Southern Arabian Brown Cobra. This is the furthest east it has been identified". I asked him if he wanted it. "Yes. But for goodness' sake don't damage the head." It was about eight feet up the tree, and all I could see was a curve of body. I took out my 9mm automatic pistol and took aim. By this time three *firks* had arrived and were watching. I took aim and fired. The sap spurted three inches from the snake. I had missed. The *firks* jeered, but I cleared the weapon and put it away – something told me that all was well. The body twitched and then sagged. I got a stick and pulled it down. The bullet had passed through the branch and severed its' spinal cord behind the head, killing it outright. Mike was amazed at such skilful shooting, and the legend of the SAS was enhanced yet again.

In 1977 a more formal expedition was mounted. It was called The Oman Flora and Fauna Survey 1977 (Dhofar). The aim was to visit representative areas of the province in order to establish what was there. The three principal environments were the Plain, the Jebel and the Negd, each subdivided into their own varying environments. I wasn't involved in the planning for it, which was a pity, because by the time I found out their plans were already set. I had little contact with them until I heard that they were having a morale crisis because they were not finding many new species known to science to give their names to. I paid them a visit when they were at Ayun pool in the Negd. This was a large pool at the bottom of a rocky wadi, and at the end of the war we had gone on picnics there. In the bottom there were visible what looked like dinosaur foot prints, and probably were. It was remote and quite spooky. When I got there the scientists were obviously hot and uncomfortable. I asked how they were getting on, and got a short answer. I went into a tent and found one of them stitching up the shattered remains of a hyrax. I asked him what he was doing. He told me that they were very rare and he had been lucky to see it. Unfortunately his shot had hit the rock in front of the creature, and the fragments had torn it apart. He was trying to put it back together in such a way that it could be mounted. I told him that I knew where there were so many of them that I used to live on them, and went back to Salalah.

There were parts of the Eastern Area that were still inaccessible by road, and too far to walk in a single day, so I arranged with some of the Firqat al Umri to spend a week walking around it in April 1977. We started at Jib Jat and headed South South East. On the third day, when east of Tawi Atair, hot and sweaty, we came upon a *sedd* at Aydawt.

This was a dam, made by the *jebalis* to collect monsoon water for use later in the year. It was full. I had seen smaller ones, but this was at least a hundred yards long and thirty yards wide. I stripped to my underpants and dived in, glorying in the cool water, despite the hordes of leeches and tadpoles. After a while I noticed a *shaiba* (old man) sitting under an overhang at the edge, holding an old Martini-Henry rifle. I swam over and greeted him, and asked him what he was doing there. He told me that his job was to stop people swimming in the water. I made to get out, but he indicated that I should stay as long as I wanted. Later that day we had reached to within half a mile of the BATT base at Kerhanawt. This base had been installed after the *adoo* had fired at us in the helicopter mentioned previously. As we crossed a track we heard unexpected movement to the east. We slipped into the bushes, knelt down, slipped the safety catches off our weapons and waited. Shortly after we saw the brown knees of a BATT patrol coming down the track, bunched together. It occurred to me that had we been *adoo* we could have wiped them out. However, that was just a malicious thought. We didn't reveal ourselves as they passed by three yards away, and when they had disappeared we continued with our stroll.

Because of the political situation I had to leave the Western Area until 1978, when the war was over. I needed a guide, and soon found one in the shape of Salem Suhail al Masheikhi, who volunteered himself. I was warned that he was a dangerous man who had committed war crimes and was trying to rehabilitate himself in the eyes of the government (When I returned to Dhofar in 1992 I was told that he had been imprisoned for his crimes, whatever they were). However, I found him to be intelligent, knowledgeable and cooperative. We drove to Sha'at on the Jebel Kamah at the eastern end of the Western Area, and then set off on foot. We gradually worked our way west, visiting all the villages in the area. We always slept with a local family, sometimes in their *baits*, and sometimes in caves. We didn't carry any more than we stood up in, apart from my note book, map and camera. By living off the local people in this way, I gained a better understanding of how the *adoo* had such freedom of movement. One night I heard them discussing the time when the Portuguese had visited Dhofar. It had been on their route to the East, and I already knew that they had constructed forts on the coast and on the jebel. A couple of days later we had descended to sea level and reached a place called *Al Hota* on the coast. There was nobody living there, just the shrine. Salem and two other *jebalis* chose to have a siesta in its shade, so I went exploring up the wadi. About 1200 yards upstream I found a stone structure. It was a tower, about twenty feet high, and consisted of four conical buttresses tapering towards the top. I photographed it, explored a bit further and then went back to Salem, and asked him what it was. He reminded me of the conversation about the Portuguese and told me that it was where they secured the end of the rope that they had used to carry supplies from the coast to the top of the jebel two and a half kilometres away, and 3,000 feet higher. I said it was impossible. They didn't have the technology, and the weight of the rope alone would have been prohibitive. He was adamant, and told me that he would show me where it had been secured at the upper end the following day. That evening we walked to the foot of the scarp and started the ascent. After a couple of hundred feet we found a family living in a cave, so we spent the night with them. The following morning we completed the ascent in the cool of the early morning, and Salem took me to where the rope had been secured. It didn't look very convincing, but he still insisted. It took us several more days on that occasion, and a second trip a couple of weeks later to complete the survey of the Western Area.

Every month there was a meeting of the Dhofar Development Committee. This comprised Sheikh Braik, the Commanding officers of the Army and Air Force in Dhofar, the head of the Police, Bob Brown (Head of the Research Department), and Martin, who was the secretary. When Martin was on leave I would stand in for him. The meetings were held in Sheikh Braik's palace on the beach, couple of hundred yards from our house. It really was a palace too – great marble halls, cool fountains etc. The thing I liked about these meetings was that they were so relaxed, despite the serious nature of the business being discussed. They always took place in the morning, and half way through, breakfast would be served at the table we were sitting around. It was a very civilised way of doing things. Sheikh Braik was always charming, and had a huge knowledge of local affairs. We used to describe him as a master of inactivity, not as an insult, but in many situations he would decline to make a decision, using his judgement to allow the situation to resolve itself, perhaps with a bit of behind-the-scenes skulduggery of his own. When he visited England he had gone to a country show and was vastly impressed by the gun dogs. He immediately bought two Labrador pups, one black, the other golden called Bob and Sunny. He brought them back to his palace, where they destroyed the place. They were completely untrained. He asked Martin if he could help. Martin asked me. Martin took Sunny and I took Bob. We agreed to house-train them and return them to him, although I think that by this time he had gone off them. About six months later Martin went on leave, leaving me with both dogs, who had learned "Sit" and "Stay". One day I was walking them in the Sultan's garden which had been built in the dunes between our villas and the sea. I became aware of a strong smell of perfume, and looking behind me saw His Majesty the Sultan and his entourage walking through the gardens towards me. I was in a quandary. To show respect, I had to get out of the path of the Sultan, but couldn't walk back past him. I walked the dogs to the edge of the garden and then stood still, facing HM. The dogs weren't on leads, and were wild with excitement, and I was muttering "Sit, Stay, Sit Stay" continuously to keep them under control. As HM approached I called out *"Salaam alaykum Seedi."* (Peace be upon you Sir). He answered, laughing his head off, because he could see the problem I was having, and walked on. On another occasion I had taken Bob with me onto the jebel, to a remote village south of Jib Jat. The *jebalis* were fascinated by him and asked what he was for. I told them that he was my bodyguard, and would do anything I told him. They didn't believe me until I told Bob to sit and stay in the Land Rover, before walking away. When I was about 100 yards away I called him, and he jumped out of the window and ran to me. They were a bit more respectful after that.

It was at Jib Jat that an interesting problem developed. The centre was on top of a horseshoe-shaped ridge, and a settlement developed along the top of it. The water well-head was on one side, together with a storage tank, and the water was distributed by means of a gravity-fed pipe. Obviously the standpipes fed by it would have to be lower than the tank. The *Mindoob,* seeing that the pipe would run below the *baits* on the far side, asked for the route of the pipe to be raised to make water collection easier. I explained why it would not be possible, and he clearly didn't believe me. When the work was completed the *Mindoob* came to me again, complaining that the water distribution system didn't work, so I paid a visit. It transpired that the *jebalis* and the *Mindoob* had threatened the Pakistani workmen, and forced them to lay the pipe nearer their *baits*, above the level of the tank. Consequently the water didn't flow. I explained again why, but they thought it was a cunning plot of mine. I left them to stew for a while, before sending the workforce back to correct the line of the pipe.

I was visiting a jebel village called Taytam, where the Royal Engineers were installing a water distribution system, when I noticed that they were working almost naked, their shorts cut to the minimum. I was concerned because there were *jebali* women around, but the *Mindoob* I was with didn't seem to notice. When I pointed it out, his response was crushing. "I don't expect slaves to wear clothes."

In April 1977 there was torrential rain. The streets of Salalah were flooded, and all air operations were cancelled. We heard that the Wadi Darbat was in flood. The Wadi Darbat was the biggest wadi in the eastern area, but its distinguishing feature was the Darbat Falls. This was a linear stalactite some eight hundred yards long and three hundred feet high. As we approached we could hear the boom of the falls from over a mile away. We drove to Sumhuram, and the scene was stupendous. The falls were in flood across their entire width, the spray formed a separate cloud over the top, and the river rushed past Sumhuram and out to sea down Khawr Rawri between the twin rocks of Inqitaat Taqa and Inqitaat Mirbat. It seemed as if the whole of Salalah had turned out to see the sight. Apparently it hadn't flooded like this in living memory.

On the 21st May 1977 a cow house at Daakhaam was struck by lightning, killing one woman and fifty cows. The villagers were asking for government assistance, so I went up to verify the matter. By the time I arrived, the woman had been buried, and the cows were being stuffed down a fissure in the limestone. I could see the damage to the cow house, but it didn't look big enough to house forty cows, even the diminutive Dhofar ones. I also didn't see how they could have got forty cows down a fissure the size of the one they showed me. Having given me time to make my report to Sheikh Braik the *jebalis* turned up, demanding their compensation. Sheikh Braik's response was masterly. Instead of getting into an argument about the number of cows killed, he asked "Are you Muslims? Was this done by man or by Allah? How can you expect me to compensate you for Allah's will?" That was the end of that, and they departed empty handed.

In June 1977 a cyclone struck Dhofar and most of the province endured heavy rain and gales. Reports of damage and death poured in. Martin was on leave, so as acting head of CAD I was responsible for coordinating the disaster relief. The Sultan appealed for international aid, and in due course ship-loads of tents, blankets and food arrived, all of which had to be stored securely. In the meantime, however, I had to ascertain which areas had been worst hit, in order to apportion the aid accordingly. SOAF flew reconnaissance missions, and it rapidly became obvious that the worst-hit was the Eastern area around Mirbat, Sudh and Jebel Samhan. I flew to Mirbat by helicopter to get the story on the ground. The scenes were reminiscent of Lord of the Rings – the peaks of Jebel Samhan obscured by lowering cloud, driving rain, the normally pale tan ground now dark brown, and everywhere the wadis flowing with torrents of water. A Defender aircraft was flying round looking for survivors, directing us to them so we could pick them up and ferry them to Mirbat. Over a hundred people had died, largely because when the rains had initially arrived they had sought shelter in the caves in the wadis. The flash floods which ensued drowned them. Ali Said Aateyq (My friend from Tawi Atair) was at Mirbat, frantic. He had lost most of his family, but there was nothing I could do to help him. The Under Secretary for Tribal Affairs was also in Mirbat, listening to the claims for aid. He was under severe pressure, and I had to produce a distribution list of tents and blankets and food as soon as possible, as every *jebali* in the country, having heard that there was to be a handout, claimed to be in most need. I did my sums, and produced the quantities of aid to go to each tribe. No sooner had I done this, and published it, when the Under Secretary immediately doubled the quantity for the Al Maasheni, because that was his tribe. I, of course, caught the flak for it, and was hassled relentlessly by all and sundry. There is an Omani saying "If you find a snake and a Dhofari in your house kill the Dhofari first." At times I was inclined to agree. It could be entertaining though. If you ask an Omani to do something, regardless of whether he is senior or junior to you, the response will be "Inshallah" (God-willing). In other words, they have the intention of complying, but if they don't, it's not their fault; it is just that Allah did not intend it. Many times when I was being hassled for something or other, I would respond *"Inshallah"*. They would say "Don't say 'Inshallah', we want a definite answer." I would say "You will get a definite answer, *Inshallah*." Some would laugh, but it infuriated others.

Sheikh Braik bought himself a big launch, and on Fridays he would go down to Rayzut harbour and play in it. On the 1st June 1979 after he had had it about a month, he managed to damage it by ramming the harbour wall. In a foul mood, he returned to Salalah and insisted on driving his Mercedes himself. Driving it at warp nine he managed to roll it, and he was taken to Salalah hospital where death was confirmed. We were having lunch with our friends Hugh and Miranda, when Martin came round and told us the sad news. Life was suddenly going to be different. As it happened Sheikh Braik was replaced by Sayyid Hilal bin Said bin Harib Albu Saidi, a member of the royal family. There was intense interest among the Omani officers at Brigade HQ when I announced this at prayers shortly after, because they would all be working out his political affiliations, and what it would mean to them.

Hugh was the doctor in charge of Salalah Hospital who had more degrees than a thermometer, and Miranda was his wife who had come to continue her Arabic studies. They had one son, Olly, John's great friend. Miranda obtained a job in CAD as a secretary/general factotum, and shortly after she joined, I took her onto the jebel for the first time. I took a circular route via Taqa, Medinat al Haq, Qatn Ridge, and Qairoon Harritti in order to familiarise her with the area. Among Miranda's many duties at CAD was the tasking of aircraft. CAD used helicopters and Skyvans extensively to move people, building materials and medical teams around the province. To do so she had to liaise with the Air Liaison Officer at HQ SOAF, Salalah. The ALO was an irascible Scotsman called Archie Archibald. Actually he was a very charming man with whom we became friendly, but he defended his empire furiously, and gave short shrift to anyone who annoyed him, especially trying to make a booking for aircraft for the following day after eleven o'clock. One day I was dashing through the CAD office, and Miranda called to me "It is nearly eleven o'clock. Do you have any air tasking?" I said "Yes, I want 200 bags of cement for Kuria Muria for tomorrow". That was a huge task, because the Kuria Murias were a group of islands off the coast about a hundred and sixty miles from Salalah. There was no landing strip, which meant that any freight would have to be flown by Skyvan to Hasik, which was on the coast about a hundred miles from Salalah, and then taken by underslung load by a twin-engined helicopter due to having to fly over the sea. There weren't many twin-engined helis, so they were in considerable demand, and it would also need its own fuel supply also transported up to Hasik, by the Skyvan. A couple

of hours later, Miranda said to me "I think I have upset Archie."
I had a sinking feeling in my stomach and asked why. She said
"I passed on your request, and he just said 'Oh Miranda, I am
so cross'". This was unheard of – Archie was far too much of a
gentleman ever to upset a woman. I told Miranda I had only
been joking. She then became upset, so I said "Don't worry, I'll
sort it." I phoned Archie. "Archie, about that cement for Kuria
Muria." I got no further. He said "Look, I can move a hundred
bags tomorrow, is it alright if the rest go up the following
day?" I grovelled and thanked him profusely. I then had to
run around buying cement, hiring labourers to load it onto
the trucks which I had to hire to transport it SOAF Salalah.
It didn't go to waste because we had a development plan for
the Kuria Murias. I just didn't need it right then. Years later I
told Archie the truth. He looked at me and his face screwed
up, but he couldn't think of anything to say, fortunately.

The Kuria Muria islands had a population of about eighty
people who eked a living out of the sea. Arab women wouldn't
go and live there, so the islanders had to go to Pakistan to
buy women for wives. There had been no live births there for
years, because the pregnant women always headed for the
mainland. When the Flying Doctor Service started visiting,
they persuaded a pregnant woman to stay and give birth on
the island, with a doctor in attendance. She duly gave birth to
a healthy girl, and the doctor departed, promising to return
the following week. When he did, he was told the baby had
died. It transpired that the local 'wise woman' had blocked all
it's orifices with rags, to stop devils getting in.

There was a hectic social life in Salalah, centred on the
military, with as much civilian involvement as possible because
they had women with them. Maggie and I were involved in
it, partly because I knew most of them from my SAF days,
but also because my position in CAD meant that as I had to

liaise with them, socialising was useful to oil the wheels. One Friday lunch time there was a mess party at Umm al Ghawarif. Maggie and I were there in the gardens where the trees were festooned with Weaver bird nests, sipping our Pimms, when I became aware of signs of consternation and disapproval from the other end. I realised it was caused by the presence of a *jebali* approaching under the trees. It was my old friend Ali Said Aateyq. I went over and greeted him in Arabic, and offered him a *Loomi* (Fresh lime iced drink). This didn't go down well with the assembled throng, and there were loud mutters, which Ali, having been taught English by me, understood. He declined the drink, and said that he had been looking for me for days. His camels had been suffering at the claws of a leopard. He had lain up over the carcase of its latest victim, and when it appeared, shot it. He produced a sand bag from behind the tree, opened it and out rolled a magnificent leopard skin. "It's for you." He immediately became the centre of attention again, but for a very different reason. "Can he get me one?" was the general cry from the mob. Ali stood there listening to them before saying in perfect English "I only give these to my friends." He departed with dignity.

Because Maggie and I were going out at night two or three times a week we had to get a babysitter. I mentioned this to Trevor, my previous incumbent, and he said he knew just the person. It turned out to be a young Zanzibari girl called Raadia. She seemed very nice, was always punctual, and John liked her. We used her for some months until we noticed that she was always picked up by one of her brothers. She seemed to have hundreds of them, and it dawned on us that she was using our house for her own purposes, for which she charged a fee. We didn't use her again.

Ali Said Aateyq was a frequent visitor to our house. We would find him there, having been let in by John. He would be teaching John *jebali* games, and encouraging him to smoke cigarettes, which we put a rapid halt to. Shortly after this he joined the Oman Research Department, and was sent up to Muscat on a course. When he came back I asked him how he had got on. He said initially he had been put up in the Intercontinental Hotel. I was gobsmacked. The thought of Ali in a place like the Intercon! He said he hadn't liked the food, so I asked him what he lived on. He told me that he had found boil-in-the–bag fish in the local supermarket, which became quite palatable after being left in the sun on the balcony for several days.

In 1977 it was decided to run the Dhofar Road race again. I wasn't going to be able to run because the date chosen coincided with the arrival of a Kuwaiti delegation who were going to finance the construction of black-top roads on the jebel. Colonel Ken Wilson offered to sponsor Maggie for nearly a thousand pounds if she took part. Maggie had no choice, so to get her fit enough I took her for runs on the jebel, she running, me escorting in the Land Rover. On one occasion we were stopped by a group of curious *jebalis*, who commented "If you make her run like that she will never have babies!" I explained that there was going to be a race and since I could not run in it, she would have to. "Oh, that's alright then!" When the day of the race came, I kept an eye on Maggie for the first few miles, but then had to leave to meet the Kuwaitis. John D, a friend said that he would follow her. The Jordanians had fielded their Olympic marathon runner, and clearly expected him to win. Instead, a former colleague of mine from D Squadron came in first, much to their obvious displeasure. When he heard that Maggie was still out on the road, he turned and ran back over five miles to escort her in. Years later, after he had qualified as a doctor, he shot his girlfriend with an AK47. Such a terrible shame. When

I returned from the Kuwaiti meeting I found several vehicles parked outside the house. Inside were my friends drinking my beer. Maggie was in the bath, soaking off what was left of her toenails. She went to a party that night. Amazing!

My meeting with the Kuwaiti delegation had been interesting. In order to prepare for the meeting I had driven along every road in the province, and recorded the distance between every village and junction. I had transposed this information onto a London Underground-style map, so that I could quickly work out the distance between any two points in Dhofar. The meeting took place in the Government Guest House in Hayy al Shaati. The Kuwaitis arrived in their shimmering white robes and *shemaghs*, and were very arrogant. We were all introduced, and sat down on the soft chairs. James, the Wali's American financial advisor, commenced the discussion, and it all went very well until they started asking about distances. The distance between adjacent points wasn't a problem, because I could just read off my map. When they asked for distances between several points, then of course, I had to add them up. I was doing this when the leader of the delegation started snapping his fingers and saying in English "Come on. Come on." James was seated between me and them. I said to James loudly "If he snaps his fingers again I am going to put his lights out." It wasn't very diplomatic, but it worked. James went white and put his hand on my arm to restrain me, and the Kuwaitis adopted a more conciliatory manner.

Maggie had got a job working as a nurse in the Field Surgical Team (FST) at Salalah airfield. The FST's principle function was to deal with war casualties, and one day a member of the Firqat Southern Mahra was brought in, having been shot through the abdomen with an FN rifle. They said that he had accidentally done it to himself, but this was manifestly impossible. Somebody else had done it, but they weren't saying, and they were hostile and defensive. He had surgery which removed most of his gut. When blood was needed, half the tribe came down and offered. They brought with them gallons of camel's milk, which they believed to have almost magical properties. Maggie complained to me that they were rude to her, jostled her, and at times, physically prevented her from treating him, if they felt like it. I was furious, and went to the FST to confront them. There were half a dozen of them there, and they looked at me with the same dull hatred I had only seen before on the faces of *adoo* I had encountered on the jebel. I knew that there was to be no reasoning with them. I said "This is my wife. You have shown her no respect. You have touched her. If any of you touches her again, or stops her from working I will smash your faces, and stop her from coming here to nurse your brother." There was no reaction, just the same dull stare, but they never interfered again. The patient later died, and I resolved to watch my back when I was in Mahra territory.

One day Maggie called me from work. She said that the local hospital had asked them for blood for a pregnant woman. She was O positive. Maggie knew that I was. Would I donate? I went to the FST, and was lying on a bed giving blood, when the Government Garage deputy manager rushed in, asking if the blood was ready. I realised that it must be his wife the blood was for. He suddenly saw me: "Oh Mr Paul, what is the matter with you?" I said "I am giving blood for your wife, and it is full of whisky and pork." He looked at me for a moment, as the import of what I had said sank in. He didn't say another word, and when the blood was ready he rushed off with it. He never mentioned it again, but it must have worked, even if it was contaminated.

Andrew Booth, who had spotted my *shemagh* in the

fighting in Wadi Ashoq was a frequent visitor to the house, and we spent many a happy hour drinking brandy sours and arguing over war games or backgammon. He decided not to renew his contract when it expired in early 1978, and as part of his farewell, he invited several of his closest friends on a dhow trip (The word *dhow* isn't actually used by the Arabs. They have specific words for particular types of boat, in this case a *sambuq*, about fifty feet long, with a low, scimitar-shaped stem piece, and powered by a diesel engine). On the appointed day we assembled at Rayzut harbour, as Andrew was completing the negotiations with the two fishermen who owned the *sambuq*. It was moored out in the harbour, and we went out to it two at a time in a *huri* (A small dug-out canoe made from mango wood exported from the Malabar Coast, widely used in Dhofar). I was delighted to see Andrew capsize it with the two fishermen in it. Unfortunately this set the tone of their relationship for the rest of the day. When we cast off, Andrew insisted on taking the helm, and reluctantly, the fishermen agreed. Andrew aimed for the harbour entrance. We became aware that an empty freighter was also heading for the same place, and we were on converging courses. Andrew refused to give way, shouting "Steam gives way to sail." The fact that we didn't have sails seemed to have eluded him. The freighter towered over us, and tiny angry faces shouted abuse at us from the deck. The two fishermen, realising that their livelihood was about to finish up at the bottom of the harbour, wrested the tiller away from Andrew and we breathed again as the freighter headed out to sea. We cruised west down the coast, watching dolphins, whales and hosts of seagulls. We fished with hand lines and rods, and didn't catch much. Late in the afternoon, just before we turned back, the fishermen decided it was time for their prayers. One of them produced a small enamel bowl, which he filled with sea water for his ritual ablution, and prayed, while his partner kept the tiller away from Andrew. When he had finished they swapped over. The little bowl was filled with water again, and just as he was about to wash, Andrew decided to cast his line. The hook came back, caught in the rim of the bowl, which then described a delicate arc across the heavens as the fisherman looked on in disbelief. It landed about thirty yards away, right side up, bobbing in the waves. They knew he hadn't done it on purpose, but it was par for the course. When we eventually returned to Rayzut the fishermen demanded more money for the mental trauma they had suffered, and we left Andrew to argue with them, having had a most enjoyable day.

A month after Andrew had left Maggie and I decided to drive to Muscat. We had made the trip several times before. The distance was over a thousand kilometres along a graded road. We had to carry all our own petrol and water and provisions. We normally took two days for the trip, and rested up during the hottest part of the day, because as the tyres grew hotter, they were more likely to blow out, as they vibrated over the corrugations in the road surface caused by the wheels of other vehicles. The road was really interesting, because it passed close by the huge sand-dunes on the southern side of the Empty Quarter, or *Arrimaal* (The Sands), as the *Bedu* called it. It was littered with the remains of broken-down vehicles, and bits of cargo which had fallen off the backs of other juggernauts. Once we followed a trail of freezers which had obviously fallen off one of them without the driver realising that he was losing his entire load. On another occasion, I even found a box full of armoured car main armament ammunition. When I reported it to Dhofar Brigade HQ, they then had a squabble with Northern Oman Brigade HQ about whose responsibility it was. On another occasion, a wagon had lost its load of nails along the length of the road. A major recovery operation had to be mounted, because the road was littered with vehicles with multiple punctures along its entire length. Sometimes people died there, because when their vehicle had broken down, they tried to walk out, instead of waiting for help.

We usually camped about half way, but on this occasion I decided to push on a bit further because I knew that there would be a full moon. When there is a full moon in the desert there is enough light to read large print, so setting up camp would not be a problem. We stopped after the sun had gone down, and a few minutes after, as I was putting up the camp beds, Maggie said "The moon is disappearing." Without even looking up I said "Don't be daft." She became insistent. When I finally looked up, largely because I could no longer see what I was doing, the moon had indeed disappeared. We decided it was the end of the world, had our supper and went to bed. It was the coldest night I have ever spent in the desert, and we froze. The following morning, as the sun was rising and warming our faces, I turned on Voice of America, which announced that some places in the Middle East would have been able to see the total eclipse of the moon last night.

We often camped in the Negd, the huge relatively featureless, sand and gravel plain lying between the jebel and the Empty Quarter. We always took at least two vehicles fully equipped for desert travel. The maps we relied upon were produced by PDO (Petrol Development Oman) and had very little detail. They showed the major landmarks such as airstrips, villages and the occasional waterhole. They showed their oil-drilling sites, and the graded tracks running between them. These tracks, although shown on the maps often disappeared as they were no longer used when the rigs moved on. The trick was not to get lost. On one occasion Hugh said he knew where there was a fossilised wood, called Ghubra Woods. He said he would take us there – it was shown on the map. So, one weekend we set off, Hugh leading. For obvious reasons I kept a close eye on our direction and distance travelled. After about six hours driving it became clear that Hugh was lost. I offered to take over, but he insisted that he could find the place. We met some *Bedu*, and asked for directions, but their directions were incomprehensible, and Hugh finally admitted defeat. I had noticed that Ghubra Woods lay beside a wadi. I knew where we were at that particular moment. I did what you always do when trying to find a spot on a linear feature. I drove to the wadi, and followed it east, Hugh poo pooing all the way. Every now and then I stopped, left the vehicles to prevent magnetic interference, and took a compass check. Hugh was obviously convinced that I was lost. No chance. After an hour and a half we drove into them. Hugh was amazed that an illiterate like me had such orienteering skills. Ghubra Woods was not the paradise we had imagined. There were a few trees there, some fossilised, and hordes of flies. There were some *Bedu* nearby, who came over scrounging. They quickly discovered that Hugh was a doctor, and after that he never had a moment's peace. We left early the next morning vowing never to return.

On another occasion, we had decided to go and camp at Ayn Hunoon, a waterhole north of the jebel. Nearby were several very old graves, pre-Islamic from their layout. Maggie and her friend had gone looking around in the rocks and had spotted something in a crevice. They pulled it out. It was a child's foot in a modern shoe. Clearly it was a grave which had been disturbed by the local wildlife. We carefully put it back and covered it over with rocks.

Chapter Sixteen

Camel trip and other stories

With the development of roads and air transport in Dhofar it was becoming clear that some of the traditional camel routes were no longer in use. Miranda identified one running from Sudh in the east over the mountains and on to Hasik, about seventy kilometres away. She contacted friends in Sudh and arranged the hire of the camels, together with handlers. The party comprised Hugh and Miranda, Gareth, from Dhofar Brigade HQ, and Sue and Kelly, who worked for the American Peace Corps, and myself. Maggie stayed behind to look after John and Olly. We left Salalah in two Land Rovers on the morning of the 10th of March 1978, and arrived at Sudh at midday, where we had a lunch of spicy fish and rice followed by dates and *qahwa* (Coffee) with Sheikh Mohammed, the *Wali*.

During the afternoon six bull camels arrived with the handlers, and were duly distributed amongst us. My camel had a mane like a lion and was called Hofayth. The handler was called Said Aateyq – related to my old friend Ali Said Aateyq. Our belongings were strapped to our camels, the handlers being relieved that we didn't have much. They were surprised that we had brought food. They said there would be enough to eat on the way, but we doubted this, and said that we would eat ours, and they could eat whatever they found. Much to the delight of the assembled crowd, which had gathered to watch seven lunatic Brits making fools of themselves, we mounted rather unsteadily and set off in the late afternoon on the dusty, rocky track.

There was no moon, and by early evening we reached a deserted village by the sea called Haap. It had taken me one and a half hours to get even remotely comfortable – ease forward uphill, lean back downhill. By the time we reached our campsite at a quarter to eight, my behind was so sore that I was dreading the next morning. The campsite was in a shallow wadi by a spring called Ayn Mahmood, the water of which tasted soapy. Nearby were some *Bedu* tents, but unusually, they didn't bother us. The handlers were helpful, collecting firewood, and I made a curry for my supper. I slept well, though lightly, being disturbed by the camels groaning.

Early the next morning we arose and set of. The handlers were never in a hurry, and we suspected that they were trying to spin out the trip so that we would pay them more. The camels groaned and grated their teeth continuously making a noise like a dungeon door in a Hammer film. Whenever they scented females, they inflated their tongues and foamed, making a bubbling noise like someone being terribly sick. Hofayth had a huge abscess on his left shoulder which looked like a large breast. It suppurated continually, and after my initial revulsion, soon became bored with trying to keep my knee out the blood and puss. Some of them had the anti-social habit of urinating while walking and thrashing their tails back and forth between their legs causing stinking urine to spray over their backs, much to the discomfiture of the rider. I was delighted when Hugh's did it to him, but not so pleased when I had a dose of the same the following day.

At midmorning we arrived at Wadi Fooshi, where the water was sweet. It was beautiful rocky scenery, the rocks glinting with mica. Whales were splashing in the sea, and our handlers amazed us by the quantities of fish they caught with hand nets while on the march – literally. Whereas we would have stopped and made a job of it, they just walked through the sea parallel with us and caught them in their stride. When we stopped, Hofayth decided to have a fight with Hugh's camel. At night and at midday they were allowed to graze untethered. For some reason the two began fighting and the handlers climbed trees and ran up hills to stay out of the way until they stopped, as quickly as they had started, with no serious damage done. Most of the sores on the camels were from infected wounds.

After lunch, having photographed the saddling of Hofayth, we set off for Hadbin. At the end of each ride I felt as if I would never walk again, but each day I rode a bit further and felt more comfortable.

Our line of march was mainly along the coast, and we were kept fascinated by the fantastic shapes of the rocks, and sea-life, which was in abundance; whales, dolphins, hammerhead sharks etc. Late that afternoon we reached Hadbin, a little fishing village with a well and only five cement houses, the rest living in tents, which were probably more comfortable in summer. That night was less comfortable, there being hordes of mosquitoes. I saw a black and yellow striped snake. The water here was the sweetest we tasted anywhere, although it came from an unlined well two feet deep in the sand of the wadi-bed, three hundred yards from the sea.

The following morning we departed along the coast again, and were surprised to find a waterhole near Ra's Nuss in the rocks by the sea. We reached Ra's Nuss at midday, where we rested the camels, and departed later that afternoon. By early evening we reached Ra's Samhan, where we spent a cool and windy night.

The next day we departed late, having been delayed by Hugh being called away to attend to a patient who had miraculously appeared. We reached the foot of the mountain late in the morning and stopped to rest the camels before tackling the climb ahead. When we set off, it was on foot, climbing towards a saddle in the mountain range, the handlers leading their camels. It took us half an hour to reach the saddle, where we waited a further half hour for the camels to catch up. The descent was slippery and difficult, and we were delayed an hour when Miranda's sandal broke. We reached a *khawr*, which had a surprising number of birds on it, including five flamingos and four grey herons and spent the night there.

The following morning we passed the three old Hasiks. Quite why they had relocated was never made clear, although the new Hasik we were aiming for was on a plain, and so had an airstrip. When we stopped for lunch I walked back to photograph the old villages and noted that the oldest was the most advanced with large houses of dressed stone and well-carved headstones in the graveyards and by the tower, and that each successive site was more primitive than its predecessor, including the present Hasik whose saving grace was the work carried in the previous ten years. There were masses of hermit crabs clacking on the beach.

We eventually reached Hasik in the late afternoon, where we had supper with the *Naib Wali* (Deputy Mayor), before sleeping in the clinic. We paid off the avaricious camel men that night and tried to arrange a sea trip back to Sudh. However the price they were asking was ridiculous (Forty Riyals), so we returned by Skyvan the following morning.

During the trip Said Aateyq had coveted my rather handsome Puma knife, and at the end he asked to buy it. We agreed a price, but he said that his money was in his house in Sudh, and that he would send the money via Ali Said Aateyq. Foolishly I agreed, aware that I might never see the money. I never did.

It was on this trip that I discovered that the chief source of income at Hasik, Hallaniya, Sudh and Gingari had been pearl fishing until the pearls had been fished out at accessible depths, when they resorted to abalone (*Safeelah*), which then fetched 250 Baizas each. Pearls are still collected however, and shortly after this I bought approximately 40 pearls, ranging from dust to 3mm in diameter for five Omani Riyals from a fisherman between Mirbat and Sudh.

As the country became more and more used to peace, so the expats wandered further and further off the beaten track, to explore this beautiful country. Sometimes I was surprised at just how far some of them wandered, because there were still a lot of *adoo* around and I still made a point of carrying my rifle. On the 1st of June 1978, a group of seven from Airwork Services (They maintained SOAF's aircraft) went on a fishing trip to Khawr Rawri, and were camped by the sea at the bottom of Darbat Falls. Dhofar Brigade HQ had had several picnics there, but they had always had a company of Baluch soldiers watching over them. During the day a group of *jebalis* came and visited them, chatting and cadging cigarettes. The Airworkies had used a SOAF minibus as their transport, and the *jebalis* obviously noticed the blue SOAF badge painted on the front. That night they returned with their Kalashnikovs and murdered five of them, only two escaping to Taqa. They had been *adoo* carrying out a reconnaissance, and seeing the SOAF badges had identified the Airworkies as pilots. I later saw the minibus in the workshops, and it had been riddled.

Later that year, on 17th June, a helicopter piloted by Adrian Winterbon crashed on the jebel. One of those killed was Stan Standford, a much respected crew member. I went to his funeral in the Christian cemetery in Muscat, and apart from the sadness of the occasion, I had to stop myself from laughing. It was like a scene from a spaghetti western. The cemetery was in a dry, rocky valley, the vicar was a young fair-haired American with a beard, and there were Egyptian vultures circling overhead. If the vicar had had a cheroot hanging out of the side of his mouth, it would have been complete. When I went to visit Stan's grave some years later I was surprised to note that it didn't have a headstone. I repeatedly contacted the officer responsible in Northern Oman Brigade HQ, but got nowhere. Eventually I wrote to the commander of SOAF, Eric Bennett, and told him. A gravestone was erected in 1983, and I was sent a photograph of it in place.

In 1978, a senior member of SAVAK (The Iranian Secret Service) and an aide visited Dhofar to see where the Imperial Iranian Forces had been fighting. I was asked to accompany them to identify the battlefields. We boarded the Heli 717 on the 31st July 1978, which had been rebuilt after the incident of 30th June 1976. The pilot was Peter, who had flown in Vietnam, and the co-pilot was Martin, the Commanding Officer of SOAF in Dhofar. I was sitting in the back on the port side facing the rear. It is quite a long flight to the Western Area, and from time to time I pointed out a few things. We landed here and there, and then we carried on down towards Khadrafi, near the border with South Yemen. It was hot and I was bored. It was all taking a long time. After a while I looked over my shoulder and was surprised to see a large town which I didn't recognise. There are no towns in Dhofar between Dhalqut and the border. I shouted into the intercom "We are over Hauf", a heavily defended town in South Yemen. At that moment I heard the 'BOOM BOOM BOOM' of anti aircraft fire, and saw streams of tracer going by. Peter took immediate evasive action, flew straight to the nearest SAF position at Sarfait and landed to inspect for damage. As it happened we hadn't been hit, so we refuelled and flew back to Salalah. The Iranians were very upset. Diplomatic incident etc. I was asked to write a report which placed us within Omani territory at the time we were fired on. Thus it was the wicked Yemenis who had precipitated the incident. A year later I was drinking malt whisky with Bob Brown (The head of the Intelligence Department in Dhofar). Referring to the incident he said that we had been very lucky. I said "I know". He said "You don't know just how lucky. I had an SEP (Surrendered Enemy Personnel) in today. He was a member of an anti aircraft team at Hauf. He said that on the day of the incident the regular crews had been stood down for some Rest & Recuperation, and the number two crews were on. He said that if they had been on we would never have got away with it". I quite believed him. Hauf was a hotbed of light, medium and heavy antiaircraft guns and SAM missiles. They were highly effective, and had only recently shot down an Iranian Phantom which had strayed too close. This had been my second experience in Heli 717. It had previously been the subject of a painting by David Shepherd, and a print of it hangs on my study wall.

In 1979 I wanted to visit a village on the southern end of Jebel Bait Safteer in the central area, called Ereshat. I had seen it in the distance, but it was relatively inaccessible, and I hadn't been able to visit it previously. When I arrived there, the people were hospitable and surprised at seeing a European in such an isolated spot. We had lunch, and during the course of it, one of them pointed out an old man with leprosy and said that he had been Bertram Thomas's guide (The famous explorer) when he traversed the jebel in the 1930s. I used my usual ploy of disbelieving him in order to get him to say more. He said he could prove it. Thomas, he said had drawn pictures on the rocks in the wadi bottom, and pointed to a spot over a thousand feet down below us. I said that Thomas would never have drawn such pictures. He said that he would show me, but not today, because it was too hot. We would go in the cool of a morning. We arranged to meet the following week at a village called Haydayk, just off the Ghadaw road. We set off north going down into the wadi bottom. After about an hour we rounded a corner, and triumphantly he pointed out the drawings. They were high on a rock, and looked like the universal picture of a man, obviously drawn by a European. However, somebody had defaced it, and it was hard to make out. I asked who had done it, and he blamed 'naughty children'. It was out of the reach of children, and it was probably the *adoo* who had done it during the war, as they had defaced the memorials to aircrew whose aircraft had crashed near Donkey's Head in the fifties. I photographed them, and made a note of the grid reference, before returning to Haydayk. I subsequently lost those photographs, so when I returned to Dhofar in October 1991, I made a point of going back and photographing them again.

On another occasion, I was driving through Bait Khashawb territory when I noticed a lone tent on the side of the hill. Nobody normally lived there, so I went over. As I approached a man came out, and after the usual greetings asked me to help. His family was inside, clustered around a bundle of rags on a thin foam mattress. It was his twenty year-old daughter. She was emaciated, and the flies buzzed around her face despite the efforts of those around her to keep them off. Her eyes were unnaturally bright and she looked at me beseechingly. She had been taken ill and had been admitted into Salalah Hospital. He said that after some tests they had been told that nothing could be done for her. Would I help? I took her details, and returned to Salalah. She had indeed been admitted, but inoperable cancer had been diagnosed. When told, the family had said that they would take her to the jebel and feed her meat and camel's milk to aid her recovery. I returned to the tent and told them that nothing could be done. When I went back the following week, there was only a mark on the grass and a cold fire-place to mark where the tent had been. She had died, and the family had moved on.

In 1979, civilian contractors started work on a large site near Zeak, on the central jebel. There was a lot of conjecture about what it was to be. We were told that it was a 'goat farm'. If it was, it would have been the biggest goat farm in the world. It soon transpired that it was to be the headquarters of the Sultan's Special Force, which was to be formed. When it was about half built, I was told that His Excellency the British ambassador would be visiting Dhofar; he was to carry out a tour of the jebel. I would accompany him to explain the civilian side of things, and an officer called Errol from Dhofar Brigade HQ would explain the military side. On the appointed day, HE and his wife arrived, together with the First Secretary and his wife. We boarded a Huey 205 at SOAF Salalah and headed east. We stopped and looked at various places, and eventually finished up at Tawi Atair, where we planned to have lunch. It was a hot day, so they didn't want to walk very far. We decided that the best place to eat was on the remains of a wrecked Skyvan, so they wouldn't have to sit on the ground. They perched like a row of sparrows on the wing, while Errol and I opened the brigade-sized cold box and distributed lunch. Lunch consisted of pre-plated salads covered in aluminium foil, cold beers and fresh fruit. When Errol handed HE his salad, HE asked "Which way is up?" To which I facetiously answered "Try it and see." He did, and his salad fell out onto the ground. I had never seen anything so silly in my life, and he represented Great Britain. While I was laughing, Errol said "Never mind sir, there is a spare." And promptly handed over his own. A man with a great future. We continued with our tour, and as we were flying east, HE asked if we were anywhere near the "Goat Farm." I said we were, and asked the pilot to go there. We were flying at about five thousand feet, and HE's wife was in the co-pilot's seat. When we arrived over the "Goat Farm" we circled to descend, the "Goat Farm" appearing to revolve and getting nearer and nearer. As we did so HE leaned over to his wife and said "Take pictures! Take pictures!" She took out what looked like a Brownie Box camera and started clicking away. He suddenly realised that we were going to land, whereon he panicked and said," Don't land! I can't be seen here." I thought it was ludicrous. We continued on our way, and headed towards my old base Ghadaw. We landed and went over to the *Firqat* position. My friend Masaud was there, and as soon as he realised what was going on, the cry of 'Dhabeeha' (Slaughter) went up. They were going to kill a goat in our honour. I said "No, we don't have time." But it was too late. Masoud had produced the knife I had given him and slit the throat of goat tethered nearby, much to the horror of the group. Other *firks* were lighting a fire to have one of their usual barbecues. While the hapless goat was being butchered I explained in greater detail to Masaud why we wouldn't be able to stay, whereon he skewered one of the goat's kidneys on his knife and went around the horrified group, waving it, still dripping blood, under their noses. For some reason or other they all refused. When he got to me, I couldn't refuse, so I took it and ate it raw, while Masaud ate the other one similarly. It was soft, and tasted fine, and the blood trickled from the sides of my mouth where I had bitten into it. From the expressions of disgust exhibited by the rest of the group, I realised that I didn't have a future in the Diplomatic Service. We returned to Salalah without further incident.

On the 12th of May 1978 BATT left Dhofar by RAF VC 10. I immediately shot down to Umm al Ghawarif, scavenging. Needless to say, there was little left of value, except in the cookhouse, where there was a huge roll of cling film, and a carving knife and fork. The cling film lasted us for three years, and I still have the carving knife and fork, which is still used regularly.

Salalah had a thriving fish and vegetable *Suq* (market). One morning as I was driving out to work, I noticed that there were huge heaps of prawns on sale. The sale of prawns wasn't unusual in itself, but the sheer quantity and size was amazing. Each prawn was about six inches long. I stopped by one heap of prawns, still in the net, and asked the fisher-man how much? He said Ten Riyals (About twenty pounds). There was over a hundredweight. I gave him his ten riyals, and asked him if I could borrow his net to get them home, to which he readily agreed. I staggered to the Land Rover, and took them home. We managed to get two thirds of them in the freezer, so we gave the rest away. We spent hours cooking and shelling them until our fingers bled, but it was worth it. We lived on prawns and white wine for months.

On another occasion, Maggie had asked me to buy some potatoes. I went to the *Suq*, and seeing that they were for sale by the sack, bought one, having ascertained from the stallholder that they were fresh. When I got them home and emptied out the sack, about a third of them were rotten. I took them back to the stallholder who refused to either take them back or compensate me. Although the stalls were owned by Dhofaris, they were staffed by Pakistanis, who were under very strict instructions as to what they could and couldn't do.

Giving money back obviously wasn't in his remit. I went to the Wali's Office, to the Department of Agriculture, where I was ushered in to see the Director of Agriculture. I explained the situation, and said that all I wanted was my money back. I went with his deputy to the *Suq*, who asked me to identify the stall concerned. I did so, whereon he told the hapless stallholder who he was, and demanded the money, which he gave to me. He then called out to some of his employees in the *Suq*, who came over, and, on his instruction, turned the whole stall over, and spoiled all of the stock. I was appalled. This was not what I had wanted. When I turned to go, he said "You still don't have your potatoes." And started looking along the line of stalls, where rows of terrified stallholders tried to avoid eye-contact. He selected one, and quizzed him about the quality of his potatoes. He produced a sack from under the counter which he assured us were his very finest, and they were.

The Wali's Office staff could be very bureaucratic, and a fine example of this was when the Finance Department decided that instead of my salary being paid directly into my bank account, I would have to go their office and queue up with everybody else, find my name on the payroll, and sign for my money which would then be given to me in cash. I argued against it to no avail, so when I went over to collect my pay, I noticed that on the top of each sheet, over the column for signatures, the Arabic actually said "Signature or thumbprint." I spotted the inkpad, inked my thumb, and quickly pressed it in the required space. They were up in arms. "You can't do that," "Yes I can, it says so." "But you can write!" "So what? The choice is there". They went back to the old way.

Some times, if I was not going up the jebel, I would walk to work. It was only about six hundred yards, and entailed walking along the road from the front of the house towards Sheikh

Braik's house and the Palace, parallel with the beach, and then turning left past the Government Guest House towards the office. There were frequently dignitaries staying at the guest house, and their presence was always signalled by the presence of a fleet of Mercedes Benz saloon cars with Palace number plates. The drivers were always Omanis in immaculate shining white *distashas* and *shemaghs*, carrying *khanjars* in their belts. There was one who I particularly remembered, because he had a chin like Jimmy Hill. I always greeted him, and we often had a little chat before I moved on. Because we lived in the Palace Compound we were affected by their security arrangements, none more so than when they issued passes to all the people living there, and said that only those with passes were allowed in. This made it very difficult for us because it meant that our friends could not come and see us. The *askars* (Guards) were always very polite, but adamant. I made enquiries as to whom I should see to allow our friends in. I was told that the only person who had that power was the Minister of the Diwaan (Palace Office). I asked for an interview, and was given a day and a time. I duly turned up, and was shown into a huge waiting room with a row of opulent chairs down one wall, and a large desk in the corner where the keeper of the door was ensconced. I greeted him politely, and explained why I was there. He ushered me to a seat, but I only had to wait a few minutes before being shown in to the minister. He was in an even bigger room, with an even bigger desk. As I walked in, he rose to greet me, and we looked at each other in amazement. It was none other than Jimmy Hill! After the usual pleasantries I told him what the problem was. He said there was no problem, picked up the phone and told someone that anyone asking to see me should be allowed in. Easy as that. I thanked him profusely, and left. It just went to show that in Oman you never know exactly who you are speaking to, because with their universal dress they can all look just the same. The fact that I had routinely been polite to someone who I had thought to be a humble driver paid dividends in the end.

The social life was hectic for those who chose to take part. We were quite picky, because there was a lot of social climbing. A good example of this was the Ambassador's Cocktail Party. Every year the British Ambassador would visit Salalah. There was tremendous competition to get on the guest list. One year, two neighbours of ours were outraged to find that they had not been invited. They wrongly assumed that the person who prepared the guest list was the financial advisor to the Wali, an American called James. They went to him, and complained bitterly. He could have very simply denied all knowledge, but instead he asked "Tell me, when you are in England are you normally invited to ambassadorial functions?" Marvellous! In fact, the guest list was prepared by a friend of ours in the Ministry of Information, so we were always invited.

Every National Day the Sultan came to Salalah for the celebrations. There was always a fire power demonstration, as previously described, a naval review, a chance to shake HM's hand in the Palace, a fire work display and a garden party. This last was considered to be the height of the season by the expats, who went to great lengths both to be invited, and to obtain suitable hats, outfits etc – very much like Ascot. It never bothered us, because we weren't particularly interested. I always went to the fire power demonstration and the fire work displays, and that was that. In 1979 as National Day approached, the invitations were sent out. The program was in English and Arabic, and the invitations to the specific functions were ornate and heavily embossed, and in *Arabic*. Being able to read Arabic I saw that I was invited to shake HM's hand in the Palace, and that we were both invited to the Fire Power Demonstration and the Firework Display. Fine. The expats were in a buzz of excitement, and we were at a party where a group were talking about their invitations to the Garden Party, and what they had ordered from the UK to wear, when they noticed that Maggie and I weren't saying very much. Someone asked us if we had been invited, and when we said no, they were amazed. We obviously weren't as important as they had thought! I asked them if they were sure they had been invited. Had anybody translated the invitations for them? It fell on deaf ears. Of course they were all going! Some said that if we weren't going, could we look after their children for them – no problem. On the appointed day, fleets of cars pulled up outside our house to drop off the children, their parents in all their finery feeling sorry for us that we were obviously such peasants that we hadn't been invited. Our friends Hugh and Miranda hadn't been invited either, and they had come round to join us. We opened a bottle of wine, and waited. About an hour later the cars returned. The occupants variously furious/in tears/shouting etc. They had been turned away at the gates of the Palace. They didn't stay very long, and I didn't say very much.

I found it quite interesting that these people, whose social status was clearly so important to them, were dropped by their erstwhile friends, the moment their contracts were terminated for whatever reason. It was then that they came to us for assistance for their exit from Oman. We never refused them, but at the same time, were not surprised to never hear from them again once our usefulness had passed.

It was on one of these National Days that the culmination of the firework display was to be a huge firework picture of the Sultan. The crowds cheered as the face was gradually revealed, but they fizzled out when the face which was completed was that of King Hussein of Jordan.

Towards the end of 1979 I was asked if I wanted to help in the development of Musandam Province in the north of Oman. I was interviewed by Salem Ghazali, who at that time was Under-Secretary to the Ministry of Defence. The development of Musandam had been contracted to an American company called Tetra Tech International (TTI), and the organisation it formed to carry out the job was called the Musandam Development Committee (MDC). TTI had been founded Jim Critchfield, a former senior CIA official who had played a prominent role in anti-soviet intelligence after the Second World War. At the time, nobody knew this, but the British military in Oman certainly suspected that most of the senior figures in TTI were CIA, to the extent of circulating a warning to all staff not to give them any information. I was directed towards Cliff Andrews, who was the Vice-President. We discussed my contract, and I subsequently resigned from the Wali's Office. The Wali gave me a Rolex watch as a thank-you, and I became an employee of TTI with effect from 1st February 1980.

We packed our belongings into boxes which were loaded onto the al Sultana, a Sultan of Oman's Navy landing craft, at Rayzut on the 8th January. We said our goodbyes and flew by SOAF BAC 111 to Muscat. I had a feeling that one part of my life had finished, and a new one was starting. I felt sorry to be leaving Dhofar, but excited at the prospect of a new challenge.

Chapter Seventeen

Musandam

The Musandam Peninsula is the northernmost part of Oman and forms the southern side of the Straits of Hormuz at the entrance to the Arabian Gulf. The governorate of Musandam is separated from the rest of Oman by the United Arab Emirates, in the form of Ras al Khaimah and Fujairah. Musandam begins where the mountains rise to the north from the plains of Ras al Khaimah.

The population consists mainly of a tribe called the *Shihuh*. They are smaller, darker and more lightly-built than many Arabs, and speak Arabic. Those in the north, especially from Kumzar, speak a dialect which contains many Farsi words. The men carry a walking stick, called a *Yurth*, the distinguishing feature of which is the handle. This consists of a small axe-head, about two inches long, which, traditionally, they bury in the heads of anyone who annoys them. The communities living in the mountains have been isolated for centuries and the coastal villages can only be reached by boat. Agriculture in the mountains is of the 'postage stamp' variety, tiny isolated fields producing poor crops. The population of Musandam was estimated in 1982 at approximately 15 – 17 thousand, of which the majority is concentrated in the capital, Khasab in the north. The second largest town is Bayah (Known in the emirates as Dibba) on the east coast. Fishing and date harvesting are the principal economic activities together with government employment. Smugglers from Iran make frequent trips across the straits to Iran, only 55 kilometres away at the narrowest point, heavily laden with cigarettes and other Western commodities.

The mountains rise straight out of the sea creating fiords. Musandam looks very like Norway, but without the snow. These mountains are extremely rugged, and the paths which exist are exposed and difficult to follow. The highest mountain is Jebel Hareem, at 2087 metres Embedded in the rocks are shell fragments and fossils. Musandam is on a tectonic plate which is gradually slipping under Iran. Consequently there are earth tremors from time to time. The scattered villages have small terraced fields surrounded by low walls to facilitate the trapping of rainwater and its accompanying silt. Rain water is collected in large *birqats* (Cisterns), either dug out of the ground, or formed by blocking off fissures in the rocks.

There are date-groves in the larger coastal settlements, the largest being in Khasab. Khasab also has a large Portuguese-built fort, which is used by the Governor as his office. Close to Khasab is the Elphinstone Inlet (Named after Lord Elphinstone, governor of Bombay from 1853 to 1860) known locally as Khawr Shamm. When the British laid a telegraph cable from India to Basra in the 19th century they established a base here on Telegraph Island. Conditions in summer must have been appalling, and sailors attempting to escape had to 'go around the bend' of the inlet, hence the expression.

Musandam had largely been left alone as the states around it developed. Consequently most of the adult male population worked in the Emirates, and had little or no interest in Oman.

In 1970 there had been an attempt by the *Shihuh* to create their own state, but this had been suppressed, with British involvement. However, the rumbling unrest continued.

Chapter Eighteen

Musandam Development Committee

When we reached Muscat we were accommodated in the Falaj Hotel, close to the TTI offices. I was given a nice Toyota car, and orientated to the ways of TTI. The Vice-President was an American called Cliff Andrews. His assistant, and my immediate boss was another American called Jim Simons. Cliff's brother, Fred, was also there. At this time the MDC was very much in a formative stage. The MDC had been created by Royal Decree Number 60/79, dated 19/11/1979, and its role was to develop the activities of the Ministries of Agriculture and Fisheries, Commerce and Industry, Electricity and Water, Posts, Telegraphs and Telecommunications, Information and Youth Affairs, Municipalities and Land Affairs, Communications, the Department of Public Works, together with the creation of central facilities such as marine engine and vehicle repair workshops. My title was "Director of Operations" based in Khasab, and essentially my job was one of liaising between the departments of the seven ministries listed above, the Ministry of the Interior, in the form of the Governor in Khasab, the military, who controlled air access, and the local population. I was also the senior MDC member in Khasab, and as such, responsible for supervising the other expats in MDC up there.

When I arrived in Khasab, there was another American called Bob there, who had been representing MDC. It very quickly became apparent to me that he thought that I was there to help him, not the other way round. With my knowledge of Arabic and my Dhofar experience I soon took over, much to Bob's disquiet. When I complained to Cliff that Bob obviously had not been informed, his response was "I thought I would let the two of you fight it out. The best man has won." I was soon to discover that this was a normal TTI strategy. Bob was a decent sort of chap, and we got on very well, but he wasn't very happy with TTI's way of doing things, and he eventually left.

I was allocated one of seven earthquake-proof villas in Wadi Khasab, and given an allowance to furnish it. Maggie and I spent several days choosing furniture in Muscat, before seeing it loaded onto *Alnims*. *Alnims* (The Weasel) was a landing craft which was the sole means of transporting anything too bulky or heavy to be transported by Skyvan. At that time there were no harbour facilities in Musandam, so everything had to be off-loaded on the beach at Bayah or Khasab. Initially there was considerable interference from the Omani Police and Customs who tried to arrest the crew, and Cliff, for smuggling. This was sorted out in time by HE Haroon al Hassab, the Minister of Electricity and Water, who at that stage was Chairman of the MDC. Some of our possessions were spoiled by seawater in transit, but at least they got there. The crew of *Alnims* were Philippinos headed by Captain Mike. They were a cheerful bunch and we got to know them well. They supplied us with ice-cream and other goodies, and we gave them beer. The Americans disapproved strongly of this. So far as they were concerned the Philippinos were TCNs (Third Country Nationals), an expression they used in a derogatory manner. You could always tell when *Alnims* was coming into Khasab because they had a huge stereo system on board, which made the vessel act like a soundbox, and the throbbing music carried for miles across the calm water. One day when *Alnims* came in, I had gone down to supervise the unloading. John was swimming in the harbour with some of the crew, and I was on the bridge with Maggie, talking to Captain Mike. When the time came to leave, I called to John to get out of the water. Seeing that I was fully dressed in shirt, and slacks, he refused, challenging me to come and get him. I handed my papers to Maggie, stepped onto the rail of the flying bridge and jumped fully clothed into the water thirty feet below, to the cheers of the crew.

Our villa was of concrete construction, and there were air-conditioners in each of the two bed-rooms, the sitting room, and the kitchen. Despite these, the heat was often nearly unbearable. In summer, the walls would radiate heat, and the only cool area in the rooms was directly in front of the air-conditioner. I kept a daily record of the weather, using a barometer, maximum/minimum thermometer, humidity gauge and rain gauge. In summer the temperature was usually above 40 degrees Celsius, and the maximum temperature I recorded was 49 degrees Celsius on the 1st July 1980. One of the curious things about the environment was that the mountains acted as giant heat-sinks. During the day they would absorb the sun's heat. The wadi would become as hot as an oven, and then in the evening the sun would go down, and it would become much cooler. Then as the sea cooled, and the temperature differential changed, the mountains would give up their heat, and a desiccating breeze would develop. In winter the temperature dropped to below 20 degrees. The rains generally came in January and February, and when they were heavy enough the wadis would flood. The clouds would hang below the mountain tops, and it would rain warm water. When Wadi Khasab flooded, it began with the water flowing at walking pace as the wadi gravels absorbed the water to a depth of several feet. The locals revelled in it, and walked along with it, knowing that this would ensure the survival of their crops. We even sat out and barbecued in the rain. As the rainwater flowed down from the mountains, so the flow would increase in intensity and become a roaring flood, sweeping away everything in its path. Not so many years previously, the wadi had flooded across its' entire width and the locals had tied their children to the palm trees to stop them from being washed away.

Wadi Khasab is about 28 kilometres long, and two kilometres wide where it reaches the sea. There was a graded track along its length, and I had a Toyota Land Cruiser to get around in. The only other way of getting around then was by SOAF helicopter. There were two Huey 205s permanently stationed there, under the control of SOAF, with whom I had to liaise closely for internal flights. Skyvan bookings were under the control of the Army, in the form the Commanding Officer Musandam detachment. We used the Skyvans to go to Muscat about every six weeks or so to buy our food, which we packed into cold boxes. There was a dirt airstrip in Wadi Khasab, one at Bukha on the west coast, and another at Bayah in the south. Strong winds called the *Shimaal* (North, although it came from the west) and *Naashi* (Which did come from the north) were powerful enough to close the Khasab airstrip for three or four days at a time, thus trapping day-trippers from Muscat. This alone was one of the reasons why people in Muscat were reluctant to visit Khasab, which increased its isolation and reduced development. Air-travel was often not comfortable because of the weather made flights bumpy. The high temperatures often reduced the load carrying capacity of the 18-seater Skyvans to three or four, and the resulting thin air made the aircraft struggle to stay aloft. The constant squeaking from the stall-warning indicator kept everyone alert. The other problem of flying by Skyvan, was that you started in the heat at sea-level, where most body water was lost by evaporation. Once the aircraft had climbed to 10,000 feet to get over the mountains safely, it became distinctly chilly, and bladders became very full. There were no lavatory facilities available, and this often resulted in considerable personal discomfort. In time, a new airstrip was built in Khasab, but unfortunately it was designed by the Americans. They sited it in such a way that the southern end of it was very close to a jebel rising from the confluence of Wadi Khasab and Wadi Mawa. Their justification was that the narrow Wadi Khasab and the proximity of the mountains were such as to prohibit any approach other than from the north. The RAF/SOAF pilots ignored this and routinely flew at low-level along the wadi, banking sharply to land, when the wind-direction dictated it. The new airstrip meant that C130 Hercules aircraft could come to Khasab. They were much more comfortable than the Skyvans, and reduced the journey time considerably. Down-draughts in the mountains had the capacity to force helicopters down. Several times I was in a helicopter flying up a wadi when we would suddenly fly into a down draught and plummet. We only escaped by the pilot turning sharply out of it. One 205 which had been forced down onto the jebel was regularly used for spare parts until its remains were picked up and taken to Muscat. The temperature differential between the ground and the mountain tops was enough to crack the helicopter windscreen on more than one occasion. The **BANG!** as it did so terrified everyone on board.

One National Day it was decided that all service personnel taking part should be Omani. This meant that all the Omani pilots returned to Muscat, and were replaced elsewhere by Royal Air Force pilots on secondment. I had to visit a place called Mudha. This was an Omani enclave south of Musandam and north of the Oman border. I went by helicopter, and to avoid flying over the Emirates we went directly over the sea. The journey out was uneventful, but the return journey was another matter. I was sitting in the co-pilot's seat, and we were over the sea when the pilot said "Did you hear that?" I said "What?" He said "That whine. It sounds like hydraulic failure. If we lose our hydraulics I will be able to keep this thing in the air for about five minutes, ten if you help me." He then turned to the Loadmaster in the back and told him to remove the engine panel to check for signs of a leak. He was frozen with fear. I tried to tell him in Arabic, without success. Then we lost the hydraulics altogether. The pilot told me to put my hands and feet on the controls and do as he said. They felt absolutely rigid, and it took a lot of effort to move them. He asked where the nearest helicopter pad was, and I directed him to Bayah, about two minutes away. There was a concrete pad in front of the fort there which he tried to land on, but he had insufficient control, and the helicopter was swinging about all over the place. He then asked if there was a landing strip nearby, so I pointed him towards the gravel strip near the MDC camp, about another two minutes away. He lined the helicopter up with the strip and approached it at about eighty knots. The ground rushed up and there was a hideous squealing from the skids as we skidded along the gravel. When it ground to a halt I let out an "*Al Humdillillah.*" (Praise be to God), and we all piled out. I borrowed an MDC vehicle and drove back to Khasab, whilst he waited for the technicians to fly up from Muscat.

259

Khasab itself consisted of decaying mud-brick buildings. At the time of our arrival, the only modern buildings were the seven villas, the MDC office in the middle of the wadi, and a shop, built by a local entrepreneur. The *Suq* (market) was very dusty, run-down sort of a place. One of the shops was an ironmongers run by a blind man. He knew exactly where everything was, and nothing was ever stolen. The *suq* was very limited in what it had available. Mostly tinned goods from the Emirates, sacks of rice, locally grown onions, dates, and frozen chickens and minced beef, which we bought from a shop owned by Mohammed Noor. He had the only freezer and air-conditioner in town, and the old men congregated in his shop in summer to get away from the heat. I noticed that the frozen chickens and sausage-shaped packs of minced beef always looked as if they had been squashed before being frozen. It was a couple of years before I discovered that Mohammed turned everything off when he went to bed. This meant that overnight the frozen goods would partially defrost, before he turned the freezer on again in the morning. How nobody died I will never know.

We didn't like going down to Muscat as often as the other expats, so we mainly bought our food in the *suq*. We had been doing this for a while, when Bob came into our house. "Guess what! Mohammed Noor is selling frozen buffalo meat. It'll be ideal for Trumpkin (Our cat)." We didn't tell him that he had been eating it in our house for years.

In the December of our first year in Khasab, we had been driving back from the *suq* when we noticed a group of boys playing football near a kitten which seemed to be staggering. We stopped to look at it. It was coal black and tiny, with a long tail. Its eyes were closed with pus. We decided to take it home and clean its eyes. If we could restore its vision we would keep it, otherwise it would be kinder to put it to sleep. We started to nurse it, but before full vision had been restored, we were due to return to England on leave. Our neighbours, Howard and Caroline kindly took him in and continued the care. On our return he was well. We called him Trumpkin, after the dwarf in "The Lion, the Witch and the Wardrobe", a book which John loved. He was affectionate and highly intelligent. Whenever we had been out, he would get up and greet us at the door. If he wanted something he would tell you, and if you tried to move without having first complied he would rest his paw and on your ankle. If you tried to move, the claws would gradually come further and further out until the pain forced compliance. He could open closed doors by standing up and pulling the handle down, and pull or push as appropriate. He was also very jealous, which we discovered when we had the temerity to rescue another kitten from the *suq*. He attacked it viciously on sight. We pulled him off and put the unfortunate kitten back into its box, which Trumpkin continued to attack. This carried on for several days, until we decided that we had to return the poor little kitten to the *suq*. For days afterwards, Trumpkin continued to attack the now empty box, and he punished us by ignoring us. So long as we had Trumpkin we never had any other animal. He would only eat fresh tuna, which was plentifully available. We would buy it by the hundredweight, and fill the bath up with tuna, cut them into pieces and freeze them. The bathroom looked like an abattoir after each of these operations. When we eventually returned to England we brought him with us. Fresh tuna wasn't available, but we found that he liked liver, to the exclusion of everything else. It was this which eventually killed him, because he developed a growth on his liver as a result, several years later.

One day a little white dog appeared by our villa. It was beautiful, and friendly. It looked like a pedigree of some kind, but I didn't know what. One thing was for sure – it wasn't a local dog. Someone had brought it to Khasab and lost it. We kept it in the house for several days while I made enquiries. It turned out that he belonged to the Sheikh of Kumzar. I paid him a visit, and when I returned the dog, he told me I could have it. I refused, on the basis that by accepting a gift I could compromise myself if he wanted a future favour from me in my position in the MDC. About a month later the little dog reappeared. It was blind in one eye, and wanted to stay. I took it back to the Sheikh of Kumzar. Again he offered it to me. Again I refused. My position hadn't changed, although I wanted him. I never saw the little dog again. The next time I saw the Sheikh I asked after him. "Oh, he died." I never forgave myself for that, and have taken care of any animal that has needed a home ever since.

The development plan for Musandam was based on creating amenities in Khasab, Bukha and Bayah and improving communications by road and air. We delivered water by tanker-ship to the coastal villages, and by road tanker to those villages accessible from Khasab. We knew that the *Shihuh* moved with the seasons, for example, from Kumzar to Khasab for the date harvest. We also knew that many of the men had moved to the Emirates for work. It occurred to me that we did not actually know very much about the *Shihuh* who lived in the mountains, so I decided to carry out a demographic survey along the lines of the one I had done in Dhofar (I also subsequently gave the Musandam survey to Durham University). The mapping of the area was poor, and initially I went to the villages accessible from Wadi Khasab. On the helicopter flights I noted the positions of the villages high in the mountains. As the roads gradually extended I was able to drive closer to some of the villages, but ultimately I had to walk to them. The mountains were extremely rugged, and the paths difficult to follow, because they were over rocks, not soil. At times the only way I could follow a path was by observing it when the sun was low in the sky, and the path appeared shiny from all the feet which had walked over it for hundreds of years. At times I lost the path, and had to free-climb over the rocks. I always went alone, because there wasn't anybody else. I was acutely aware that an accident could easily prove to be fatal. I carried a Motorola radio, and lots of water. If the villagers were in residence I was greeted with surprise and hospitality. They were amazed that a European could walk in the mountains alone, and I was always offered coffee, bread, and *dibs* – date treacle obtained by piling sacks of dates on top of one another, the pressure so-caused squeezing the treacle out underneath. I would ask them which tribe they were from, what months of the year they were in residence, and where they moved to and why etc. If the villages were empty, I would count the number of habitable houses, fields, *birqats* (Water cisterns) and fields. I gradually built up a cardex system so that I could cross-reference this information and detect any anomalies. I also returned to the villages at different times of the year for the same reason. Accessible from Wadi Khasab was a three thousand foot high plateau called Al Yemit. One winter I drove to the foot of the mountain and walked up it. It was a cold and damp day, and I was looking forward to some hospitality. When I reached the top, there was a village called Taf al Qarha, and it was empty. I was looking around for some shelter where I could light my cooker and make some tea, when I noticed a very pungent smell. It was just like the lion house at Regents' Park Zoo. I knew that there were leopards in Musandam. I also knew that if I was cold and hungry, so would any leopard up here be too. Also, I wasn't armed, having left my rifle and Smith and Wesson .38 Special in Salalah. All thoughts of refreshments vanished, and I moved rapidly north to the other group of villages I knew to be there. They were empty too, and so, not daring to retrace my steps, continued northwest and dropped down into another part of Wadi Khasab, with great relief.

The *Shihuh* lived a hard life, and weren't in the least bit sentimental about animals. With the advent of motor vehicles they abandoned their donkeys to their own devices. We would see groups of donkeys standing miserably in the wadi. Every now and then one would bray, and for no apparent reason would walk over and bite its neighbour. In summer we took buckets of water for them. The goats similarly had a hard life, although they were still herded. They were always hungry, and frequently climbed into the tops of the acacia trees to get at the buds. They would eat anything, and we frequently saw them eating empty cement bags. As an experiment I once offered one a box of tissues, and photographed it as it held the box down with one hoof whilst pulling out the tissues and eating them. Outside each of the villas was an empty oil-drum for putting our rubbish in. There was one goat which was in the habit of climbing in to eat the rubbish. We called it the Bin-Goat, and Maggie fed it titbits.

Foxes were a problem for the *Shihuh*. They were just as hungry as everything else, and particularly liked chickens. As a defence against them the *Shihuh* were in the habit of putting their chickens in palm-frond baskets at night, and hanging them from poles out of reach. They also set large traps for them, made out of stone. When they caught one, they would hang it, alive, by one leg from a tree, where it would hang, screaming, until it died. This cruel idea was to frighten other foxes, and I often found their remains on my travels.

About fifty yards from the office was a well. It was about a hundred feet deep, ten feet in diameter, and lined with stone. It was dry at the bottom, and had a low stone wall around it. One day, one of our neighbours said there was a fox in the bottom of it. We went and had a look, and so there was. Much to the amusement of the *Shihuh* we decided to rescue it. There was no way we could get down the well, so we lowered a fish-trap baited with food and waited. No luck. The fox just wouldn't be caught. We left it in overnight, and the following morning when I checked it was still empty, but there was no sign of the fox. Puzzled, I went into my office. A few minutes later the door-man appeared, a *Shihuh* called Khamis. He had a reputation as a hunter, and was said to be immune to snake-bites. After greeting me formally, he said, hesitantly "Did you want this?" He produced a sack. In the sack was the fox, alive. It was beautiful, with great big ears and bright eyes. I was amazed, and asked him how he got it. He told me that he had climbed down during the night and grabbed it. Incredible. In the dark he had climbed down a hundred foot well, caught a wild animal, put it in a sack and climbed back out, and here he was, offering it to me. I asked him to let it go. He was puzzled, but he did so.

There was a little *Shihuh* who lived about half a mile up the wadi from us. I used to see him several times a week, usually as he returned from Khasab *suq*. He wasn't very popular with the other villa residents, because he used to use a broken down, abandoned Land Rover near the end of the line of villas as a public lavatory. Whenever I saw him he was usually carrying a huge load of bits and bobs he had scavenged on the way. I got to know him, and found that he lived in poverty. His name was Sultan Ughrub as Shahi, and he was the happiest man I have ever known. He was always smiling and laughing, and whenever, in response to his questions, I told him what I was doing that day his response was always *"Miskeen, miskeen"* ("You poor thing"). When we finally left Khasab I took all the things we were leaving behind in the villa to his house

– *"Miskeen, miskeen"* was the last thing I ever heard him say.

I hadn't been very long in Khasab when I received a telex from the Royal Oman Police in Muscat asking me to pay them a visit regarding stolen ammunition. I was suddenly very worried. I had carefully disposed of all my firearms and ammunition before leaving Salalah, and wondered what it could all be about. I flew down to Muscat, and was directed to the office of a Chief Inspector. He asked me if I had issued ammunition whilst in the employ of the Wali's Office. I said I had. I used to issue .303 ammunition to the *Mindoobs* for their government-issued rifles. He then produced some yellow boxes of Kynoch ammunition, and asked me if I had ever seen it before. Beginning to think I was being set up for a long prison sentence, I said "No. All the ammunition I issued was in khaki bandoliers." He said "That's good, because these were last recorded in Aden, and were part of a consignment left behind when the British withdrew." He told me that the *Mindoob* from Jib Jat, who I knew well, had been picked up at Nizwa, in the north, trying to sell them. When arrested, he had told the police that I had given them to him, obviously thinking that I had left Oman for good. In fact they were part of a concealed *adoo* cache which he had been sitting on, waiting for an opportune moment to sell. The Chief Inspector said "You have nothing to worry about. You are free to go." I went, with great relief.

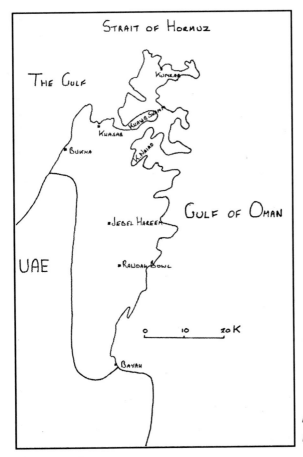

STRAIT OF HORMUZ

THE GULF

KUMZAR

KHAWR SHAM

KHASAB

BUKHA

K.NAIRD

GULF OF OMAN

UAE

JEBEL HAREEF

RAWDAH BOWL

0   10   20 K

BAYAH

*Musandam
Province*

Khasab

267

*Mountain scene.
Note cultivation*

Khasab cannon. Eid al Fitr 1983

Smugglers in Khasab harbour

Rip Reddy's memorial in Rawdah Bowl

Maggie feeding the bin goat

Trumpkin waiting for lunch

Chapter Nineteen

MDC stories

My office was on the top floor of the MDC building. About a quarter of my time was spent doing paperwork, the rest, I was out and about, checking on development work, talking to the locals and generally keeping everything moving. Initially, there was wide-spread resentment that Oman was tightening its' grip on the area, and the Musandam Development Committee (*Lijina Tatweer Musandam*) was widely referred to as the *Lijina Tadmeer Musandam* (Musandam Destruction Committee). As such, I had to know who the local personalities were, their connections and affiliations. In this respect I worked closely with the Oman Research Department (ORD), and on one occasion tracked down an innocuous-seeming shopkeeper in Dubai with links to the separatist cause. I slowly and assiduously built up a cardex containing a considerable amount of information about local people. Once the *Shihuh* realised that development was taking place they started laying claims to parts of Wadi Khasab which they thought we would want to develop. They did this in the traditional way by putting some bricks on top of each other and then announcing that it was the start of a new house. If we needed the land they immediately demanded compensation. I discussed this with the Governor, Sayyid Sultan Hamad Hilal al Samaar al Bu Saidi. We decided that the best thing was to put the whole of the wadi under Planning Control, to put an end to this kind of extortion, and I duly issued a notice proclaiming this. In my office was a pleasant cleaner and tea-maker called Khadim. A couple of weeks after my proclamation, he came to me and asked if he could have the following morning off in order to attend a meeting, to which I agreed. At about eleven o'clock the next morning I was in my office when the phone rang. It was the Governor. Could I come down to his office? "Of course." I finished pushing papers around, got into my Land Cruiser and drove sedately down the wadi towards his office, which was on the battlements of the old Portuguese fort by the sea. As I entered the town I encountered a large cheerful crowd coming up the wadi away from his office. When I reached the main gate I was surprised to see that there were no *askars* on guard. (*Askars* were the Governor's personal bodyguard consisting of old men with .303 rifles). I went up onto the battlements, and was also surprised to see the Governor before I expected to, largely because the opaque window to his office was broken. When I went in he got up from behind his desk, something he never done before, and came and sat beside me on the settee. He seemed quite nervous and I asked him what had happened. He told me that the cheerful mob I had encountered, which included my nice tea-maker, had come to protest about my Planning Controls. They had broken his window, and roughed him up. When I asked why his *askars* hadn't protected him, he said "They are old men. I got wind that this was going to happen so I sent them away for their own protection". I asked why he hadn't called the Army. He said that he didn't want anyone hurt. How wonderfully Omani. I asked him what he wanted me to do. Did he want me to rescind the proclamation? No, he would think what to do about it. We had a cup of *qahwa* *(coffee)* and I left. I was in the habit of visiting him a couple of times a week, and when I visited him the following week, the *askars* were back at their post, in the shade of the main gate, quite relaxed. Inside the gate, by the dungeon door were about twenty pairs of sandals. The dungeon door was open, and when I looked into the gloom I recognised Sheikh Mohammed Hassan, the sheikh of Kumzar, and many others. I asked him what they were doing there. He said "We are guests of the Governor". I went upstairs to see Sayyid Sultan, and asked him what was going on. He explained that he had sent a message to all the tribal leaders that he wanted to discuss land reform. When they arrived he had put them all in the slammer. I said "If they are in prison, why is the door open?" He said "It is too hot for it to be closed." I said "But they could all just walk out." To which he responded "Where to?" He kept them there for a few days to make his point before letting them all go.

On another occasion when I visited him, he told me that he had a big problem. It was after the corniche road had been opened up along the coast from Khasab to Ra's al Khaymar and beyond. Instead of going to Muscat, we were able to drive to Dubai for our fresh food and supplies. Dubai was a wonderful place, and it was less than two hours away by road. We went there frequently, as did many others, including the locals. On this occasion, a group of off-duty policemen had gone to purchase alcohol, and bring it back into Musandam, which was illegal. When they reached the border post, their friends on duty recognised them, and knowing what they were doing, waved the car through. One of the policemen, more drunk than the others, was outraged. Insisted that they did their duty and search the car. Knowing what they would find, they refused. The drunk became more belligerent, and an argument ensued, which culminated in him saying that if they did not do their duty and search the car, he would report them. They duly searched the car, found a load of alcohol, and had to arrest them. They were currently in the nick. That was the last I heard of the problem, and I didn't like to enquire.

There was an extensive road-building program and another of the projects in addition to the corniche to Ra's al Khaymar, was one through the centre of the province to Bayah. This was a huge feat, because from Khasab the road initially followed Wadi Khasab before rising into the mountains around Jebel Hareem, and then descending into Wadi al Bih, near the Rawdah Bowl, climbing again, before descending into the Wadi Khabb Shamsi before arriving in Bayah. In Rawdah Bowl there is a cairn with the words 'FOR RIP' on it. Most people, when seeing it would remark that you didn't normally put the word 'FOR' before 'RIP'. What they didn't realise was that this 'RIP' was not *Requiescat In Pace*, but a memorial to an SAS soldier called Rip Reddy who had been killed whilst free-fall parachuting there in 1970. We had been on the same free-fall course at Pau in 1968. The stretch along the Wadi Khabb Shamsi was very impressive because it was like the bottom of the Grand Canyon, with towering walls, in places only yards wide. When the wadi flash-flooded large stretches would be wiped out, and have to be rebuilt. The highest point on the road was about five thousand feet, and as the crow flies, the distance was about 70 kilometres. In actual terms, with all the switch backs involved, it must have been five times that. The roads were built by the Ministry of Defence (MOD) Roads Division. While this road was being built I was driving along it with Cliff when we came across a low-loader with a huge generator on the back. Two English engineers were struggling to offload it, using a wooden beams and a block and tackle. We watched as they sweated, and cursed the incompetence of the seniors who had sent it to them, knowing that they didn't have the means to unload it. Looking at them, Cliff commented "Well, that is what I would call good old-fashioned Yankee ingenuity." The retort was "Well, that's what we Brits call a fxxx up."

Driving along this road early one morning Maggie and I noticed a plume of smoke ahead. As we got closer we saw fire as well. It was half way down a hillside, and there were no locals about. We got out to investigate, and found that it was a bush, on fire. There was no obvious source of ignition. When I asked the Governor about it later, he said that bushes frequently spontaneously combust, and we found several more in the time that we were there. I hadn't come across burning bushes before, except in the Old Testament, and wondered if there was a connection.

In November 1983, I was driving back up the road, alone, from Bayah, on a narrow ridge, when around the corner came an MOD Toyota Pickup, travelling at warp nine, on my side of the road. There was nowhere for me to go and we collided head-on. I had been wearing my seat-belt and was unhurt. The two Pakistanis hadn't been, and their heads had starred their windscreen, although they didn't seem to be hurt. I called for assistance on my Motorola radio, and in due course the police arrived. They took photographs and statements, and told me it would go to court. It never did, because the MOD did what it always did in those circumstances, and sent them back to Pakistan, never to return. Their unstated rationale was that since the two Pakistanis would be found guilty they would be fined. They would lose all their meagre savings, and so they were made inaccessible to the court, in order to preserve what they had.

The border check points were a problem for as long as we were there. Previously on the West coast there had been no road, consequently there had been no need for a check-point. When the corniche was opened, the Emirates reacted first by installing a check-point. Sometimes they let foreigners (Us) in and out, sometimes not. It was very frustrating, so I appealed to the British ambassador to help when he visited. We had to go through the check-point when he visited because the Khabb Shamsi route was closed due to heavy rain. He was treated churlishly by the guards, even after I explained who he was, and that he was accompanied by the German ambassador. It probably wasn't worth a diplomatic incident, and eventually they relented and let us through. Other expats made a scene, but I knew that that does not help matters in the Arab world. I returned later and had a chat with the guards, who suggested I made an appointment to see the head of the Ra's al Khaymar Police and Immigration Department, which I did. When I went to see him, I was shown into a large office, where, in true Arab style we discussed everything bar the matter in question. Knowing what was going on, I was careful not to show any signs of impatience, and it paid off as usual. After about half an hour, after the *qahwa* and dates had been consumed, he abruptly asked to see my passport. He took it without comment, and passed it to his secretary, who took a photocopy of it. He said "This will be posted at the check-point. You will have no further difficulty." I thanked him profusely and left. He didn't offer the same concession to the others, and it had clearly been my reward for being polite.

The other check-point which was a perennial source of problems was on the northern Omani border at Khatm al Milaha. Again, the problems were intermittent depending on who was on duty. One day, travelling north out of Oman, the Immigration officials refused to stamp my passport, saying I was a frequent traveller, and they knew me, and that my passport would soon fill up if they stamped it every time. When I reached the Emirates side they refused to let me in because I had not been stamped out of Oman, so I went back to the Omani side. They then refused to let me back in because, on paper, I had never left Oman. I returned to the Emirates side, but their position hadn't changed, so I drove back to the Omani side, stopped the car short of the post and walked over. I explained the situation, whereon they relented and stamped me out. The simplest things could be so difficult.

On the other hand, they could be supremely practical. Now that Khasab had road access to the Emirates it was important that everyone had a driving licence. Up until then it hadn't been important because the roads were practically non-existent, but now that they had access to the outside world they would have to comply with the law. The prospect of carrying out a hundred driving tests was out of the question, so the Police sent up a tester from Muscat. The relevant forms were filled in, and all the applicants were told to be at the *Suq* with their vehicles at nine o'clock in the morning. A police car drove up and told the applicants to follow them, and about a hundred cars did so. They drove all around the town, and licences were given to all those who survived the course.

On another occasion, a 60 foot yacht sailed into the harbour. It was crewed by a Brit from Salalah. He was part of a consortium which had financed its' construction, with aim of selling it at a profit. He had sailed the Gulf without success, and when I went to see the Governor I mentioned it, but I had forgotten the Arabic for "Yacht", so I said to him "There is a wooden boat in the harbour which is driven by the wind." "Oh" he said, "You mean a yachcht." I burst out laughing. I hadn't realised that 'yacht' is a universal word.

His deputy Sheikh Hamaid was a lovely, cheerful man. We were having lunch one day, sitting around a tray of rice and boiled mutton. He reached over and took the goat's skull and tried to break it to retrieve the brain. It just wouldn't break, and eventually he gave it a mighty blow and it shattered. There was nothing inside. "Look" he laughed, "We have been eating a mad goat!"

At the end of *Ramadan*, (The Muslim month of fasting) is *Eid al Fitr* (A feast, like Christmas). In Khasab, the end of *Ramadan* is announced by firing an old cannon in front of the Governor's office. There were several old cannon lying without carriages in the sand, and I noticed one day that one was being cleaned out. Several *askars* were working at something nearby, and when I enquired what was going on, they said they were making gunpowder. I knew *Eid* was close, and asked them when it was. "On the dawn after the new moon appears" was the somewhat enigmatic answer. I decided I wanted to see this, and kept a close eye on the situation. When I worked out when it was going to be fired I told the other expats, and several of us went to the Governor's fort the following dawn. There was no sign of life as I set up my camera on a tripod a few feet away from the cannon, a good thing, as it turned out, and went and banged on the door. Silence. I banged again, this time more forcefully. I heard movement inside. A sleepy *askar* stuck his head through the peep-hole "What do you want?" he asked grumpily. No other greeting. No nothing. "We have come to see the cannon being fired." "You are early." "No we are not. It is dawn." "Wait a minute." More scuffling. He came slowly out, picked up a dried palm-frond, lit it, threw it at the cannon, and scuttled off. There was a deafening roar as it went off, slewing around in the sand. The others threw themselves on the ground, while I hung onto the tripod and squeezed the shutter. A huge shower of sparks came out of the muzzle, and a chunk of wadding flew far out into Khasab Bay. We picked ourselves up and went home.

Fortunately, my picture came out beautifully.

In April 1980 our friends Hugh and Miranda had paid us a visit. We were standing in the blinding sun on Khasab airstrip awaiting the arrival of their Skyvan. It stopped with the usual roar as the engines reversed thrust, and the rear ramp slowly raised. John and Olly ran delightedly towards each other. Unfortunately they didn't stop, and there was a sickening thud, as their heads crashed into each other. They quickly recovered, and went off exploring.

John made friends all over Khasab. One, in particular, was a Gurkha diver called Thappa who was working on the harbour project, supervising the placement, underwater, of the breakwater. He taught John to dive, initially by putting him in a *burmail* (Oil drum) full of water so that he could practice using the air tank and demand-valve. When John was competent, Thappa took him diving in the harbour. John was too small to wear the oxygen tank, so he pushed it in front of him as he swam. Thappa was doing this one day with the son of one of the engineers. A large shark appeared, and the boy bit through the mouth-piece of his demand valve in his terror. Thappa sat him on the sea-bed and shared his mouth-piece until the shark lost interest.

There was no English-speaking school in Khasab, so education for John was a problem. We sent away for a home education course, the idea being that Maggie would teach John at home. This didn't work out because the two of them were effectively trapped within four hot walls while John wanted to be outside exploring. The heat caused tempers to fray, and we decided, reluctantly, that John would have to go to boarding school. We chose *The Elms*, at Colwall, near Malvern. This was a small prep school, and seemed ideal. We employed an agency called Universal Aunts to escort him to and from Heathrow Airport when he came out to us in holiday time. We noticed that he was always ravenous on arrival, and it took a lot of coaxing to reveal that the charming lady who collected him in London used to take him to her house in Chelsea until nearer the time of the flight. She always offered him food and he always politely refused. He had noticed a wart on her nose and he knew that witches had warts on their noses, ergo she was a witch, and trying to poison him. After his first term we visited him, and while we were having a pub lunch in Colwall we spotted a group of Morris dancers forming up, with their bells and blackened faces. When we pointed this out to John, he lowered his Daily Telegraph, studied them for a moment. "Probably striking miners" he announced as he raised his paper again.

Chapter Twenty

More MDC stories

When we returned from leave in 1981 I was told that His Excellency Sayyid al Musalim Bin Rashid al Busaidi had taken over as chairman of the MDC. He was a lively, charismatic man, and I had first met him when he was a platoon commander in the Muscat Regiment at Hajeef in Dhofar, in 1976. I had taken Maggie and John there during the monsoon. Al Musalim had put a rat in an army mug and given it to John 'to show mummy'. Maggie, being a country girl, hadn't reacted in the way he had hoped. When he became ADC to the Sultan a couple of years later, he moved into a villa two doors down from us in Salalah. John had let the hand-brake off his Mercedes in his driveway, and it had rolled into his garage doors, without doing any damage, fortunately. Al Musalim brought John back to the house with a box of chocolates. When he saw Maggie he said "Remember me? I am the rat from Hajeef."

By this stage Al Musalim had become a Minister of State, and the first thing he wanted to do was to have a tour of Musandam, incognito. His aide, Abu Rusail, had bought some camping kit, and we drove north in two Land Cruisers. We camped outside Bayah, and waited for a reaction from the locals. In due course a *Shihuh* spotted us and came over. Al Musalim offered him *qahwa* (Coffee), and he sat down for a chat. Eventually, Al Musalim asked him what he thought of the Government. The man thought for a moment, then said "Well, the Sultan's alright, but his Ministers – what a load of wasters!" I looked into Al Musalim's eyes as he received this, and I saw them twinkle, but he didn't respond. We continued with our tour, and returned to our campsite. After supper we settled down to play backgammon, and the skies opened up. It poured and poured, so we put on our waterproof jackets and carried on playing, tipping up the board from time to time, to empty it. This had been going on for some time when we saw vehicle lights approaching. It was the head of our Bayah office, Habeeb. He had known that we were in the area, and, concerned for the Minister's well-being, had come out to offer us accommodation. He was standing there explaining all this as the rain water dripped off his nose, and I could see that he had difficulty taking in what he was looking at, Al Musalim and I sitting out in the rain playing backgammon happily. Al Musalim thanked him gracefully for his kind offer, and declined. Habeeb, baffled, disappeared into the night. The following morning Al Musalim decided that he had found out enough, and announced that he was going to hold a *majlis* (Meeting) with the locals. The word went around like wildfire, and, at the appointed hour, over a hundred people turned up at the Deputy Governor's office. Amongst them was the little *Shihuh* we had met at the camp. Al Musalim was resplendent in his robes, looking very much the minister. Our little *Shihuh* wasn't in the least put out, and attacked Al Musalim furiously for the lack of development in the province. Al Musalim was diplomatic, but he wasn't having any of it, and gave as good as he got. This was al Musalim's style. He would listen, but he was autocratic, and didn't tolerate whingers.

When the Khasab Youth Club had demanded a proper football pitch they hassled me relentlessly. They weren't children, they were young adults, in their early twenties, and they hassled Al Musalim as well, so he diverted a grader from the roads program and made them a pitch. Then they complained that it wasn't big enough, so he enlarged it. Then they complained that it didn't have goal-posts, so Al Musalim supplied those, but they said that they didn't like them. Then they said that they wanted it turfed, like in the Emirates, even though they knew that Khasab was acutely short of water. The complaints were endless, and ultimately Al Musalim phoned me. He wanted the entire youth club to assemble at the football pitch, and he wanted a Roads Department earth-grader standing by. The youth club assembled in great expectation as Al Musalim got off the plane and came straight over. It wasn't what they expected. He gave them the biggest dressing-down they had probably ever received, and then told the grader driver to tear up the pitch. He stood there until the job was completed, and then came with me back to the office for *qahwa*.

Al Musalim decided that he wanted to visit all the coastal villages with a view to assessing their needs with regard to the supply of water tanks. We had a Boston Whaler in Khasab, powered by twin outboard engines, and decided to use it for the trip. When Al Musalim came up, he was accompanied by John and Terry, from head office, who clearly didn't understand his style. They had safari suits and coats, although Al Musalim had decided it was to be a camping trip. They were miserable, and huddled up against the spray as it came over the side of the Whaler, and their safari suits weren't ever meant to be slept in either. We spent two days on the survey, and when we approached Bayah, Jim and Terry clearly thought that was the end of their purgatory, but no. Al Musalim insisted on camping for a third night by the giant sand-dune at the north end of Bayah beach. I think he was enjoying their misery. The following morning Al Musalim insisted that they bury him in the sand by the water's edge, and their misery was complete when a wave caught them from behind and soaked their safari suits.

Al Musalim and I got on well, and he knew that we were in the habit of visiting Dubai so he decided to come along with his wife. Although there were many first-class hotels in Dubai, our favourite was the Al Bustan. This was a much more modest establishment, and a haunt of the local Palestinians and Lebanese. The manager's name was Mansoor, and he ran it with a fist of iron. When the Lebanese had a party the room would be decked out with flowers. There would be a bottle of Black Label on every table. There would be a cabaret. One of our favourites was a singer called Mike Hayek who had a spinal deformity, but he could play the guitar very well, and had a very distinctive booming voice. The families would arrive, all ages, and after the food had been cleared away they would dance on the tables. On the occasion that we went with Al Musalim there was an excellent belly-dancer. She would come, when called, and dance on your table in exchange for cash being tucked into her bikini bottom. Al Musalim was so impressed that he called over Mansoor and much to the irritation of his wife, said that he wanted the table cloth to use as the MDC flag.

In April 1982 I was summoned to Muscat. TTI had a problem with their well-drilling contract in Dhofar, and wanted me to sort it out. Apparently the jebel tribes were refusing to cooperate. They had demanded that their old men be employed as guards, and the Americans, recognising a scam when they saw one, had refused. I could have solved the problem for them there and then, but never looking a gift-horse in the mouth, agreed to pay a visit. Maggie and I drove direct from Khasab to Salalah, a journey of over eight hundred miles on gravel roads, the first time this had been done. We arrived in Salalah on 21st April and visited our old friends. It transpired that the problem was that the Americans had alienated them by their arrogant approach, and lack of understanding of the local culture. They just didn't realise that it is a tradition to employ old men as guards. This benefited both sides; on the one hand it showed good will on the part of the company, and on the other, the whole tribe could be held accountable if anything went wrong. We spent an enjoyable week in Dhofar, the culmination of which was the agreement by TTI that they would employ two old men at each drill-site for the duration of the contract. Gareth, from the camel trip, asked for a lift back to Muscat with us. We had intended to stop at Nizwa, a town in northern Oman, but it started to rain. Concerned that the wadis may flood, thus trapping us, we had to drive past Nizwa, which was a pity, because after that it succumbed to the development going on all over the country.

On our return the French oil company ELF had established a rig in the sea north of Khasab. It was felt incumbent that the chairman of the MDC should pay it an official visit, and that I should arrange it. We flew out to it by helicopter, spent several hours being shown around it, while Al Musalim tried to look interested, had a meal, and then departed. The most memorable part of the exercise for me was that ELF had to send its senior officials up as hosts. The previous night they had been accommodated in the Khasab Guest House, an MDC-run hotel. I visited them as they sat down to dinner, and one of them asked me to recommend a main course from the menu. I suggested the Veal Mornay, which they all chose. Afterwards I asked him if he had enjoyed it. He glowered at me. "Do you know what *mort* means in French?" "Of course" I said, "It means *dead.*" "Yes" he said, "Do you know what *née* means in French?" I said "Yes, it means *born.*" "Yes he said "That is what it tasted like – *mort née*, dead-born, a still birth." I took it from that, that he hadn't enjoyed it. On the other hand, he was probably disgruntled at having been dragged away from the four star hotels of Muscat.

Relations with TTI were becoming strained. They wanted me to liaise with all local agencies in order to ensure the implementation of the strategic plans for the Province, which I did. However I did not lose sight of the needs of the local population, and so, if I saw that a particular plan could adversely affect a particular group, I would argue for a change in order to accommodate them. The Americans could not understand this. An example was rubbish disposal. At that time large pits were dug in the wadi bottom and the rubbish simply dumped in. The local goats would go in to feed, and become injured on the sharp tins. I asked for them to be fenced off, without success. A prestigious youth club had been built at Bayah, and I noticed a contract had been given to a company to build a fence around it. I sent a telex saying "Reference fence for Bayah youth club. I consider fencing rubbish tips to be more important. With immediate effect I will commence dumping all rubbish in Bayah youth club." The following day I was given funds to fence all tips. I was later told that when my telex arrived, they had run round saying "Paul has gone mad". I also used MDC resources to improve access to villages in the area. I never diverted plant away from an existing project, but, if a grader was sitting idle in the yard, I would put it to use. This also went down like a lead balloon.

TTI issued an edict. The TCNs (Pakistani/Indian employees) of which there many, were banned from talking in their own national language on the Motorola radios. This was stupid, because they communicated more effectively that way. It was just that the TTI, in their paranoia, wanted to be able to understand what they were saying, even though they themselves were rarely in the Province to hear them. I discovered that we Brits were also considered TCNs. Whenever we visited Muscat we were accommodated in a simply-furnished guest house. There was a Pakistani servant who did a good job of keeping the place clean and tidy. TTI decided to relocate him to a well-site in the middle of nowhere, and we could do our own cleaning. He didn't want to go, and I fought to keep him, but I lost. This incident got me wondering where the Americans went when they visited Muscat. I found out. It was a luxurious villa on a smart estate, with many serving staff, and a buffet breakfast every day. I was furious at the difference in treatment, but it was par for the course. I discovered that my deputy in Bayah had been given a new air-conditioned state-of-the-art Toyota Land-Cruiser to ride around in while I had kept a battered old Toyota. Nothing had been said to me. They tried to justify it by saying that he needed it so that he could drive down to Muscat in comfort. My response was that I had more need to visit Muscat than he had, and had further to travel, and that unless I was given one I would not visit Muscat again. They sent one up straight away.

On the rare occasions that TTI management visited Khasab, they would be assailed by the locals demanding improvements in services, especially the supply of electricity, which was extremely limited, and had now become essential since the *Shihuh* had discovered air-conditioners. They would make all sorts of promises, knowing that there was no way they could be fulfilled. They also knew that they would be safe in Muscat and I would get the flak. I became so fed up with this one day, that I told a group of *Shihuh* that I was powerless, and that in order to get whatever it was that they wanted, they should go to TTI head office in Muscat. I described to them exactly how to get there, and booked them on a SOAF flight. They caused mayhem in those luxurious ivory towers. The offices were completely disrupted for half a day. When I received a message I denied all knowledge of the incursion. All their requests had been granted and I took great delight in telling TTI why what they had acceded to was impossible. When the *Shihuh* complained to me after that, I was able to refer them to TTI in Muscat. They would say "But there's no point." I would say "Exactly, but I will do what I can." At least I was straight with them.

One project was to extend the Khasab electricity grid to Bukha. This entailed building a power line over the mountains. To place the poles in position required a helicopter, and Bristows were given the contract. The skill that the pilots employed to lower the poles into the holes bored into the rocks, was impressive, with the rotor-tips only feet away from the mountain-side in gusty conditions. When I decided that I wanted to visit another, more remote plateau, called Salistam, SOAF said they could not guarantee collecting me because of the weather conditions. The Bristows pilots they said they would collect me regardless. I would need to spend several days on Salistam in order to do the job thoroughly. I didn't know if there was anybody there, so I would have to carry everything I needed with me, including five gallons of water. The five kilometre, three thousand foot high, walk from the wadi-bottom was gruelling, and when I reached the plateau, it was deserted. The plateau itself is four kilometres long, with several scattered villages. I stayed up there for three days, and the weather was miserably cold and wet. I had agreed a time and place for a pick-up point with Bristows before I left. It was to be the western end of the plateau, in a village overlooking a precipitous drop down to Wadi Ghumdah on the west coast. The weather was so foul I didn't think that Bristows would make it, and I sat hunched against a wall, watching the eagles riding the air currents over the cliff only feet away. Then, right on time, I heard the distinctive 'whoopwhoopwhoop' of the Huey as it came over the plateau. I threw a smoke grenade, and the Huey delicately put one skid on the roof of a convenient house, enabling me to climb on board.

To keep fit I used to go running in Wadi Khasab, ten to fifteen miles was my usual distance. The heat was incredible, and in summer I had to pre-position bottles of water with salt added, along the way. The *Shihuh* got used to seeing me, and ceased to be alarmed. In that part of the world someone running is a sign of a major problem. One day, when I came back from Muscat, one the office clerks, ran up to me. "Oh Mr Paul, thank goodness you are back." My heart sank. What disaster had happened? "There is to be a road race today, and we have entered you to represent the MDC." "Thank you very much" I thought. As it turned out, it had been well organised. The route was about three miles, starting in the *Suq* and finishing at the Boy's School. All those taking part had to have a brief medical examination by the doctor, and there were about fifty runners, all much younger than me. We jostled good-naturedly at the start, and then there was a shot, and we were off. They took off like maniacs, and I thought there was no way they would keep that up. I settled into a rhythm at the back, and after about half mile started to overtake some of them. As the race progressed I gradually overtook the field, until there were only two in front of me. The leader ran with his hands held at shoulder level. I had never seen anyone run like that before, especially at that speed. Even so, I thought that if the race was a couple of miles longer I would be able to overtake him. We ran through the crowds outside the school, and there on the veranda was the reception committee. It consisted of the Governor, Deputy Governor, Director of Education, Chief of Police and others. They waited until every one was in, and then the speeches started. They seemed to go on forever, and then came the prize-giving. The high-handed *Shihuh* winner was given a watch. Number two was given a pile of blankets. I suddenly realised I was in line for a prize. This hadn't occurred to me, and when my name was called out, I made my way through the cheering crowd. The Governor said a few words, and then the Director of Education lugged a large box across the veranda. It was three feet long, by two feet wide and a foot deep. As he gave it to me he whispered "It would be better if it was a watch." I hoisted it onto my shoulder and staggered back through the crowd. When I got home I opened it. It was a gas cooking range! Hence the whispered remark. I gave it away.

Apart from running, walking and swimming, the only other means of keeping fit in Khasab was the squash court. This was located behind the villas. It had no roof, and the temperature in there used to soar, hence its' nickname 'The Oven'. I considered myself to be quite a good player, certainly the best in Khasab. One day I bumped into a little fat Welshman I hadn't seen before. He was looking for someone to have a game of squash with, and asked me if I would play with him. I looked at him with barely concealed contempt. Of course. We went onto the court and he absolutely thrashed me. He didn't move off the 'T', and didn't even break into a sweat. When he had reduced me to a gibbering heap, he told me that he was a county champion from South Wales. A quick lesson in humility there. Later we managed to have a roof put on it, and air-conditioning installed. As usual, in that environment, the air-conditioning wasn't very effective, and it was probably the cause of a fatality. Alasdair Campbell, former professional footballer turned electrical engineer, collapsed and died in there shortly after we left. We had had our last meal in Khasab with him and his wife in their house.

In 1982 a team of Royal Engineers was dispatched to Musandam to carry out small local projects. They clearly hated the place, and when the Omani Minister of Defence, HE Sayyid Fahr was due to fly up and pay a visit, a helicopter pilot flying over a few days before, noticed that in Rawdah Bowl they had made a sign out of rocks, painted white, legible from 8,000 feet. It said "I am so happy I could shit". They were told to rearrange it to form a helicopter pad. Before they left, a football match was arranged in Khasab between them and the local youth club. The average weight of the *Shihuh* was about eight stone. The average weight of the Sappers was nearer fourteen stone. The *Shihuh* ran rings around them in the heat, and in frustration, one of the Sappers took the legs away from one of the *Shihuh*, leaving him in a crumpled heap in the dust. He promptly jumped up, ran to the side-line, borrowed a *yurth* (*Shihuh* axe) from one of his friends and buried it between the shoulders of his assailant. The match was called off.

While driving up the corniche road from Bukha one day I noticed a dead buffalo on the beach. There was a trade in these from India, and presumably this one had been washed overboard in a storm. The head and horns were magnificent, so I decided that I wanted it. I left it where it was, and waited for the natural decay process to make it more manageable. Every time I drove by in the ensuing weeks, there it was. One day I stopped again to see how it was getting on, and seeing that it was just a skeleton, decided that the time was ripe to recover the skull. When I went to move it, I found that it was still attached to the body by the hide, which by this time had been hardened by exposure to the sun and salt air. I didn't have a knife on me, and worried that the next spring high tide might wash it out to sea again, searched up and down the beach for something suitable to cut it with. All I could find was a whisky bottle. I broke it, and set about using the razor sharp glass to cut through the hide. It was at this point that a group of *Shihuh* came along and stopped to watch me. What they made of it I don't know – the head of the MDC in the province, crouched on the beach using a whisky bottle to cut off the head of a dead buffalo. Probably thought I was mad. I took it home and cleaned it, and it graced our gate until we finally left.

In February 1983 I was told that the British and German ambassadors, together with their wives would be visiting Musandam, and I would be hosting them. I met them at the Holiday Inn at Khawr Fakkan in the south. I had been intending to drive up the new road in the Wadi Khabb Shamsi. This wadi was like a small version of the Grand Canyon, and the scenery was magnificent. Unfortunately heavy rain had been forecast. The likelihood of flash flooding in the wadi made it too dangerous, so we went up the west coast to the Ra's al Khaymar check-point I described previously. Amongst my staff in Khasab was a Norwegian-American who had served in the Norwegian army. He had announced his intention of climbing the six thousand feet high Jebel Hareem that weekend. Seeing what the weather was like, and knowing the mountains as I did, I told him not to go. When we reached Khasab, I was told that he had gone up the mountain, and by this time the rain was torrential. I put the ambassadorial party into the Khasab Guest House for the night, and the following morning, as I went over to collect them, I turned on my Motorola radio to hear the climber screaming hysterically into his radio that he couldn't go on, that he was going to die, etc. I was still listening to it when I sat down with the ambassadors. The

British ambassador said "I suppose this means that the tour is off." I said "Why?" He said "Because you are going to have to mount a rescue party." I said "Certainly not. I told him not to go. He ignored my instructions. I have no intention of risking anybody else's life to try and save his. There is nobody else up here with the necessary skills, and I don't know exactly where he is. I will go and look for his body when the storm is over." I felt that he didn't agree with me, and I realised that yet another chance at a diplomatic career had been quashed. The German ambassador didn't say anything, but I could see in his eyes that he agreed with me. When we entertained them all in our house that night, we got on very well with the Germans. When they had all gone I had letters of thanks, and a nice coffee-table picture book from the German ambassador. The climber eventually got himself off the mountain, very shaken. He had reached the summit in storm conditions, and had sheltered in the small radio hut which had been put there. He had abandoned all his kit. When I went up a few days later I recovered his kit, and was angered to see that when he had left the hut, he had neglected to close the door, ruining all the equipment inside.

The Tumb Islands are a group of islands to the west of Musandam. They have been the cause of a long-running dispute between the Arab states of the Gulf and Iran. While we were in Khasab there was a further deterioration of relations, and it was felt possible that we could be involved in the fall-out. Talk of evacuation was in the air. MDC staff were understandably anxious about this, and took a lot of reassuring. At this time there was a group of Texans installing an earth satellite station in Wadi Khasab. They were some of the biggest men I have ever seen. Not just fat, but big-boned as well. Their reaction to all this was to board the first Skyvan to land, and refuse to get off. They left, abandoning all their kit, and returned a couple of weeks later when the fuss had died down. In the mean-time an American television crew arrived. I gave them all assistance, and one of the things they wanted to film was a *nidhiba*. This is a *Shihuh* custom following a feast in which they give thanks to their host. It involves a group of them standing in a circle with the skulls of the eaten goats, and blowing into them like conch-shells. It creates a weird sound, and I rarely saw the ceremony carried out. I explained that we would have to provide a feast, but the TV crew wouldn't pay for that. I negotiated with the *Shihuh*, and to my surprise they agreed to do a *nidhiba* without a feast. They would provide the skulls. I brought my recorder along, but the TV crew said they would give me a copy of their, much better, recording. They left afterwards without doing so, and my letters remained unanswered. It reminded me of a time in Salalah when I had similarly assisted a British reporter, who, knowing the sensitivity of the situation subsequently printed in the British press that 'Paul Sibley, a former SAS soldier, was working in the Wali's Office, just a few hundred yards away from the Under-Secretary, a former communist, whom he once would have hunted to the death'. Thank you very much.

The excitement prompted the Commander of the Sultan's Army to visit. I had known him in the SAS. The local detachment commander said that he would want to talk to me, and asked me to be in the Officer's Mess to meet him. I knew the general was flying around the Province, so I waited there for him. When he came in, I stood respectfully. He ignored me and sat down, picking a magazine. I sat down again and continued reading. I was aware that he was watching me. Abruptly he put his magazine down. "Well. What do you want?" he barked. "Nothing" I said, "I thought you wanted to talk to me". He thought for a moment. "What would you say if I said I was sending up two battalions of infantry?" "I said "I would tell you to bring your own water as well, because I don't have enough." He picked up his magazine again, and I walked out without another word. He probably regarded me as a traitor for having left the SAS.

The Army was obviously concerned about reinforcing Musandam in the event of a confrontation because shortly afterwards I heard that the Sultan's Navy's new logistical support vessel, Lima 1 was to pay a visit to the landing ramp in an inlet called Khawr Naiad. Lima 1 was to land on it for the first time. In the early dawn I was standing with some others on the ramp. It was a beautiful morning. There wasn't a breath of wind. The water was like a mill pond, and we could see several miles down the *Khawr* (Inlet). Lima 1 came around the corner, heading for the ramp. She came very slowly. I was standing between the leading marks (shore based navigation aids) and could see that she was off course. She finally came to rest skewed on the ramp. It was only with difficulty that the vehicles could disembark. We were invited on board for breakfast. The skipper was the former Navigation Course commander I had met in Southampton. When I introduced myself, and reminded him about the course he denied all knowledge of it. I was amazed, then I realised – he was ex Army, and all his officers were Navy – real sailors. He hadn't wanted to be embarrassed. At table I commented about the skewed landing and asked him why, if conditions were so difficult, he had not dropped a kedge anchor, thrown a bow line, and used the two to land squarely. There was a stunned silence around the table, and he muttered something indistinct. Afterwards one of his officers said to me "If you had been a member of this crew he would have had you keel-hauled for that."

One of the officers in the SAF camp was Sami Hamed Albu Saidi. He was a member of the royal family, and had once been an ADC to the Sultan. He was fun, charismatic, and spoke fluent English. I had first met him in Salalah, and he was a frequent visitor to the house. I had cause to bless our friendship when one Christmas we decided to hold a party in the club house I had managed to obtain between our villas and the army camp. We were having a great time with beer, music and fireworks, when there was a bang at the door. I was called over, and at the door was the SAF platoon commander who had been left in charge of the camp that weekend. He rudely demanded to know what was going on, showing an unusual lack of courtesy. He said that the Pakistani road workers had said that they had been shot at from the cliffs. I told him that was just our fire-works, and it was clearly a malicious complaint. He demanded that we stop, and I refused. I looked beyond him and saw his platoon deployed behind him in the dark, weapons at the ready. He demanded again, and I told him to get lost and slammed the door, half expecting a hail of bullets to come through it. We carried on partying. The following day I was told that he had got onto his headquarters, and that the matter had been rapidly rising through the Ministry of Defence, when Sami had got wind of it. He used his influence, and quashed it. Shortly after, he was lucky to survive a helicopter crash. He had been flying down to Muscat when he abruptly changed his plans and got out before the Huey reached Muscat. As the helicopter was flying over the sea, there was a malfunction which caused the main rotor to cut off the tail. All on board were killed. I was saddened to hear of his death several years later in a car crash.

My relations with TTI continued to deteriorate, and at the end of 1982, when we were going on leave, I decided to take our collection of shells and curios back with us then, rather than entrust them to a packing case when we finally left.

We wrapped every single item in newspaper, and carefully packed them in our suitcases. When we reached Muscat we were met by an official from the Deputy Prime Minister's Office. His Excellency Qais Zawawi, the Deputy Prime Minister for Financial and Economic Affairs was in London. He had been invited to a formal occasion and needed his ceremonial medals. I was asked to carry them, and was given two red velvet-covered boxes and a Letter of Introduction. When we arrived at Heathrow, we went straight through the green corridor. Customs officials were standing around, and they spotted the large Samsonite suitcases and velvet boxes. One of them intercepted us, and we went through the usual preamble of "Anything to declare etc" I said I hadn't. He pointed at the velvet boxes. "Open them." I showed him the Letter of Introduction, which seemed to impress him, so he desisted. He pointed at one of the Samsonites. I opened it. It was a sea of paper. He looked at it for a moment, and then pounced on one of the balls of paper. He opened it. It was a seashell. He repeated this several times. Same result. By this time his colleagues were taking an interest, and were gathering around. He gave up on the first case, and started on the second. No difference. He attacked the third. He was desperate to find something. His friends were taking the Mickey out of him. I just stood there watching him, silently. In the end he gave up, and we were allowed to leave.

In 1983 I finally decided to leave, and we started to make arrangements to get Trumpkin back to the UK. In March I contacted the Veterinary Section of the Ministry of Agriculture and was pleasantly surprised by their friendly and efficient service. I had been expecting all sorts of problems, but it went without a hitch. Even when we were told to take Trumpkin, in his box, to a hangar at Seeb Airport at midnight. I thought there is no way there is going to be anybody here at this time. We approached the darkened, silent hangar, and knocked at the door. Almost immediately, it was opened by an Omani policeman. There were already five other boxes containing cats destined for England. It turned out that he was from Khasab. He said "My father told me that if I wanted to get on in life I should join the Police. And here I am guarding pussycats at midnight in an empty hangar!" We went on leave later that year and visited Trumpkin in the quarantine station at Clows Top near Kidderminster. Mr Conn, the vet, was amazed that we spent over an hour with him. "Most people only come for a look," he said.

While I was making my final preparations to leave, on the 20th May 1983 400 *Shihuh* gathered in Bayah, again to claim their own state under the leadership of Sheikh Mohamed Saleh Kumzari, a former Wali of Bayah before 1970. They were from the *Salahada, Kanabila, Hamaabaja, Khanazira, Asami and Yahamra* tribes. A strong presence of ORD, and Royal Oman Police moved into the MDC camp in Bayah, accompanied by the Governor and myself, whilst a SOAF helicopter circled overhead. As it happened, Sheikh Mohammed refused to be their leader, and the whole thing fizzled out, after a few names had been taken. No arrests were made, and there were no repetitions during my time there. I realised that the political information I had collected during the previous four years could do serious damage if it fell into the wrong hands, and decided to destroy it. I burnt it in a *burmail* outside the office, and it took me two days to complete the job.

My passport needed to be renewed, so I went to the British Consular Office in Muscat. At that time it was located in the old town, and I walked down the narrow dusty streets looking for it. I was told that it was just around the next corner. I spotted a large wooden door with a highly polished brass plaque alongside, and went in. Stepping from the blinding sun into the shade, I saw a desk and went up to it. "Good morning, I have come to renew my passport," I said, offering it to the woman behind the desk. She said "I am sorry, but we can't do that." "Why not?" I asked indignantly. "Because this is the American Embassy." As my eyes adjusted to the gloom I saw the biggest American flag I have ever seen on the wall behind her. I gibbered my apologies and staggered out onto the street to renew my search.

On 21st January I supervised the arrangements for the dedication ceremony of the Bayah corniche, and spent the next few days going around Musandam saying my goodbyes. I visited the Governor for the last time at 1130 on 26th January. As usual, the Arabs couldn't understand why I was leaving them. I didn't mention TTI, I just said that I was an English *Jebali*, and needed the cold rain on my face, which they seemed to understand. We flew to Muscat on the 29th, had lunch with the First Secretary at the British Embassy, and his wife. The following day, I visited Al Musalim in his office to say goodbye. He kindly offered me a job looking after his business interests, but that wasn't for me. We had dinner with Martin and Jenny at the SAF Beach Club that evening. The next few days were a blur of farewells and on Thursday the 2nd February we boarded Flight BA 012 at 0420 and arrived at Heathrow at 0830.

Glossary

2ic	Second in command
58 pattern mug	Black plastic mug, 1958 issue
ADC	Aide de Camp
APC	Armoured Personnel Carrier
Adjutant	Assistant to the Commanding Officer
BAC-111	Passenger aircraft in use by SOAF
Bait	Jebali house
Ball	Live ammunition – as opposed to blank
Baluch	Soldier from Baluchistan
Basha	Shelter (Malay)
Bedford RL	Four ton truck
Bedu	Nomad
Bergen	Rucksack
Burmail	Oil drum, after *Burma Oil*
BFPO	British Forces Post Office
BMH	British Military Hospital
CAD	Civil Aid Department
CASEVAC	Casualty Evacuation – usually by air
Chapatti	Arab flat bread
CO	Commanding Officer
Compo	Tinned rations
Crabs	RAF
CSPEP	Carrying Straps Personal Equipment Parachutist

Distasha	Arab clothing – like a night-shirt
Dojo	Judo practice area
DMS Boots	Directly Moulded Sole Boots
DSM	Divisional Sergeant Major
Doubling	Trotting – twice the speed of marching
DZ	Drop Zone – parachuting
E&E	Escape and Evasion exercise
Falaj	Aqueduct
Firqat	Group
Fragged	Killing someone on your own side with a grenade. US Viet Nam origin
FST	Field Surgical Team
GOC UKLF	General Officer Commanding UK Land Forces
Heavy Drop	Parachuting equipment such as Land Rovers and Artillery
Hedgehog	Small fort constructed of burmails on Salalah Plain to defend RAF Salalah. There were five, A, B , C ,D and E
Hexy	Hexamine – solid fuel for cooking
Jebali	Mountain dweller
Jundi	Private soldier
Khanjar	Arab ceremonial dagger
Khawr	Inlet
Ladang	Cultivated area (Malay)
LMG	Light Machine Gun
LP	Helicopter Landing Point
LZ	Landing Zone – several LPs
NCO	Non Commissioned Officer
Medivac	Helicopter medical evacuation
MDC	Musandam Development Committee
MFV	Motor Fisheries Vessel – trawler
Mindoob	Government representative

MI Room	Army medical centre
MT	Motor Transport
NAAFI	Navy, Army, Air Force Institute – shop and club
OC	Officer Commanding
ORD	Oman Research Department – Intelligence department
O Group	Orders Group
PE	Plastic Explosive
Pink Panther	SAS Land Rover, so-called because of its colour
Prayers	Morning meeting at which the day's plans are set out
PJI	Parachute Jump Instructor
PSI	Permanent Staff Instructor
PX	American NAAFI
Qahwa	Arab coffee, strong, sweet and black
RCL	Recoilless artillery piece, either 75mmor 82mm
RPG	Rocket Propelled Grenade
RMO	Regimental Medical Officer
R&R	Rest and Rehabilitation
RSM	Regimental Sergeant Major
RTU	Returned To Unit – thrown out
RV	Rendezvous
Recce	Reconnaissance
Sabre Troop	SAS operational troop
SAF	Sultan's Armed Forces
Shemagh	Arab head-dress consisting of a square of cloth
Shirt KF	Shirt Khaki flannel
Sitrep	Situation report
Skyvan	Transport aircraft extensively used by SOAF

Stag	Guard duty
Suq	Market
Saladin	Armoured car
Sangar	Small defensive shelter usually made from rocks
SLR	Self Loading Rifle. Then current army issue rifle
SO2	Staff Officer Grade 2 – (Major)
SO2 (SD)	As above, Special Duties
SQMS	Squadron Quartermaster Sergeant
SSM	Squadron Sergeant Major
Tab	March (across country)
Tacsign	Badge on a vehicle denoting its unit of origin
Trousers OG	Olive Green trousers
WRAC	Women's Royal Army Corps
X-Ray	Previously adjusted target for artillery
Yurth	Shihuh axe

DEVELOPMENT OF
THE INSURGENCY

The influx of workers accompanying the Gulf oil boom in the 1950s included large numbers of Dhofaris. They, with others, absorbed the ideas of Arab nationalism and Marxism. In 1962 dissident members of the Dhofar branch of the Arab Nationalist Movement (ANM) created the Dhofar Charitable Association (DCA). Its politics were mixed-nationalist, Marxist, Nasserite, but primarily it was opposed to the Sultan's rule and to the British connection. Its purpose was, ostensibly, to build mosques and aid the poor; in reality it collected funds, recruited members and established political contacts for the purpose of armed rebellion against the Al Bu Said dynasty and British influence in the region. In fact the DCA was a cover for the embryonic Dhofar Liberation Front (DLF). At that time, most of South Arabia was in a state of turbulence. In September 1962, war broke out in northern Yemen, and in October 1963 an anti-British insurrection began in southern Yemen (Aden).

The first public signs of unrest in Oman came in the spring of 1963, with the distribution of anti-Sultan leaflets by the Dhofar Arab Youth Organisation, and an attack on oil company vehicles. Several vehicles were destroyed, and an escort, one of the Sultan's askars, was killed. The leader of this attack was Musselim bin Nufl, a sheikh of the Al-Kathiri tribe in Dhofar, who was formerly a mechanic on the Sultan's staff. He was arrested but escaped to Saudi Arabia where he contacted Imam Ghalib. With Saudi assistance, Musselim bin Nufl went to Iraq where he was trained in guerilla tactics and enrolled about 30 other dissidents. In 1964 this group formed the nucleus of the DLF, which had expanded following the merger of three clandestine groups— the Dhofar Charitable Association (DCA), the local branch of the Arab Nationalist Movement (ANM) and the Dhofar Soldiers' Organisation (DSO) — a loose group formed from Dhofari soldiers in the armed and police forces of the Gulf.

1964

In 1964, Red Coy of the Northern Frontier Regt and a Tactical HQ were sent to Dhofar. This was the first time that the Army had been allowed into the province. During this short first stay the Northern Frontier Regiment ranged over the whole of Central Dhofar from the desert to the coast but they found no sign of the enemy. It was assumed that the leaders had gone abroad to tout for help and that the rank and file had melted back into the civilian population. The Regiment returned to Northern Oman.

1965

In the spring of 1965 Government askars who looked after a well to the North of Raysut were attacked. Because of this two Companies of the Muscat Regiment with Reconnaissance and Assault Pioneer platoons and a Tactical HQ were sent down to Salalah. SOAF supplied two Beaver liaison aircraft and two Piston Provost ground attack aircraft in support. Information was almost non-existent and what there was, vague. It was believed that the leaders were still abroad but that there was a gang of about 30 enemy in the area of the Wadi Urzuq. Guides were provided by Sultan Said Bin Taimur. Most were unreliable and frequently came from an area different to the one in which they were required to guide. There were no maps. Communication was by 19 set (An obsolete radio) which could not be taken on foot patrols. To try and get round this Said bin Taimur lent a very unfit donkey, but the company who had it normally finished up carrying both the donkey and the set. The standard of training of the soldiers was poor. However, the enemy were also feeling their way and were very hesitant. The soldiers' battle ration was meagre and 7 days rations could easily be carried on the man. When this ran out, re-supply was by Beaver air drop and took a long time.

Two early defectors from the enemy led to a large arms and ammunition find at Thint which had been brought in by convoy from the North. (Around the edge of Empty Quarter then down through Qafa. Supplies did not come from Northern Oman)

Contacts prior to the monsoon included one enemy killed in ambush, 3 minor fire fights and some successful enemy mining with British Mark 7 anti-tank mines. A dhow carrying enemy supplies and advisors from Iraq ran aground in Iranian waters. On board was a list of enemy sympathizers in Salalah. This list was passed to the Sultanate and resulted in the arrest of about 40 people. This probably broke the back of the Salalah Town branch of the enemy.

On 9th June 1965, the driver of an oil company truck was murdered by machine gun fire while driving on the jebel. For the Dhofar Liberation Front this attack marked the beginning of the armed rebellion. At this stage the rebellion involved no political grievances. Resentment by the rebels was not directed against the Sultanate or the system, but against the reigning Sultan Said bin Taimur. Said bin Taimur was a medieval and somewhat despotic ruler who had rejected the material and cultural features of 20th century society and enforced strict isolation in Omani national policy. By his decree the import of almost all foreign goods was forbidden and among other things Omanis were forbidden to dance, play music, smoke, wear sunglasses, take photographs or wear western clothing. The penalties for disobedience were either flogging or imprisonment. Said bin Taimur also prevented any reforms in health services or education thus forcing young men to leave Dhofar illegally to obtain an education in other Gulf countries. In April 1966 an attempt by soldiers of the Dhofar Defence Force to assassinate Said bin Taimur during a military parade barely failed. The Sultan was unharmed but the Pakistani Commander of the Dhofar Force was wounded.

In mid monsoon of 1965 it was decided that one rifle company could take care of the future in Dhofar. Leaving this company behind, the remainder of the Muscat Regiment returned to the North. This company was eventually deployed in section positions, sited on water and with their own communications. These positions were spread throughout Central Dhofar and as far North as Mudhai. At this time there was no military presence in the West and, until the beginning of 1966, the Eastern Area was thought to be loyal.

1966

In early 1966, a group of enemy bringing in a re-supply convoy of Dodge trucks from the North (via Qafa) attacked the SAF section position at Mudhai. As a result, the Northern Frontier Regiment complete was sent to Dhofar. To start with only the attached Red Coy was sent to join 'A' Coy NFR who were already in Dhofar but, within a very short time, the whole Regiment was there. They had few contacts. The enemy dressed and carried the same weapons as the rest of the civil population. It was their choice whether they should remain as civilians or start a contact. The few contacts there were, were normally the result of bad tactical errors by SAF which the enemy took advantage of. SAF casualties in these contacts were high.

Work was started on wiring off Salalah town. This was as much to control food getting out as to stop enemy getting in, and this year saw a gang of enemy emerge in the Eastern area.

1967

The activity in 1967 was similar to the pattern in 1966. In addition SAF recce'd road routes into the West and established camps at Iraqi and Everest. This was an attempt to cut the enemy supply line but troops were too few to provide enough regular patrols and ambushes, and the enemy soon learned how to bypass the camps.

As early as 1965 the Sultanate had been trying to persuade the British Government to clean up Hawf, on the border with Yemen. This was not done. However, with Aden independence looming close, the Royal Navy landed a force of Guards and Royal Marines there. Unfortunately, bad weather had made a dawn landing impossible and the ship was clearly visible from the shore before the landing was attempted. Most of the enemy in Hawf at the time were able to escape to the hills.

By the end of 1967 the enemy in the Eastern area were tired, and it is possible that they would have surrendered if they had been granted an unconditional pardon. Sultan Said Bin Taimur would not agree to this.

1968

1968 prior to the monsoon was very quiet with few

contacts. At the end of the monsoon an enemy was killed in the Western area who wore a Mao Tse Tung badge and carried an SKS semi-automatic rifle. This was the first visible sign of Communist influence. From now on the majority of the enemy had automatic rifles whilst SAF still had the Mark 4 Lee Enfield rifle, and did not change over to the FN semi-automatic for at least another 6 months.

Post monsoon of 1968, the first task chosen was to occupy and hold Dhalqut by a landing from the sea. To support this, a company position was established at Defa. This company had a single 25 pounder field gun, and was in range to support the Dhalqut landing. The landing was successful but the enemy built up on the scarps which overlooked the beach. There were not enough soldiers both to take and hold these so, after some days, the company was withdrawn. This landing was followed by several successful 'in and out' seaborne operations both in the west and as far east as Marbat.

An additional rifle company was brought down from the North. This was to be a permanent arrangement until there were two battalions in Dhofar. The enemy started stand-off attacks against jebel camps in a limited way. They had 3 inch mortars and British (ex Aden) ammunition. By and large the attacks were inaccurate and badly planned.

The first battalion-sized operation was mounted at the end of 1968. The objective was Sherishitti. On the operation there were several contacts and many enemy around but, once again, there were not enough soldiers to both hold the high ground and clear the wadi. When its' water ran out, the battalion withdrew without having achieved its task.

The second DLF (Dhofar Liberation Front) conference was held in 1968 at Hamrin to the north of the Wadi Naheez in Central Dhofar. At this conference Marxist socialism was formally adopted as a platform and the name of the front was changed from DLF to the 'Popular Front for the Liberation of the Occupied Arabian Gulf' (PFLOAG). Leadership of the movement became joint, with Muhammed Ahmad al Sayl al Ghassani becoming one of the High Command. This reorganisation was followed by a period of military successes for the Front. Thirty rebel leaders were sent to China for guerilla training and Chinese advisers arrived in the Hadramaut to train the rebels.

1969

In 1969 SAF pulled out of the West completely. The coastal town of Rakhyut fell to the rebels and the same year saw most of the jebel, including the Thumrait road fall under enemy control. The oil company operating in Dhofar was forced to suspend its activities. At this point PFLOAG was composed of several hundred Dhofaris and other Arabs, a few escaped slaves, and some Chinese advisers in the Hadramaut in Yemen. Many of the Dhofaris had gained military experience in the armies and police forces throughout the Gulf.

PFLOAG concentrated its attack in four distinct areas, Dhofar, two areas of northern Oman, and The Union of Arab Emirates. The West was declared a 'Liberated' area. Having pulled out of the West, SAF had two companies on the Midway road in camps at Mount John and Aqabat Jasmine. There was a company at Mughsayl and a company at Umm al Ghawarif. The companies on the road were mainly committed to picketing the road and had little time for ambitious, aggressive patrolling. Enemy small arms and machine gun stand off attacks increased in frequency and were better planned. As was normal practice at that time SAF pulled companies out of the monsoon belt for the duration of the monsoon. At the end of the monsoon, when SAF re-established the positions on the Midway road, there was quite heavy opposition from the enemy.

The Midway road was a graded track which had been maintained by the MEKOM Oil Company until they pulled out in 1967. Thereafter it slowly deteriorated.

1970

In 1970 the enemy announced that they governed the Jebel in the Central area. This was not completely true. SAF forces could go where they wanted provided they were strong enough and mindful of tactical principles as the enemy could not stop them. However, sooner or later SAF would have to leave for some other task, and then the enemy would re-emerge and take back control of the area.

In March 1970 it was decided that the two companies holding the Midway Road could be more gainfully employed elsewhere and that the future re-supply of Salalah would be done by air and sea. The Midway road was abandoned. One of the companies thus released moved to Marboosh in yet another attempt to cut the enemy supply route.

An abortive attack by the rebels on an army garrison at Izki in Central Oman on 11 June 1970 triggered off a reaction both in Oman and Britain. In July 1970 Qaboos Bin Said, Bin Taimur's only son assumed power and his father retired to England where he remained until his death in October 1972 in the Dorchester in London. The new ruler of Oman, Sultan Qaboos bin Said was born at Ma'murah on the Salalah plain in 1941. His mother was a Dhofari from the al Maasheni tribe. As a boy he was educated privately in Salalah and later went to the Royal Military Academy, Sandhurst. On commissioning he joined the Cameronians and served with them in Germany. Before leaving England in 1964 he took a course in local Government at a technical college.

Following the succession, Sultan Qaboos began to put into effect the necessary reforms in education, health services and development. He declared an amnesty to the rebels and opened up Salalah to all Dhofaris. The coup and subsequent developments removed much of the motivation behind the rebel movement and precipitated a crisis amongst their ranks. PFLOAG was forced to threaten its members with execution if they attempted to surrender, and to place Salalah Town out of bounds. Resentment of the methods employed by the communist-dominated front mounted and on 12 September 1970 fighting broke out in eastern Dhofar between PLOAG' s communist supporters and other elements who regarded the communists as anti-religious. The attempted counter revolution was ruthlessly suppressed by the communists and resulted in mass defection to the government. Between September 1970 and March 1971 a total of 201 rebels surrendered to the Government. In late 1970 the first Firqat was raised by the SAS (BATT) and began training at Marbat. It was a multi-tribal Firqat and elected to call itself the Firqat Salahadin. Expansion of the Firqat Forces continued. Sultan Qaboos used his oil revenues to buy modern weapons and equipment, and vigorous efforts were made to recruit Omanis into the Sultan' s Armed Forces in preparation for carrying the fight back onto the Jebel.

1971

In 1971 a second battalion (Northern Frontier Regiment) was sent to Dhofar. This battalion was initially based at Haloof (Hagleet) in the Central Area. In these early stages, the enemy believed that they could take on the battalion on equal terms. A series of battalion operations were mounted. At the start of the series all three companies of the battalion could be in contact with the enemy at the same time with contacts lasting for 8 hours or more. But by the end of three months, the enemy's determination was broken and the battalion could patrol right up to and in to the Wadi Nahiz without opposition. NFR was then withdrawn and sent to establish a new position at Akoot in the Western area.

In a show of strength PLOAG held its third congress in occupied Rakhyut on 9 June 1971. A resolution was carried calling for the amalgamation of PFLOAG with the National Democratic Front for the Liberation of Oman and the Arabian Gulf (NDFLOAG, the organization responsible for the attack at Izki on 11 June 1970).

In October 1971 Operation Jaguar was mounted to clear the Eastern Area of enemy. This was a combined operation with SAF, BATT and Firqat. Despite some successes the aim was not achieved and Jaguar (with several changes of name) dragged on after its planned end. Op Jaguar saw the establishment of permanent SAF and Firqat bases in the Central Jebel, at White City (Medinat al Haq). Waterhole (Ayn) was withdrawn to Jibjat.

1972

Before the monsoon of 1972 the Simba position (subsequently known as Sarfait) was established on the border. The original plan was to build a wire obstacle down to the sea but, for a variety of reasons, this was not achieved. SAF entrenched itself on the top whilst the enemy still had relative freedom of movement between the scarp and the sea.

The Leopard Line was set up in November 1971 and consisted of Line of picquets running from Mughsayl into the interior of the jebel to the north east. The line was withdrawn during the 1972 monsoon. Following a meeting held at Ahlaish in the 'Ho Chi Min' area between 14th and 20th December 1971, it was announced that PFLOAG and NDFLOAG had amalgamated to form the Popular Front for the Liberation of Oman and the Arabian Gulf (also known as PFLOAG). During the same month, Musallim bin Nufl surrendered to the Government authorities in Muscat. In early 1972 Chinese backing for the rebellion in Dhofar waned and Russian weapons and supplies began to appear on the jebel.

Pre-monsoon in the Central area, Salalah town was fully wired in. A thousand yards and plus from RAF Salalah a semi-circle of five strong points - known as "hedgehogs", had previously been constructed and connected by a wire fence. At this time, SAF in the Salalah area were very defensive and patrols and ambushes seldom went outside the hedgehog perimeter. Despite radar (ZB 298 manned by RAF Regiment) and artillery, the enemy mounted several stand-off attacks against the hedgehogs and RAF Salalah itself.

1972 saw the arrival of Iranian help. This started with an airlift of equipment and weapons, much of it very dated. A Special Force unit also arrived and stayed on. During the monsoon a large rebel force numbering over 200 collected from all over Dhofar attacked the town in Mirbat with the intention of capturing it. Defending the town were a group of askars, Firqat, a BATT team from 'B' Sqn and Dhofar Gendarmerie and a 25 pounder field gun.

The attack was put in with the utmost determination and only failed because the equally determined and heavily outnumbered defence gave time for 'G' Sqn 22 SAS who had armed up to go on the range in Salalah, to be flown in and attack the enemy in the flank thus relieving the town. The enemy suffered Over 30% Killed In Action and never again attempted an assault of this nature.

Successful follow up operations were also conducted by the Government Forces in the following weeks. By the end of the 1972 monsoon the rebels had been successfully driven from all the areas east of the Jebel Samhan and in the autumn of 1972 operations began in the area of Jebel Aram and the Wadi Khishayn.

Operation Hornbeam, between Adonib and Manston, was a mobile, one company operation. It was the forerunner of the Hornbeam line, which was intended to cause considerable hindrance to enemy resupply.

Operation Sycamore and Hawk were combined SAF, BATT and Firqat operations in the White City, Wadi Darbat and Tawi Ateer Area. They carried on from where Operation Jaguar had left off. Although they had some success and made the enemy reinforce from the Central area, they did not destroy the enemy in the East.

In late 1972 successful operations were conducted in the area of the Wadi Darbat by combined forces of Firqat and regular troops. In December 1972 some 80 members of PFLOAG were captured in Central Oman and Abu Dhabi, and Chinese arms smuggled into the old pirate port of Sur were also captured.

During the 1973 monsoon, Government forces remained on the jebel at Jibjat, Medinat al Haq and all positions on the Hornbeam Line but Tawi Atair was again withdrawn.

This was a turning point in the conflict. There had been a virtually bloodless coup and where there had been nothing, development was taking place. An all-weather harbour was being built at Rayzut, because no ships could come to Salalah and off-load during the three month monsoon period. Tarmac roads were appearing inside the wire of Salalah Town and to the new port at Rayzut thus lessening the threat of mines. New weapons, new and more aircraft gave mobility and killing power at longer ranges. With the introduction of the British 81mm mortar and the GPMG (Machine gun), ideal weapons, SAF became the hunter instead of the hunted. There was an injection of new personalities into the leadership of the force and new ideas materialised. There was a constant flow of Surrendered Enemy Personnel (SEPs) which brought in the information and intelligence, so very much needed in this type of conflict.

Jebel bases had been established at:

Marbat:	1 x Rifle Company, Firqat and BATT
Tawi Atair:	1 x Rifle Company, Firqat and BATT
	1 x Troop of 25 pounder field guns.
	A fixed wing airstrip allowed supplies to
	be flown in, except during the monsoon.
Jibjat:	1 x Rifle Company, Firqat and BATT
	A Fixed wing air strip
White City:	1 x Rifle Coy, FQ and BATT.
	A fixed wing airstrip.

There were SAF troops in Taqa, Ayn Arzat, Arzat, UAG, Rayzut, and Adonib (which included the Iranian Battle Group (IIBG) Manston, Simba, Midway and Habrut.

The main enemy dispositions were as follows:

Eastern Area

North and South-East of Tawi Ateer/ Wadi Ghazir, Jebel Ashawr, Wadi Darbat, Wadi Raythawt, Wadi Arzat, Wadi Lenin and Wadi Khashayn.

Central Area :

Wadi Risham and the deep wadis astride the Midway Road.

West:

Kaftawt, Shershitti, Safkut, below the scarp at Simba and along the border.

The Plain

The enemy were pushed off the plain back into the Scarp and their activities were limited to small scale stand off attacks and a number of mining incidents outside the wire.

The Hedgehogs, as they were called were the outer airfield perimeter defence posts (manned by Baluch Guard, Cracker Battery Royal Artillery and the RAF Regiment).

Following the monsoon of 1973, extensive operations were carried out by Government forces in eastern Dhofar. Later in the same year, following an enemy attack on Salalah with 122mm Katyushka rockets, positions were set up at Adami, Hattel and Aqabat al Sheikh (Operation Diana) to prevent a recurrence.

The Plains Battalion mounted continual patrols around the plain and below the Scarp. Zulu Company, an Independent Baluch Company, searched roads and tracks and cleared mines. Salalah was now secure, and the *adoo* had been pushed back to the jebel

SAF moved forward to the West from Adonib to Mugsayl and set up a line of pickets eventually some 35 Kilometers long from Mughsayl to the Wadi Amat. Called the Hornbeam Line, it consisted of a blocking system of patrol bases at Company and Platoon Level, some with fixed wing airstrips and with their own artillery support flown in by SOAF Skyvans and Caribous. Their main supply base and Tactical HQ was set up at Mughsayl. The aim was to cut the enemy's main camel supply routes, thus denying the enemy in the Central and Eastern Areas the necessary supplies of arms and ammunition to maintain attacks on Government. forces. This it did effectively – as the enemy camels probed north so did the line until they were in an area where there was no water for the animals and they ceased to attempt the crossing. Attempts to breach the line were made, but few were successful. It further allowed operations to be mounted into the areas east and west of the line. By 1974 this had become an impressive wire and mined barrier. SAF stayed there throughout the monsoon, or khareef as it is known, until 1975. With the effectiveness of the line the enemy in the Central and Eastern Areas had to move to gain access to supplies and caches and some useful contacts ensued.

1974

By 1974 SAF had formed two further Infantry Battalions and by so doing gained more troops for mobile operations against the enemy on the jebel. Simba continued to be maintained from an airhead at Manston and soaked up much of the enemy's hardware. By this time the Iranian Forces now at Manston and Midway had built up to Brigade level. Their heavy air and fire power allowed SAF to do things that they could not have done before. The Midway Road was opened by an operation starting simultaneously in the north from the Midway end and in the south from Mount John. It was a joint SAF/Iranian operation. After a certain amount of opposition the track, as it was at that time, was opened to traffic from Midway and Salalah. It was kept open by a series of pickets astride its axis and developed into a tarmac road in 1975

By this stage a Civil Development programme had been introduced to complement the military campaign on the jebel. Civil Action Teams had been established in several Government locations notably Jib Jat and Medinat al Haq which provided clinics, shops and schools for the local inhabitants. Drilling for water in certain jebel locations was also underway, but at this stage the Civil Development programme lacked both the organisation and the finance to be really effective and was also hampered by the lack of 'safe' routes to move plant and supplies.

In August 1974 the name of the Front was changed to the Popular Front for the Liberation of Oman (PLFO) in an attempt to gain political support from the Gulf area. Although Russian support for the rebels continued, evidence of Cuban and Libyan support also began to materialise. In October 1974 Government troops and the Firqat Abu Bakar Sadeeq moved onto the Jebel Kaftawt in the first of a series of operations aimed at establishing Firqats in their tribal areas. Enemy reaction was almost negligible and by the end of December new positions had also been set at Zeak, Ayun, Burj, Kushaat and Ashinhaib. The civil development programme achieved a new emphasis with the reorganization and expansion of the Civil Action Department, the inauguration of a concerted road building and water drilling programme and the re-emphasis of the military aim to achieve and maintain a suitable climate for civil development on the jebel. This emphasis was supported by comprehensive financial backing by the Government. Military Engineers built over 200 kms of motorable tracks on the jebel.

On 2 December 1974 Iranian Forces began operations in Western Dhofar in two battalion strength. The operations were directed against major terrorist bases in the Sherishitti and Bait Handob areas. After some hard fighting during which both sides sustained many casualties, a change of plan was ordered. The Iranians were given the task of recapturing Rakhyut on the coast, and SAF was given the original Sherishitti caves objectives.

Rakhyut fell to the Iranians on 5th January. The Iranians constructed a line of positions running north of Rakhyut; the Damavand Line. The SAF operation to reach Sherishitti was only partially successful although a large quantity of enemy ammunition was found in the nearby area. During December and January the heaviest casualties of the campaign were sustained by both sides.

On 21st February 1975, Operation Himmar was launched to the west of the Hornbeam Line which resulted in an enemy regimental headquarters (9th June Regt) being captured and the find of a very large quantity of arms and ammunition. The remainder of the campaign season up until the monsoon was taken up with a series of major operations in the central and eastern areas. The previously unentered Wadi Risham area to the West of the Midway road was subjected to a battalion operation and met little opposition. It was proved not only that the enemy were unable to oppose SAF in strength anywhere east of the Hornbeam Line but also that SAF could go everywhere they wished.

The next step had to be further to the West and a plan to take out the Shershitti cave complex and the access route along the Darra Ridge was made. A diversion operation was to be mounted in the West and Simba to break out south below the Scarp via Capstan. Its aim was to draw the enemy from the east and the cave areas and to catch them off balance, while SAF's main attack and effort was to be put in on Shershitti itself. However, there was little or no opposition to the breakout at Simba and no real retaliation from the western border because the enemy were convinced that the main thrust would be from Defa.

June – December 1975

The monsoon period was quiet, and by patrolling, SAF maintained dominance over the enemy. Operations between August and October established further positions west of the Damavand Line, and a line of positions between Sarfait and the sea. Another wire obstacle was built linking these latter positions so that the major supply route used by the guerillas and their People's Democratic Republic of Yemen (PDRY) Regular Army advisors was cut. Due to this success the plan was changed, and it was decided to put in a permanent block from Simba to the sea, again wired and mined to cut off completely the supplies coming in from over the border. This probably ended the conflict some six months earlier than had been expected.

Three stages had been completed - Hornbeam - Damavand -Simba - more ground seized from the enemy, held dominated and developed. Finally mopping up operations in the west were mounted. Shershitti collapsed and the PDRY troops fled over the border rather than be captured. The enemy could have been hit during their withdrawal but were allowed to go back in order to decrease the likelihood of retaliation. Their withdrawal caused the irregulars left behind to collapse. Further operations in the Central and Eastern areas accounted for more enemy surrenders and equipment, including several complete caches. In 1975 the province was declared safe for civil development leaving some 50 - 60 enemy to be accounted for.

On 1st December 1975, the coastal town of Dhalqut was recaptured with no enemy resistance and two days later the troops advancing from the opposite directions met up. For the first time in ten years the entire province of Dhofar came under Government control and peace was declared. However enemy artillery from across the border in PDRY continued to bombard SAF positions at Sarfait nearly every day, despite a temporary lull in October, brought about by cross border air strikes. The bombardment was ineffective and did not hinder operations. The flow of surrendered enemy persons increased markedly in November and December. Between the 14th October and the end of the year 222 former terrorists gave themselves up; this was a higher total than during the amnesty of 1970-71.

Casualty List

Enemy casualties from 1970 to May 1977:-

Reported Killed   620, of which 509 were

confirmed.

Reported Wounded   528, of which 199 were confirmed.

Sultan's Armed Forces casualties from 1971 to May 1977:-

Killed in action   191
Wounded in action   67
Missing   2

Total confirmed casualties for both sides, 1579, plus 440 unconfirmed casualties on the enemy side.

Total possible casualties for both sides, 2019.

(These figures do not include SAS or Iranian Forces)

FIRQAT NAMES as at 1976

Firqat	Full Name	Location/Tribe
FSD	*Firqat Salahadeen*	Mirbat 1971, mixed tribe, then 1972 *Ali bin Badr* (W) at HH Delta & *Mohammed bin Ahmed* (E) at HH Bravo
FKW	*F Khalid bin Waleed*	*Taqa 1971, Al Maasheni*
FAU	*F Al Umri*	*Mirbat 1972*
FAQ	*F al Qaboos*	*Jaaboob. Ma'murah, 1971*
FAA	*F al Asifat*	*Jib Jat, 1972*
FAM	*F al Mustajila*	*Tabawk (W), Kashawb (E)*
FBS	*F Abu Bakar Sadeeq*	*B. Said Kaftawt*
FAS	*F a'Saaiqa*	*B Qatan, HH Alpha & Umbushuq*
FGAN	*F Gamal Abdul Nasser*	*Sudh & Sawb*
FAB	*F al Barama*	*Hajeef*
FAN	*F a' Nasser*	*Mughsayl*

FAI	*F al Istikshaaf*	*Mudai*
FOK	*F Omar bin al Khattab*	*Ayun & Huloof*
FSM	*F Southern Mahra*	*Shihan & Habrut (then toSheleem – Barakat!)*
FTZ	*F Tariq bin Zaid*	*Western Mahra*
FHG	*F Hadood al Gharbiya*	*Mudhai & Heeron*

BIBLIOGRAPHY

"OMAN: Insurgency and Development" by D.L. Price. The Institute for the Study of Conflict, 1975, No. 53.

"Condensed Notes on the Dhofar War 1964-1978" found in Dhofar Brigade HQ. Author Unknown.

"Military Press Brief Dhofar 1976" by E.J. Ward, Advisor to The Dhofar Information Office which later became part of The Ministry of Information.

Personal Notes by P.R.Sibley.

APPENDIX 2

Military Courses Completed

Survival
Resistance to interrogation
Parachute Course
Signals, Basic & Advanced
Medics, Basic & Advanced
Demolitions, Basic & Advanced
81 mm Mortar
GPMG SF
Coastal Navigation
Astro Navigation
Junior NCO's Section Commanders Battle Course
Free Fall Parachute Course
Arabic
Mortar Fire Control
Forward Air Controller
Psychological Operations
Forward Observation Officer
Jungle Training
Tracking
Gemini Repair

Lightning Source UK Ltd.
Milton Keynes UK
21 November 2009

146575UK00001B/29/A

9 781412 086356